The *Collage* Compendium

2,000 IMAGES TO CUT OUT & COLLAGE

—BY—

Roomytown

CHRONICLE BOOKS
SAN FRANCISCO

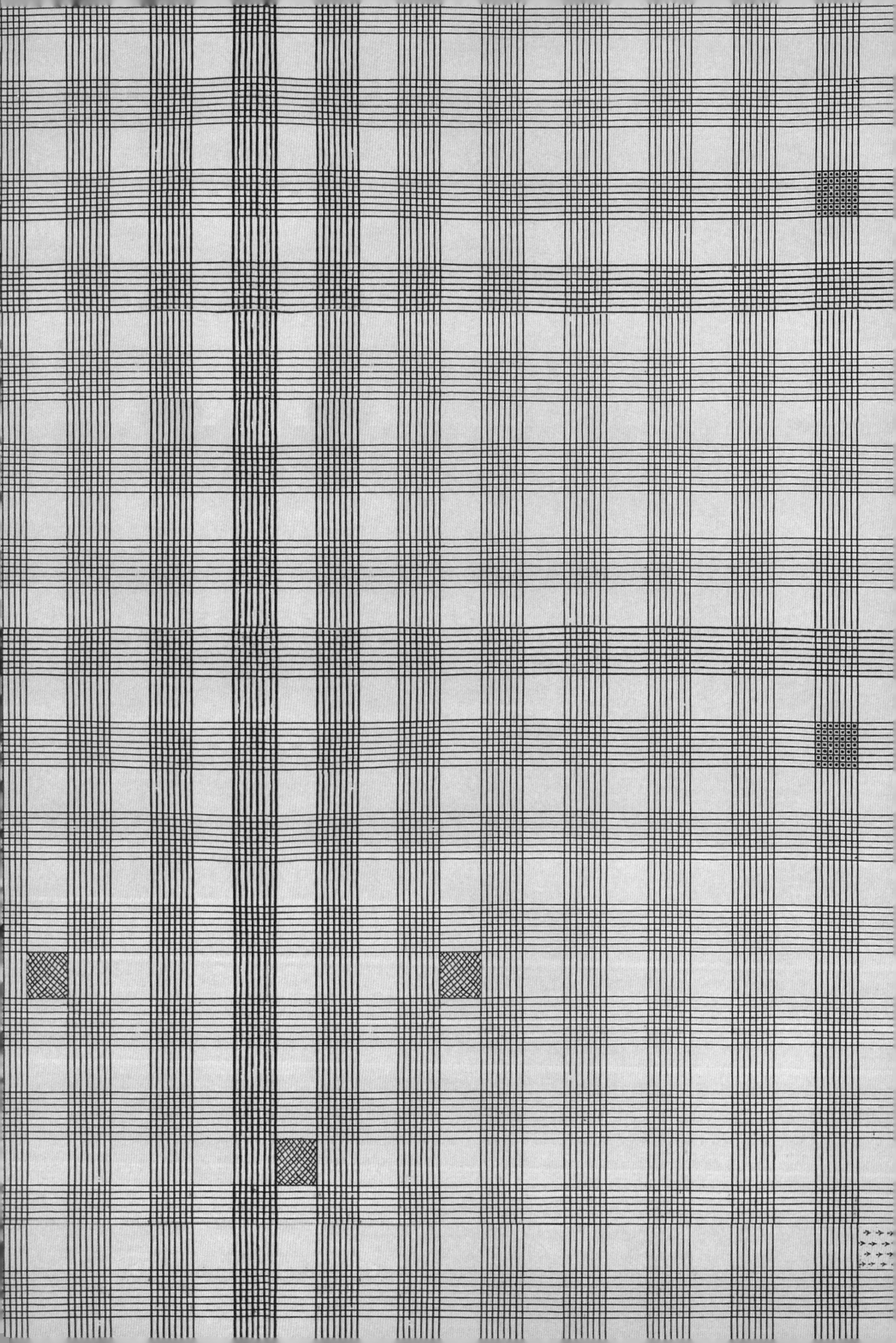

At Roomytown, design starts with discovery.

That means sifting through time—forgotten archives, museum libraries, vintage markets, antique bookshops—in search of the unique, the beautiful, the unexpected. It's how we create every product in our gift collection, and it's exactly how *The Collage Compendium* came to life.

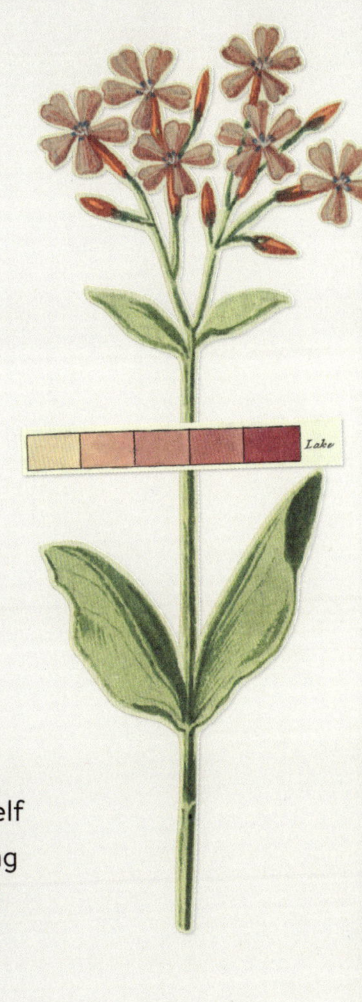

Inside these pages, you'll find a carefully curated collection of 2,000 vintage images—ready for you to cut, layer, and transform into your own works of art.

At Roomytown, we believe there's something special about slowing down, creating with your hands, and surrounding yourself with things that tell a story. We've spent countless hours trawling through hidden corners of history to find these gems. Botanical illustrations, whimsical animals, nostalgic typography, playful patterns—each piece is a fragment of design history waiting for a new chapter.

Now, it's your turn to bring them into your own creative projects.

Whether you're journaling, making art, or just rediscovering the simple joy of cutting and sticking, you'll find inspiration in this book. There are no rules—only possibilities. Use these images to personalize your journal, make special cards for friends, dream up wall art, or simply explore ideas on a rainy afternoon.

We hope *The Collage Compendium* becomes a well-thumbed favorite in your home—it's a place to peruse ideas, a source of inspiration, and a tool for uncovering the magic in old things made new.

Happy making,
The Roomytown Team

Nomenclature of Colors
for the studies of nature

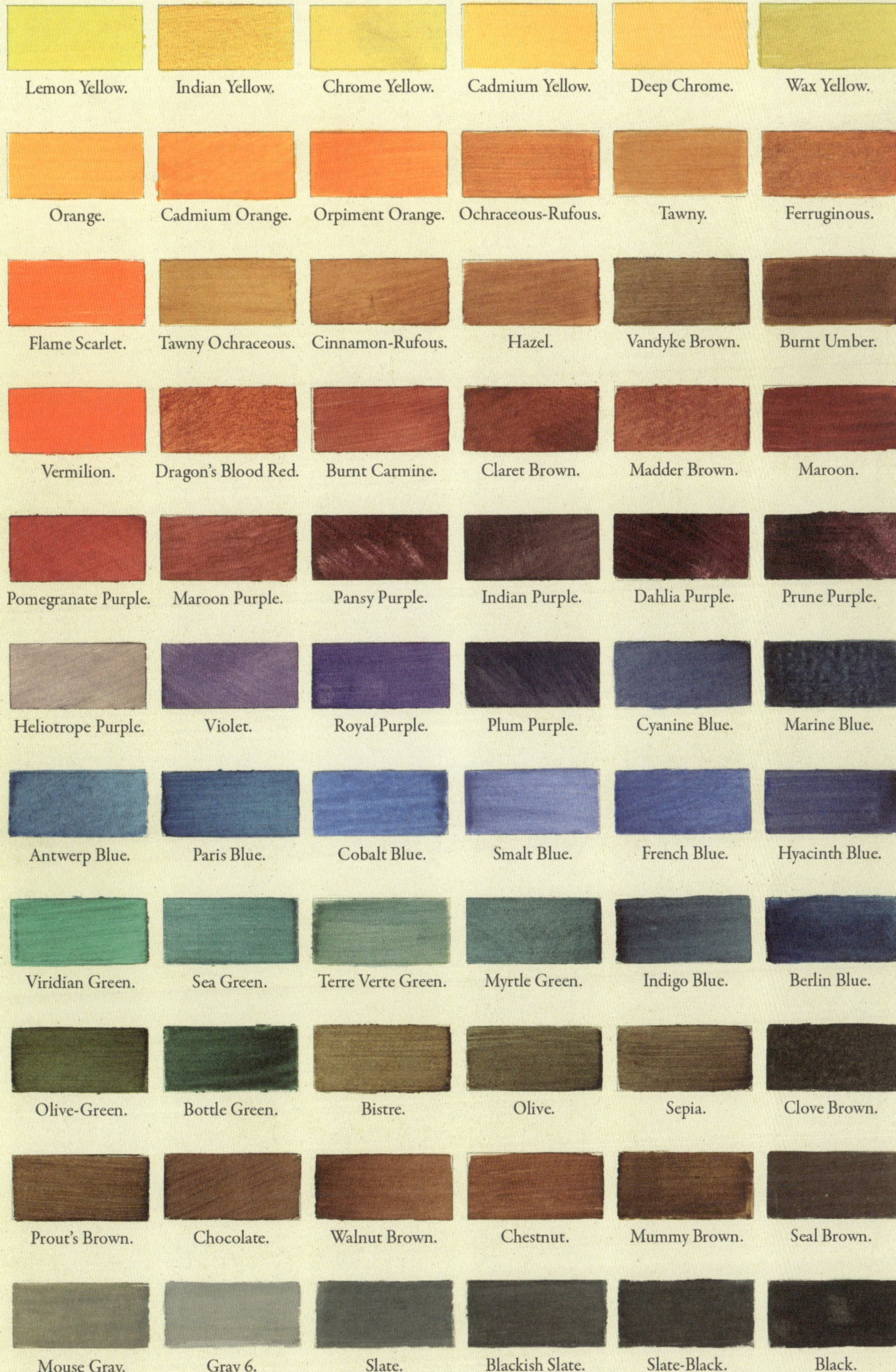

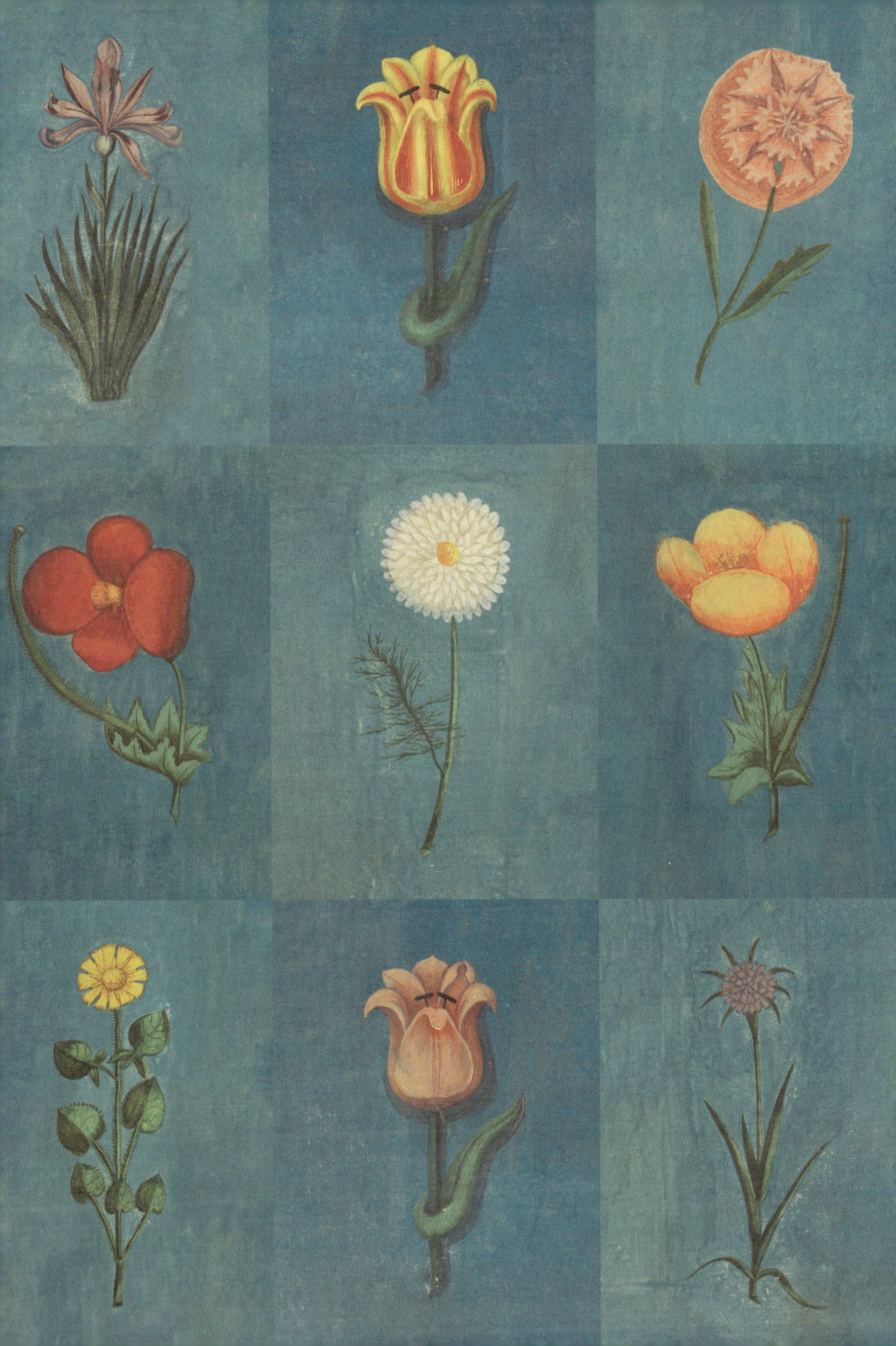

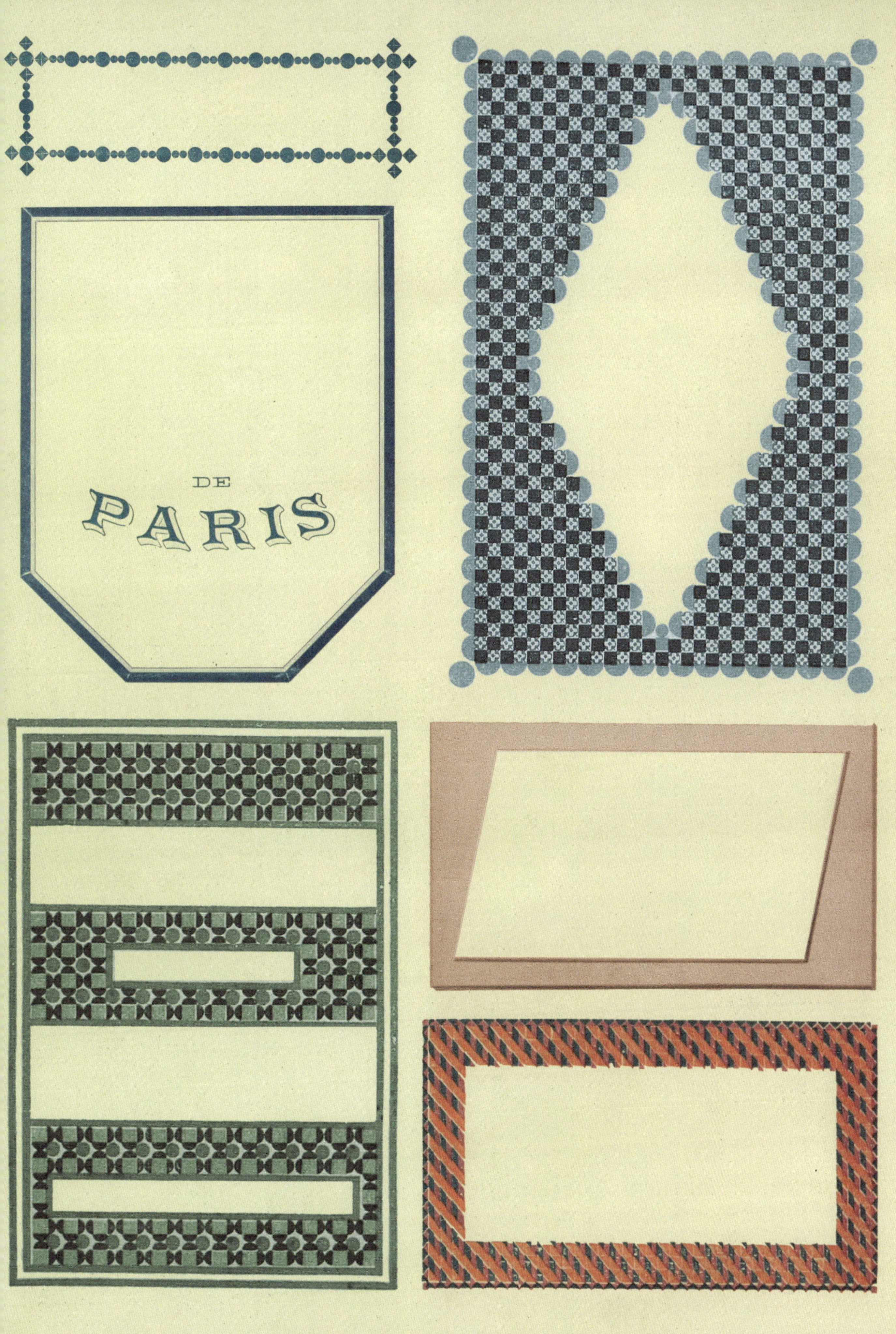
DE
PARIS

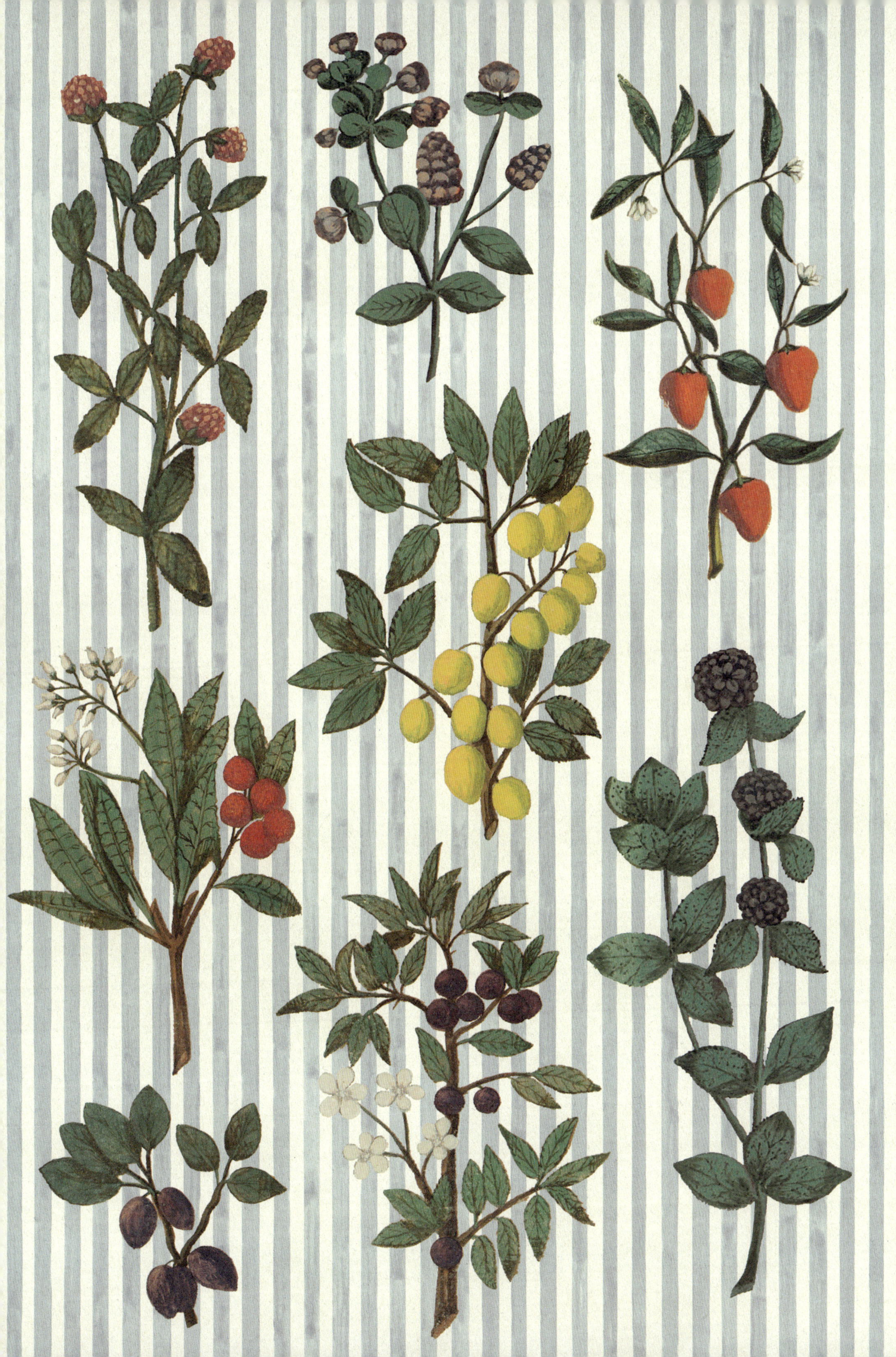

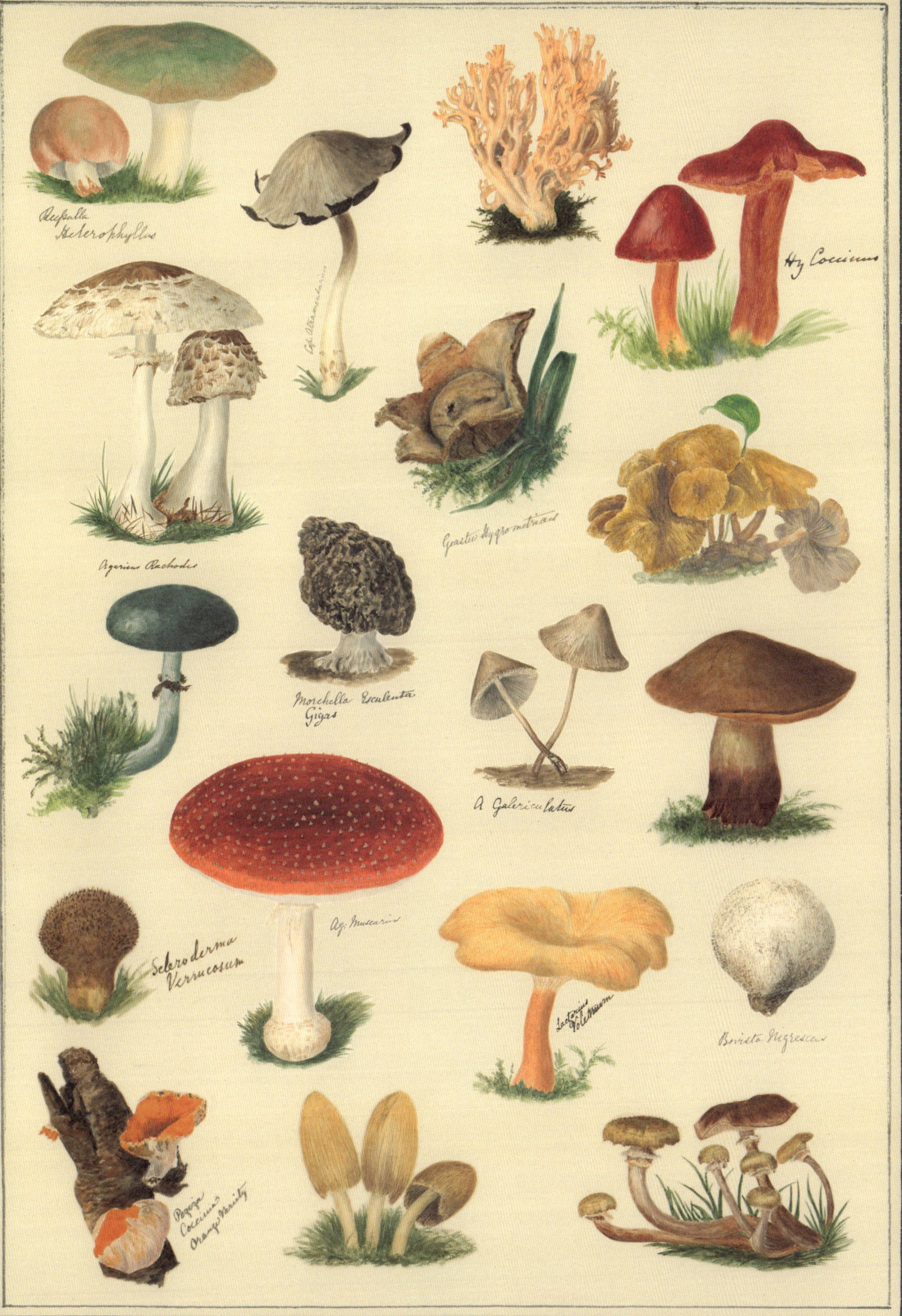
Russula Heterophyllus
Cop. Comatus
Hy. Coccineus
Agaricus Rachodes
Geaster Hygrometricus
Morchella Esculenta Gigas
A. Galericulatus
Scleroderma Verrucosum
Ag. Muscarius
Lactarius Volemum
Bovista Nigrescens
Peziza Coccinea Orange Variety

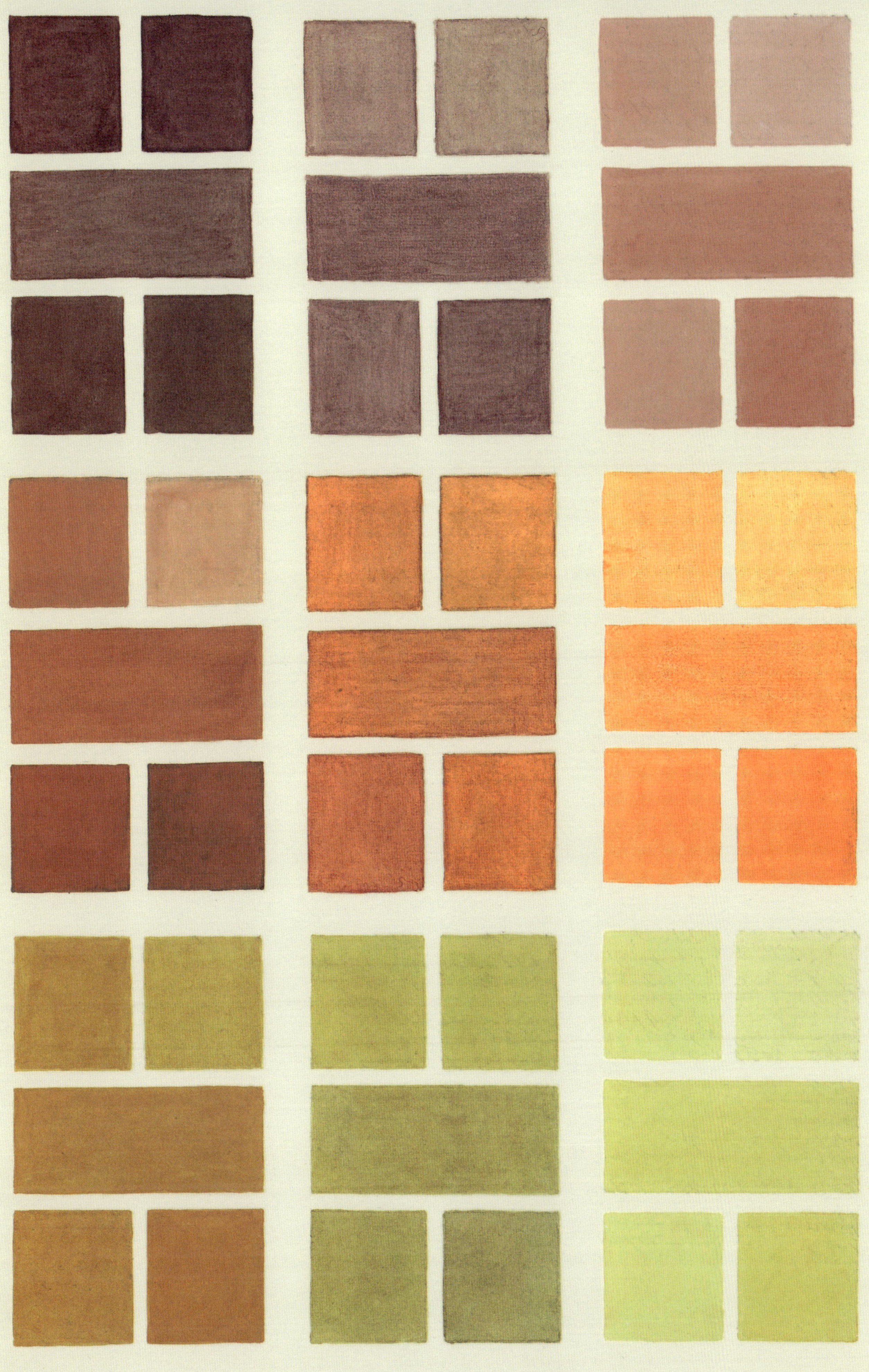

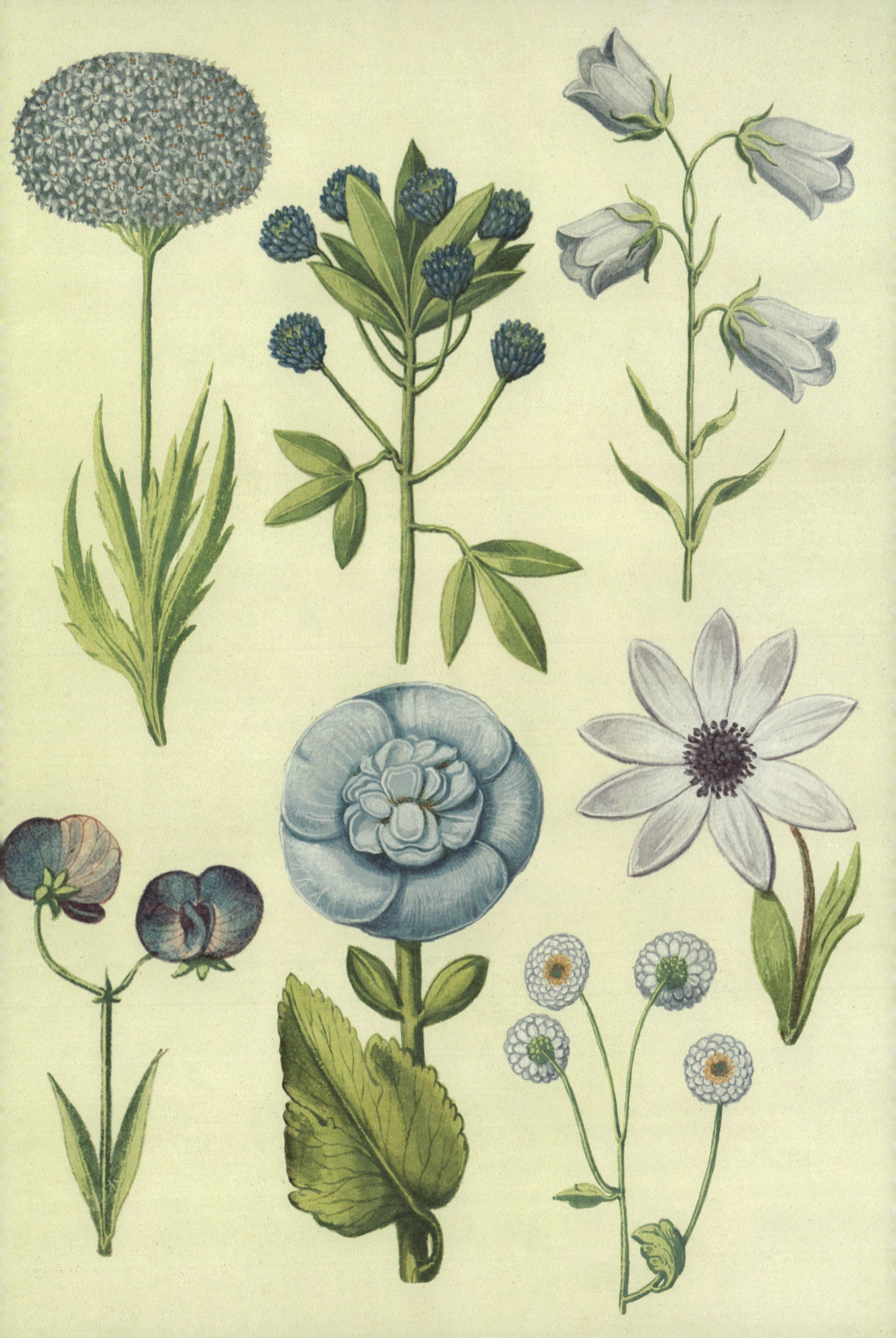

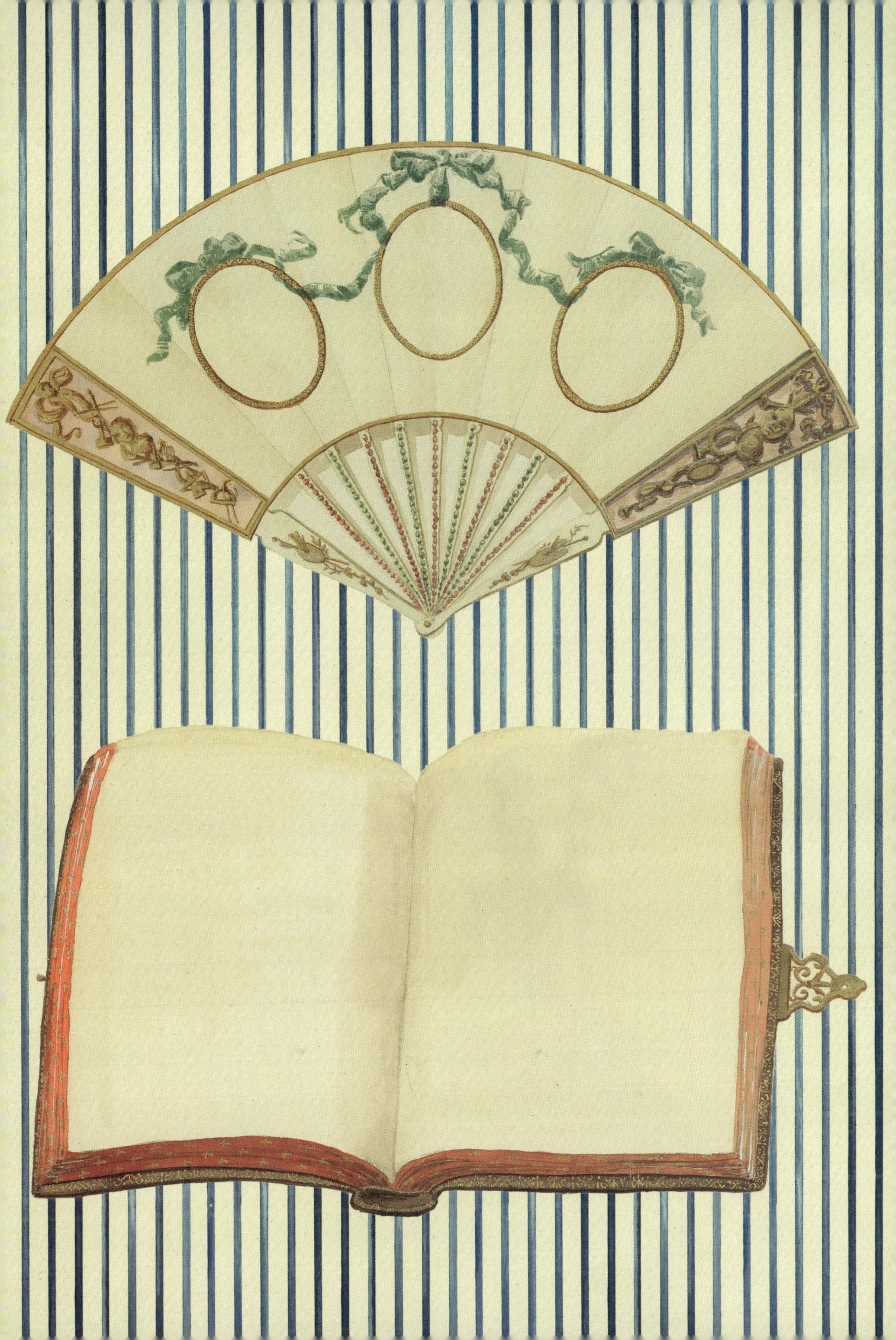

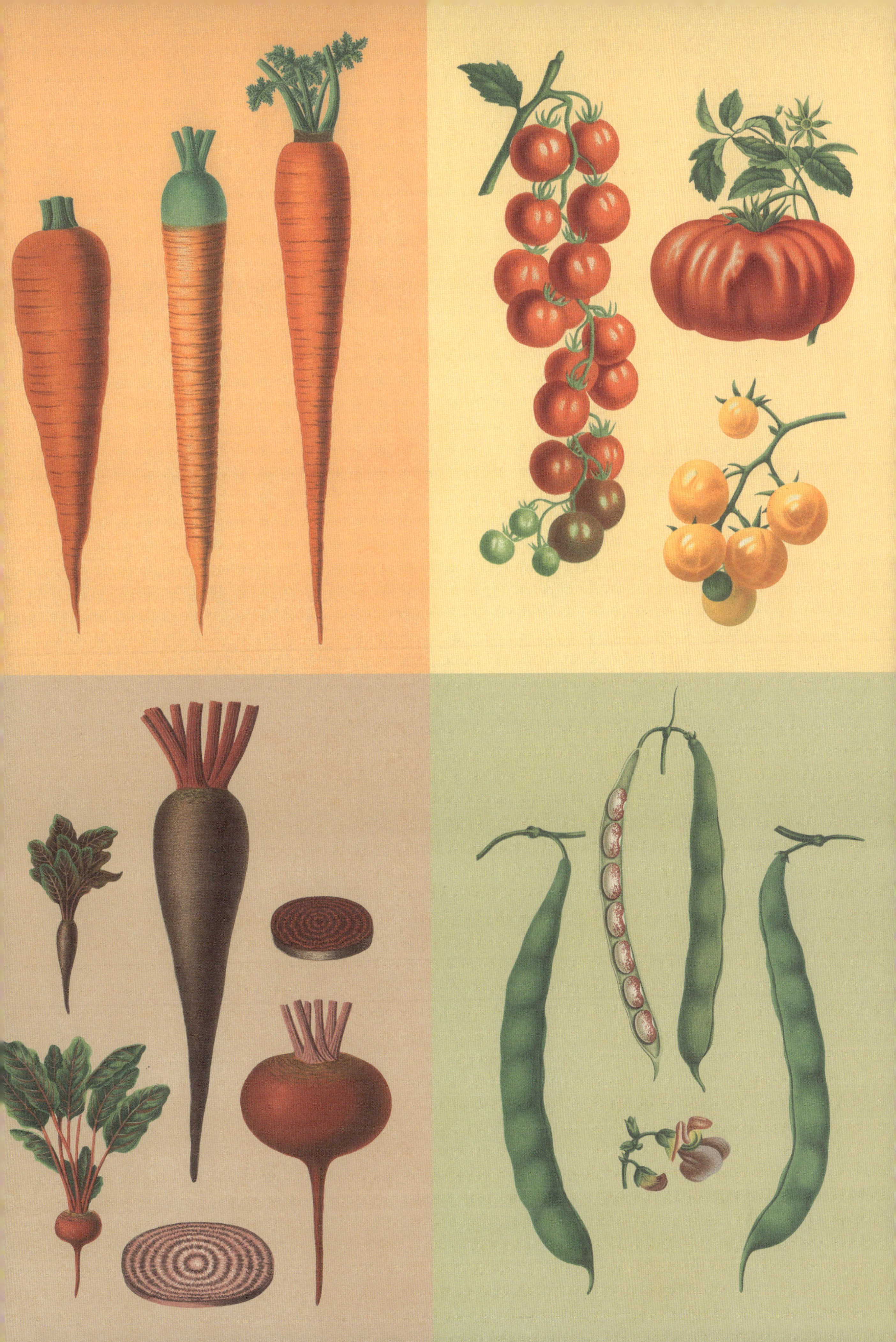

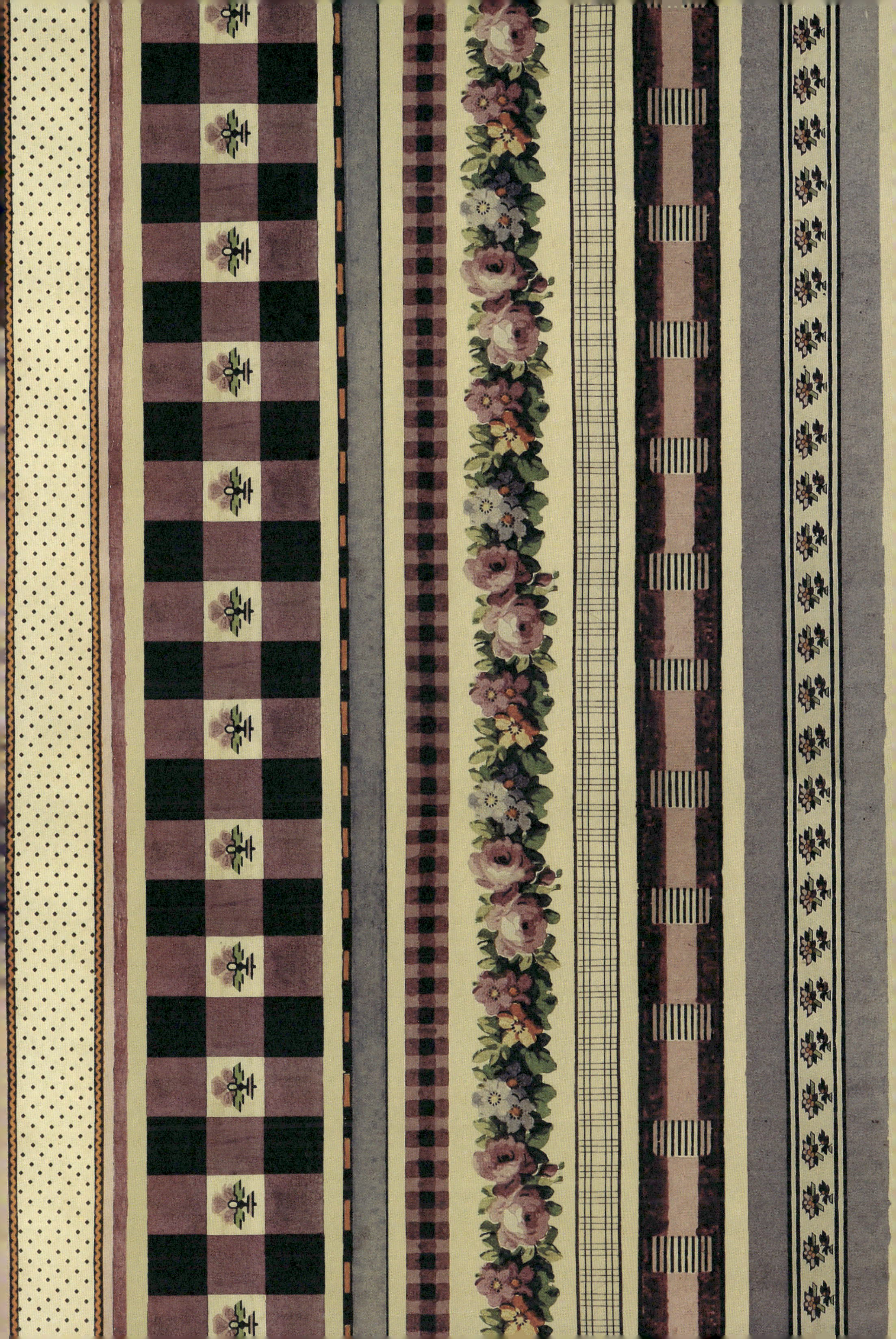

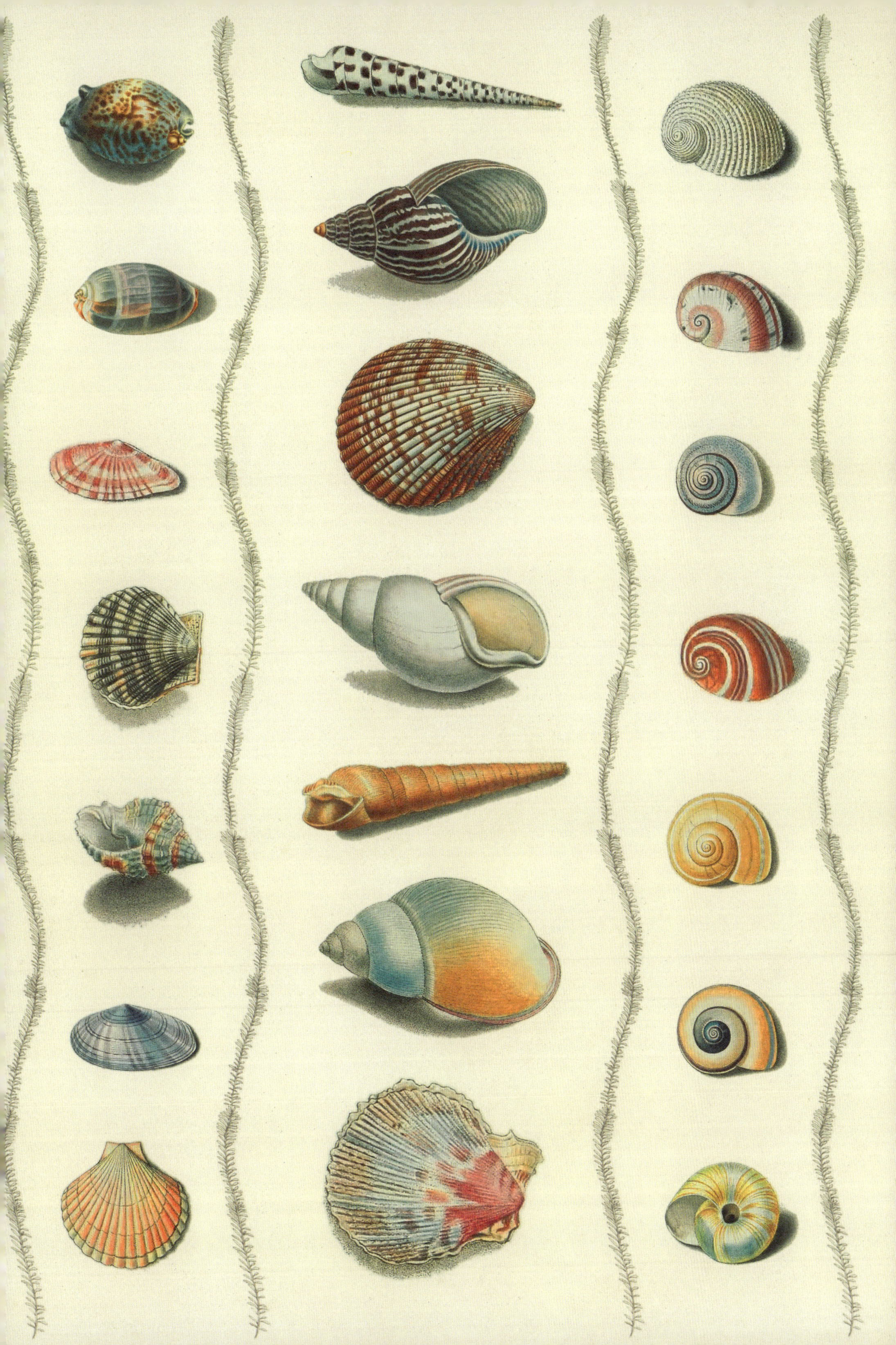

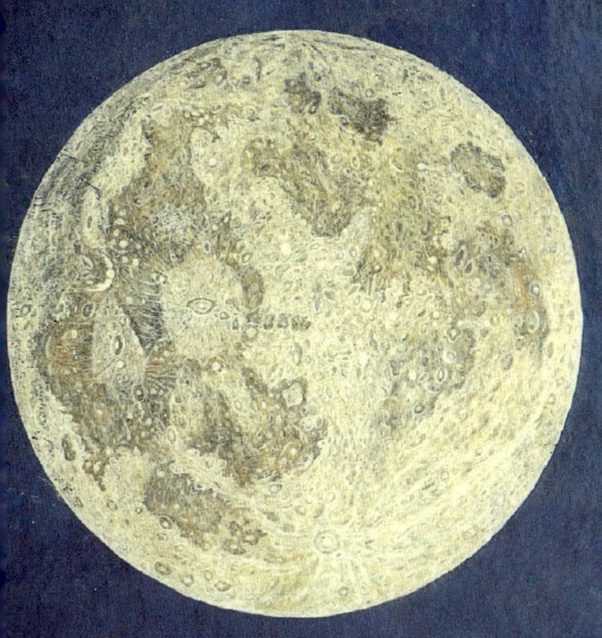

PLENILVNIVM
pinxit ad Archetypum M.C.Eimmarts Norimb.

MERCVRII Phases ab Hevelio observatæ.

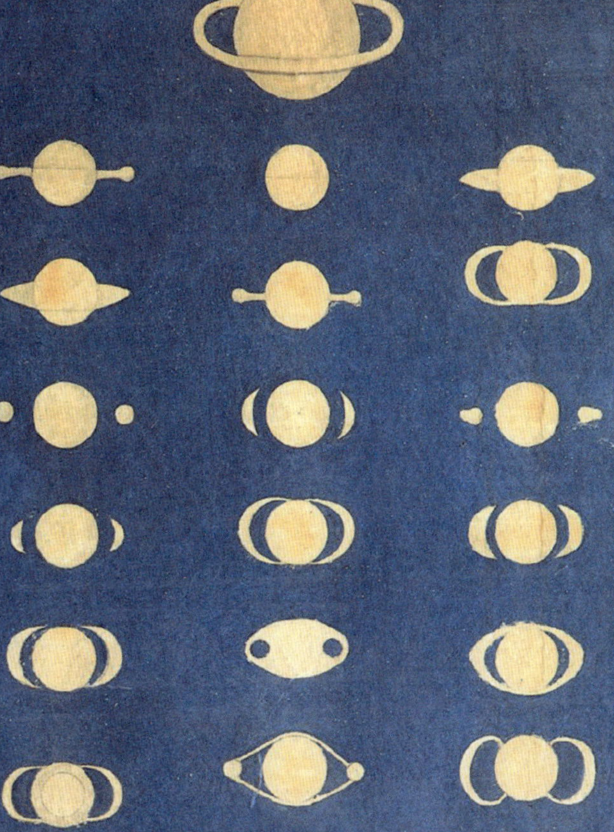

Variæ SATVRNI Phases ab Astronomis observatæ.

VENERIS diversæ Phases ab Astronomis observatæ.

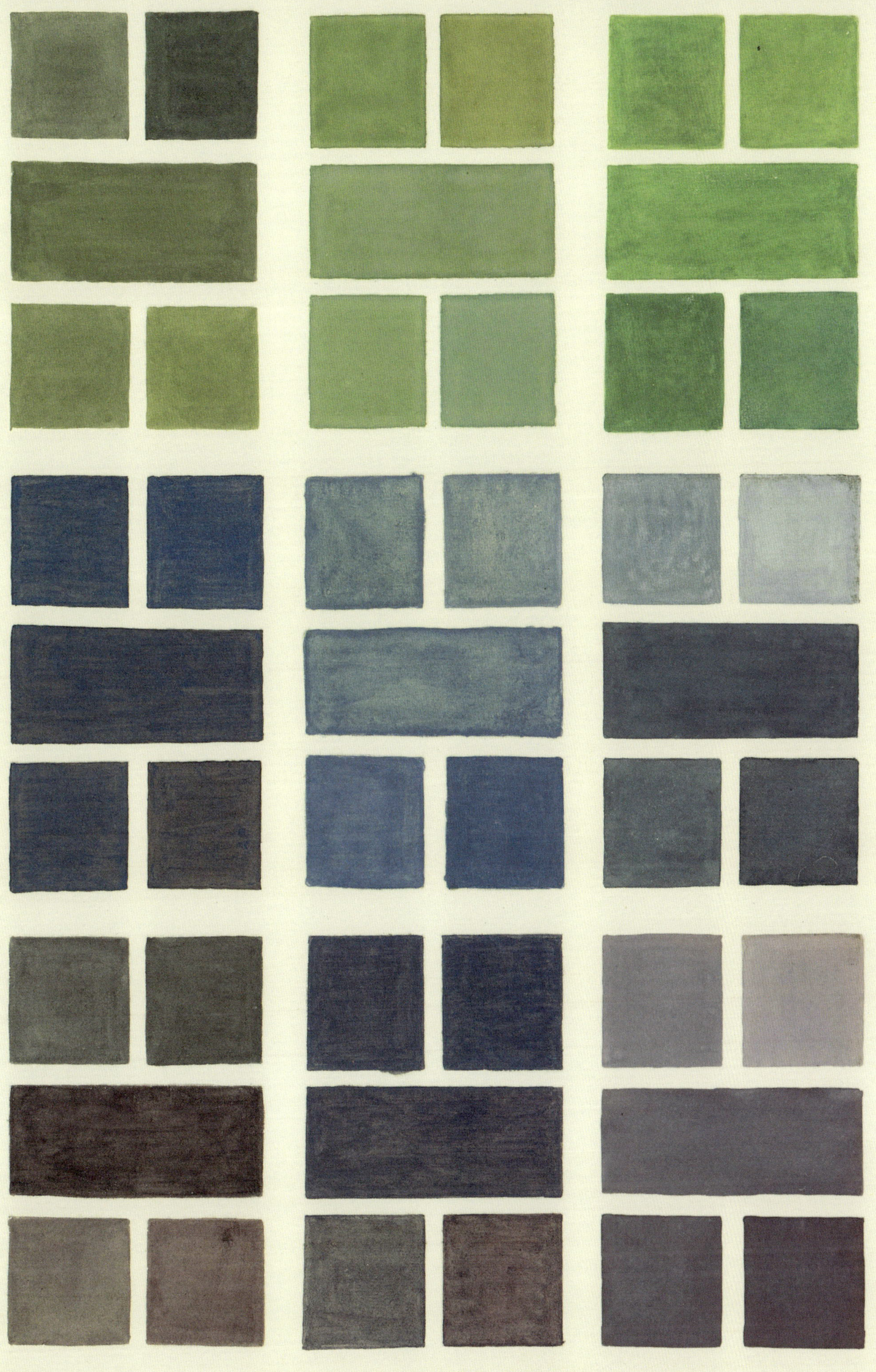

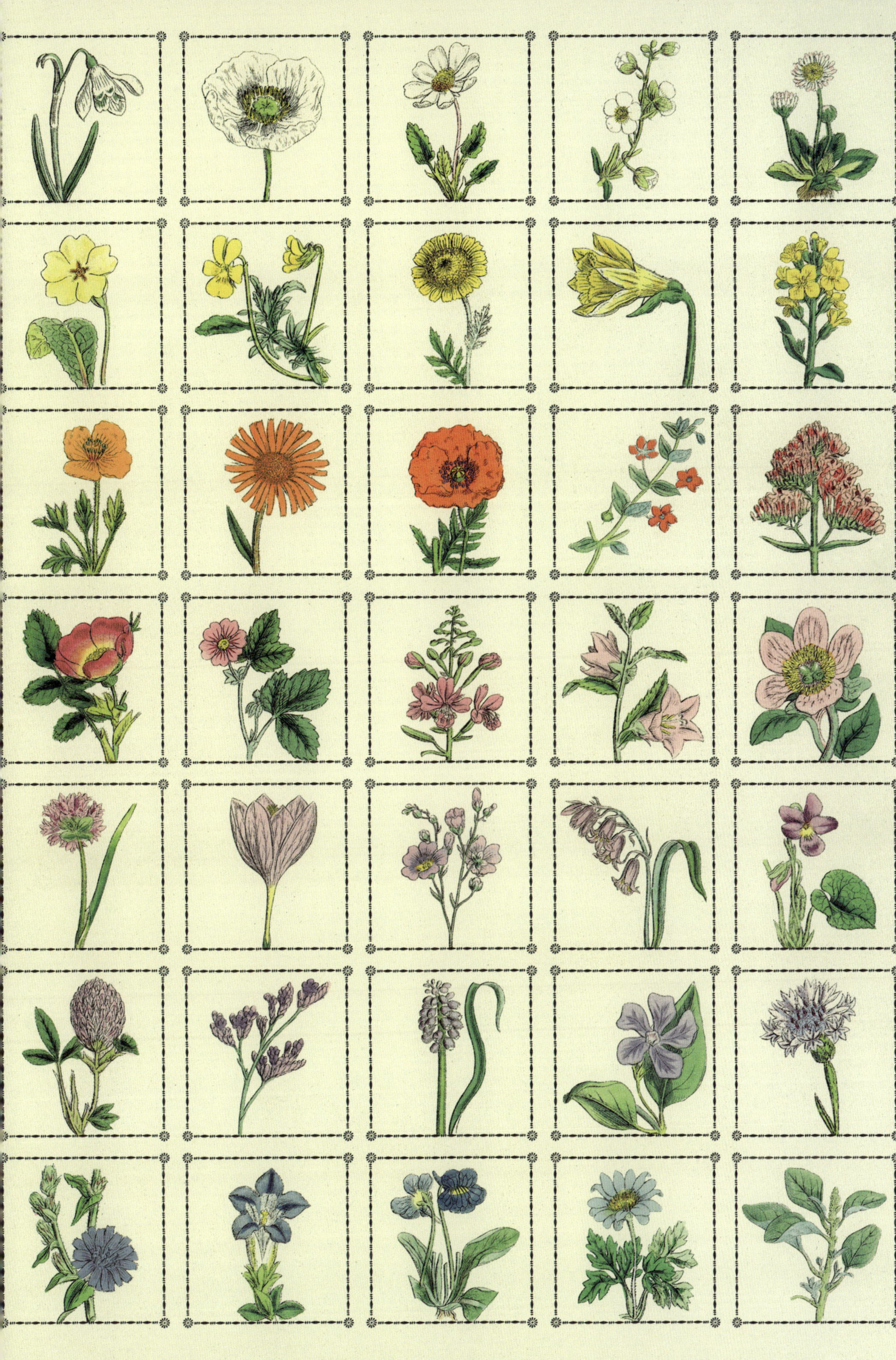

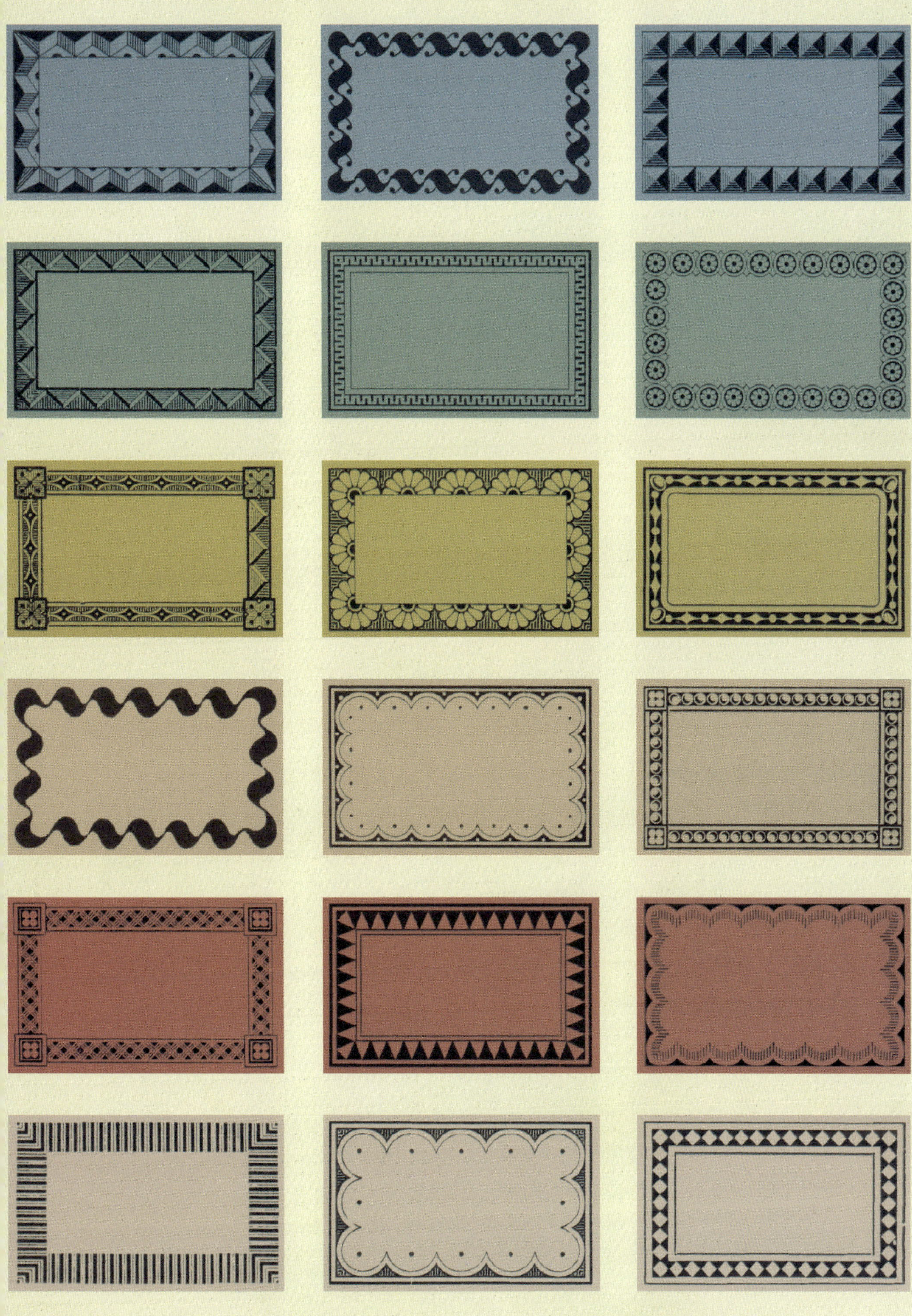

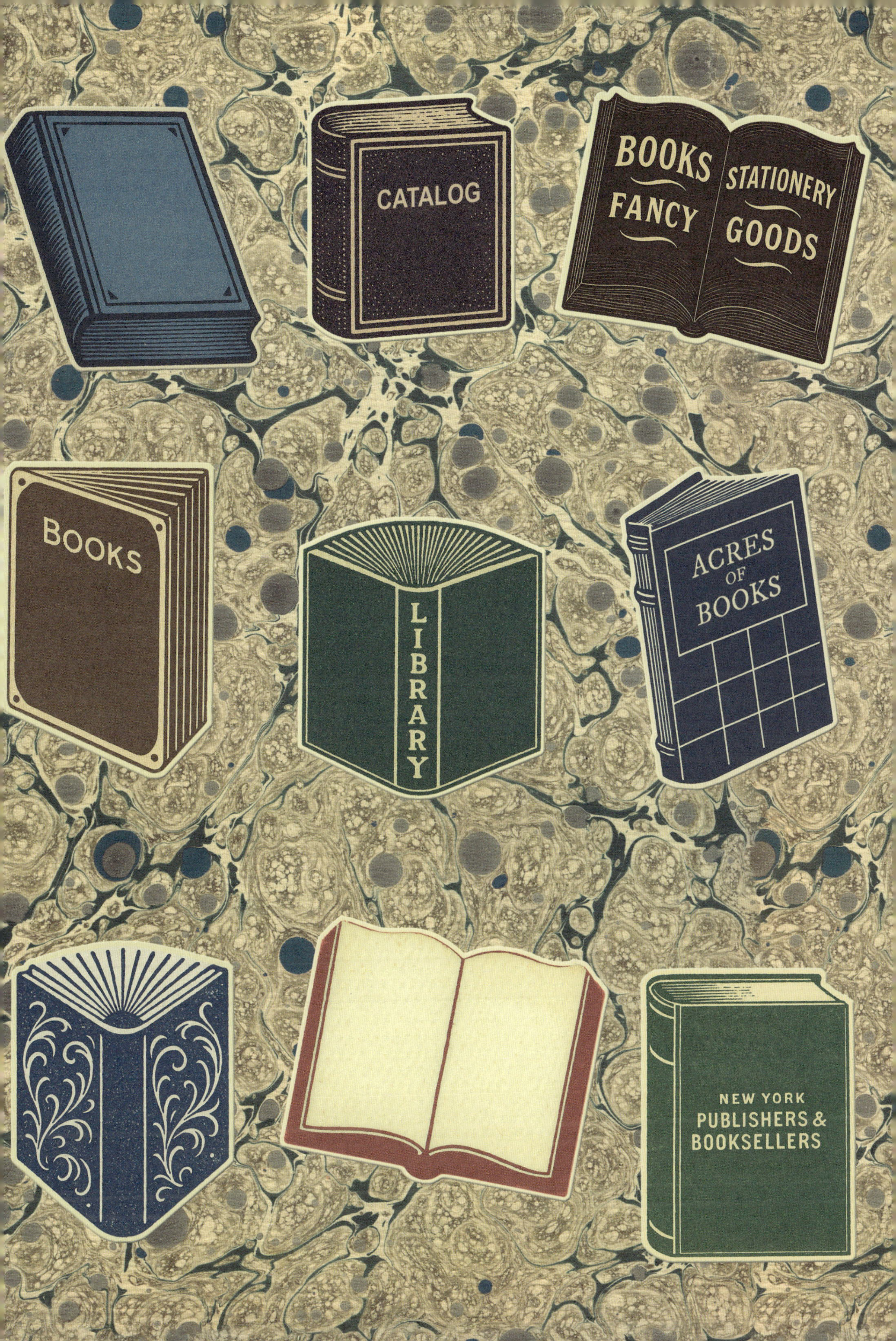

CATALOG
BOOKS
FANCY
STATIONERY
GOODS
BOOKS
LIBRARY
ACRES
OF
BOOKS
NEW YORK
PUBLISHERS &
BOOKSELLERS

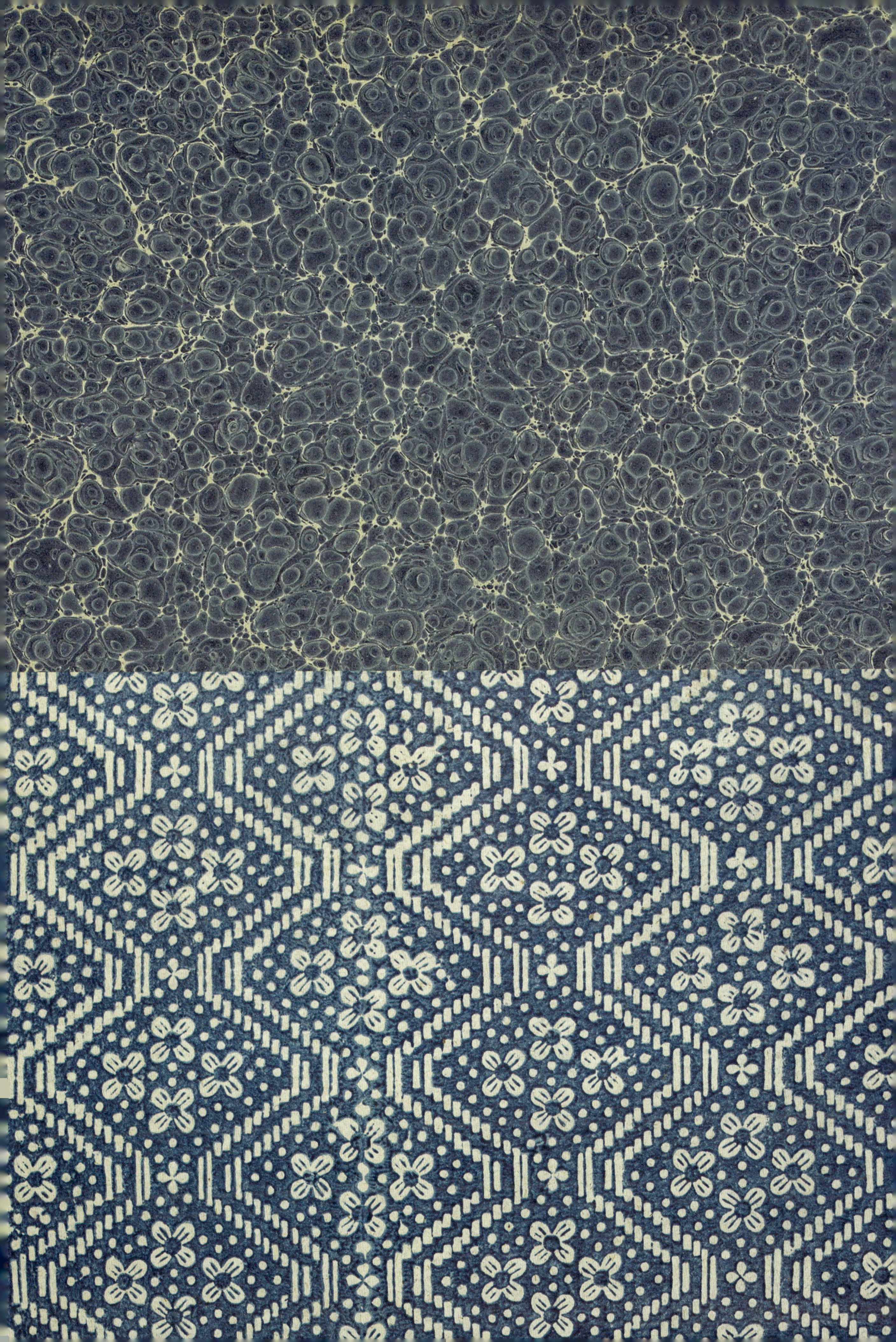

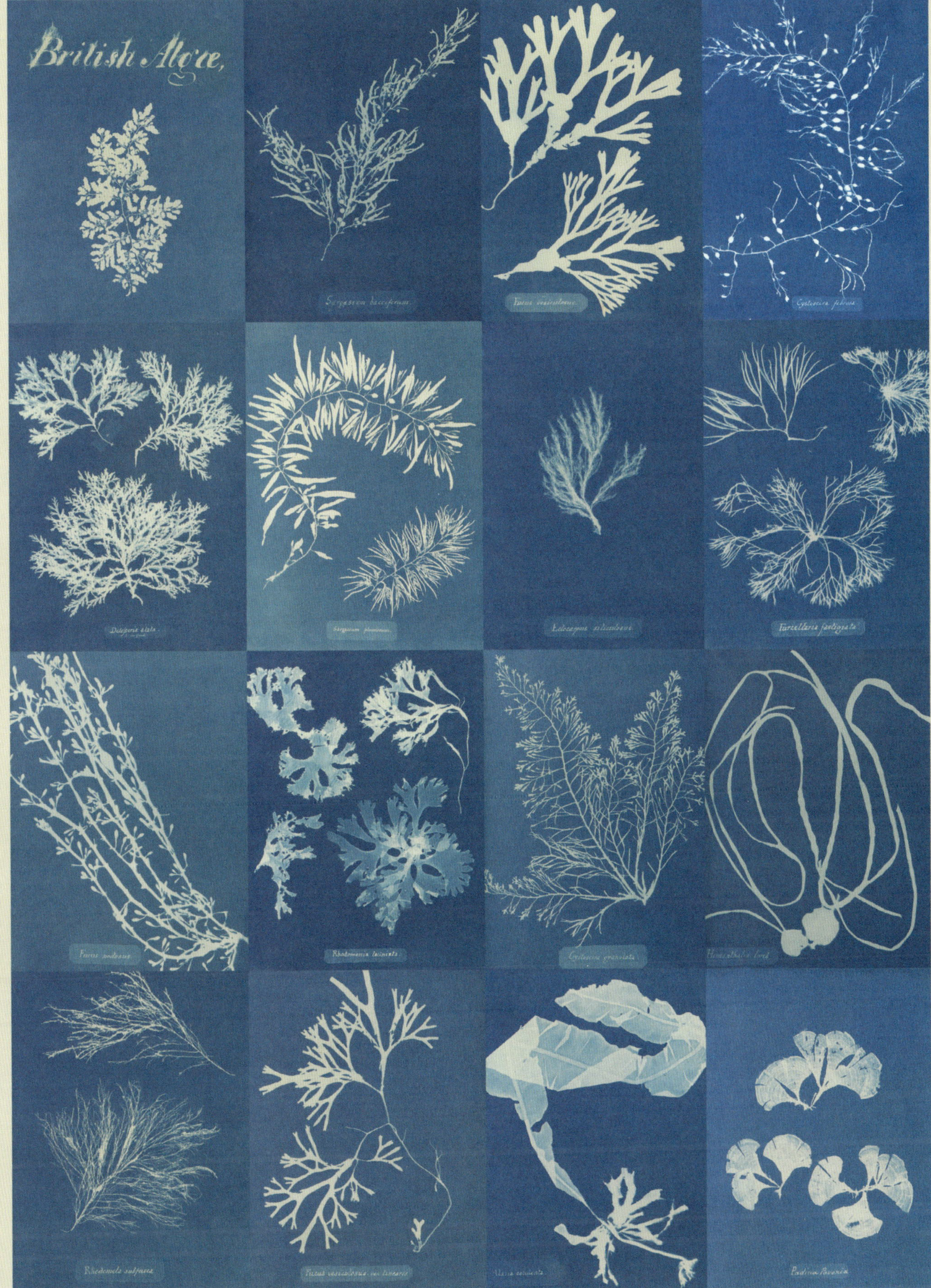
British Algæ,
Sargassum bacciferum.
Fucus vesiculosus.
Cystoseira fibrosa.
Dictyota elata.
Sargassum plumosum.
Ectocarpus siliculosus.
Furcellaria fastigiata.
Fucus nodosus.
Rhodomenia laciniata.
Cystoseira granulata.
Himanthalia lorea.
Rhodomela subfusca.
Fucus vesiculosus var. linearis.
Ulva latissima.
Padina Pavonia.

A A A A A A A A A
A B B B B B C C C
C D D D D D E E E
E E E E E E F F F
F C C C H H H I I
I I I I J J K K L L
L L M M M M M N N N
N O O O O O O O P
P P P Q Q Q R R R R
R R R S S S S S S
S S T T T T T T T
U U U U U U V V V W
W W X X Y Y Y Y Z Z

CARTE POSTALE

CORRESPONDANCE

ADRESSE

A. Leconte, 38, r. Ste-Croix-de-la-Bretonnerie, Paris

CARTE POSTALE

Correspondance

Adresse

Tous les pays étrangers n'acceptent pas la correspondance au recto, se renseigner à la poste

CARTE POSTALE

CORRESPONDANCE

ADRESSE

Imp.-Phot. « L'Abeille », Asnières-Paris

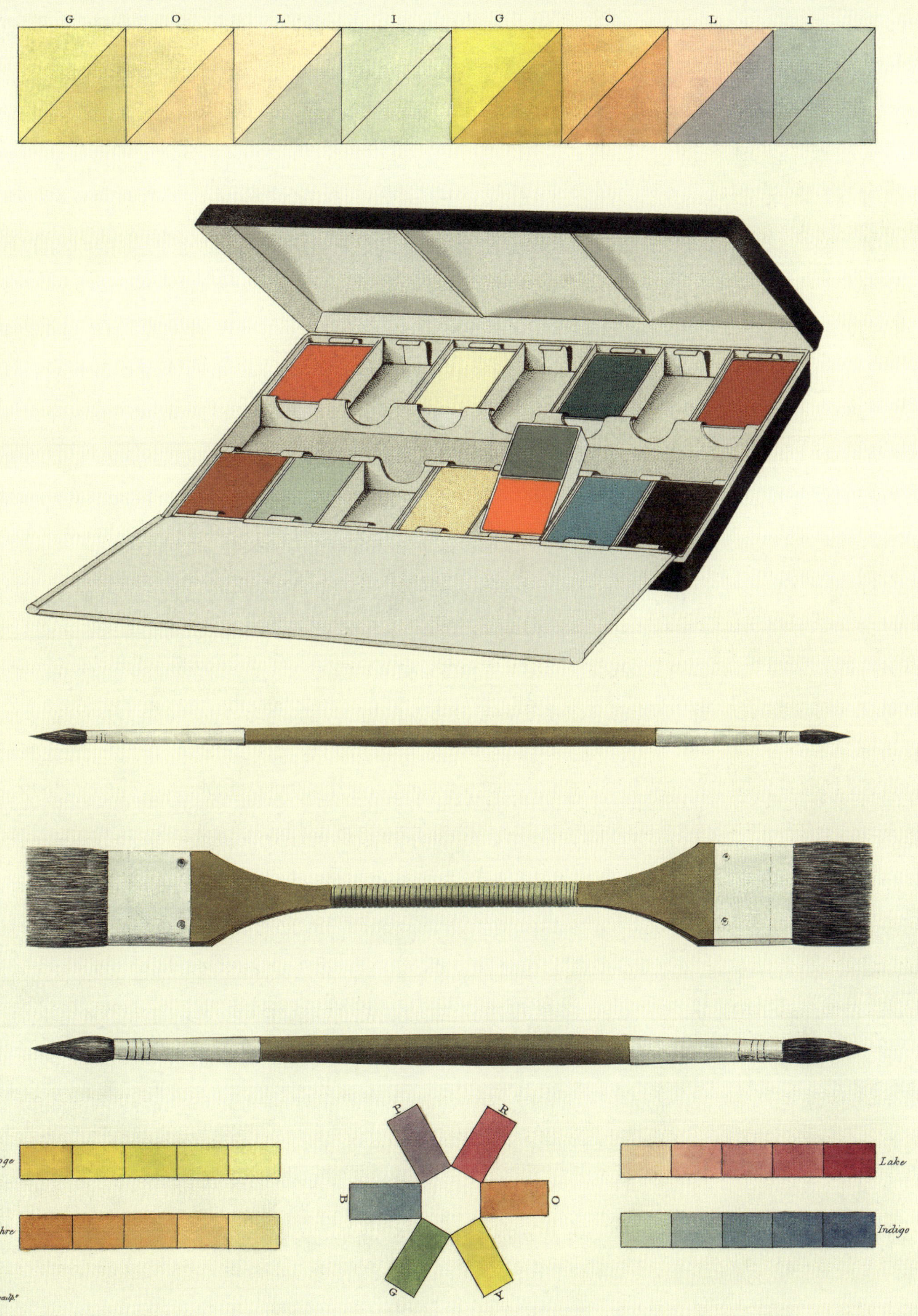

G O L I G O L I
P R
B O
G Y
Gamboge
Ochre
Lake
Indigo
Published & Sold Jan.ʳ 1.1807. by Edw.ᵈ Orme. 59. Bond Street.

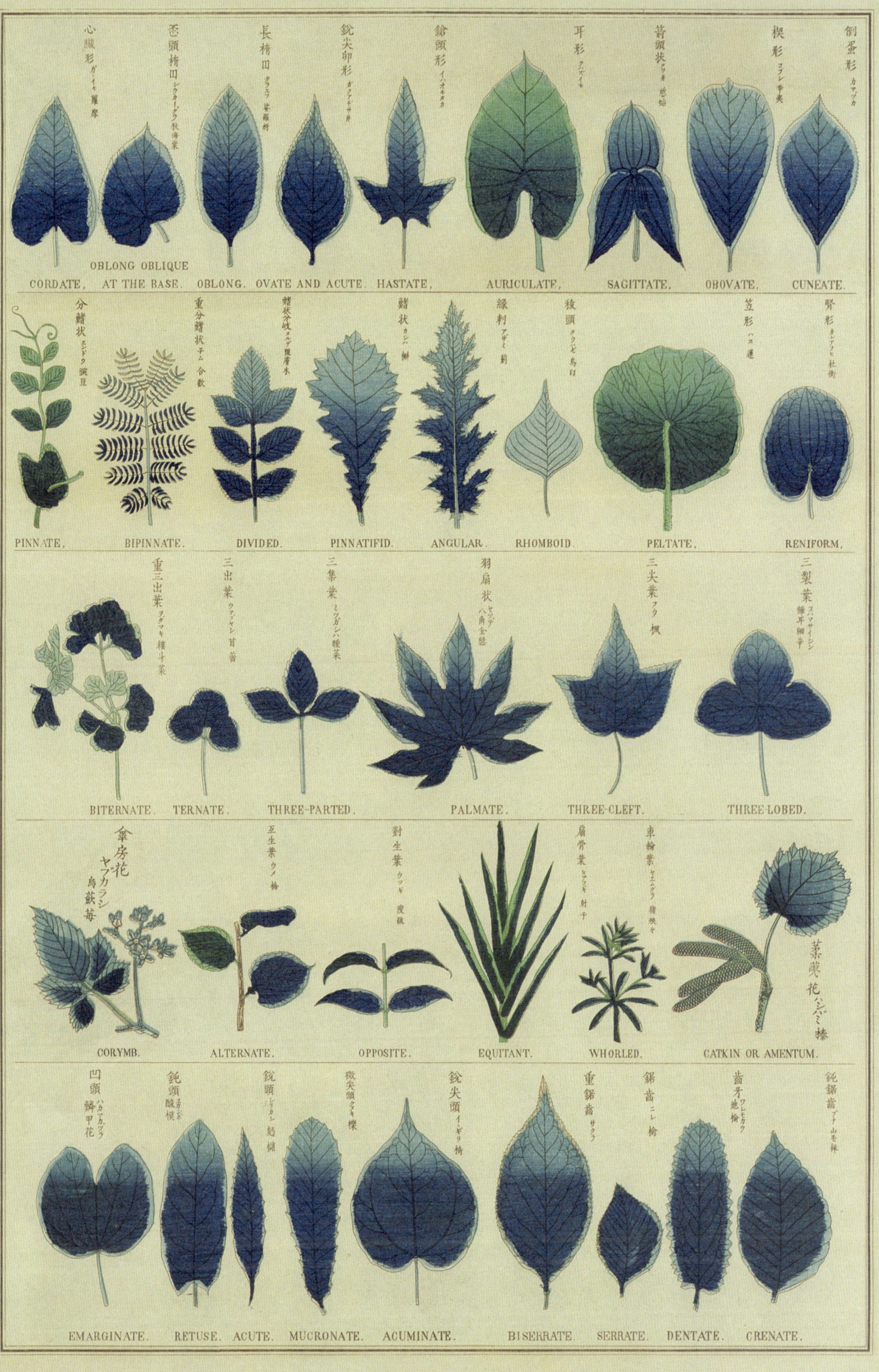
OBLONG OBLIQUE
CORDATE, AT THE BASE. OBLONG. OVATE AND ACUTE. HASTATE, AURICULATE, SAGITTATE, OBOVATE, CUNEATE.
PINNATE, BIPINNATE. DIVIDED. PINNATIFID. ANGULAR. RHOMBOID. PELTATE, RENIFORM,
BITERNATE. TERNATE. THREE-PARTED. PALMATE. THREE-CLEFT. THREE-LOBED.
CORYMB. ALTERNATE. OPPOSITE. EQUITANT. WHORLED. CATKIN OR AMENTUM.
EMARGINATE. RETUSE. ACUTE. MUCRONATE. ACUMINATE. BISERRATE. SERRATE. DENTATE. CRENATE.

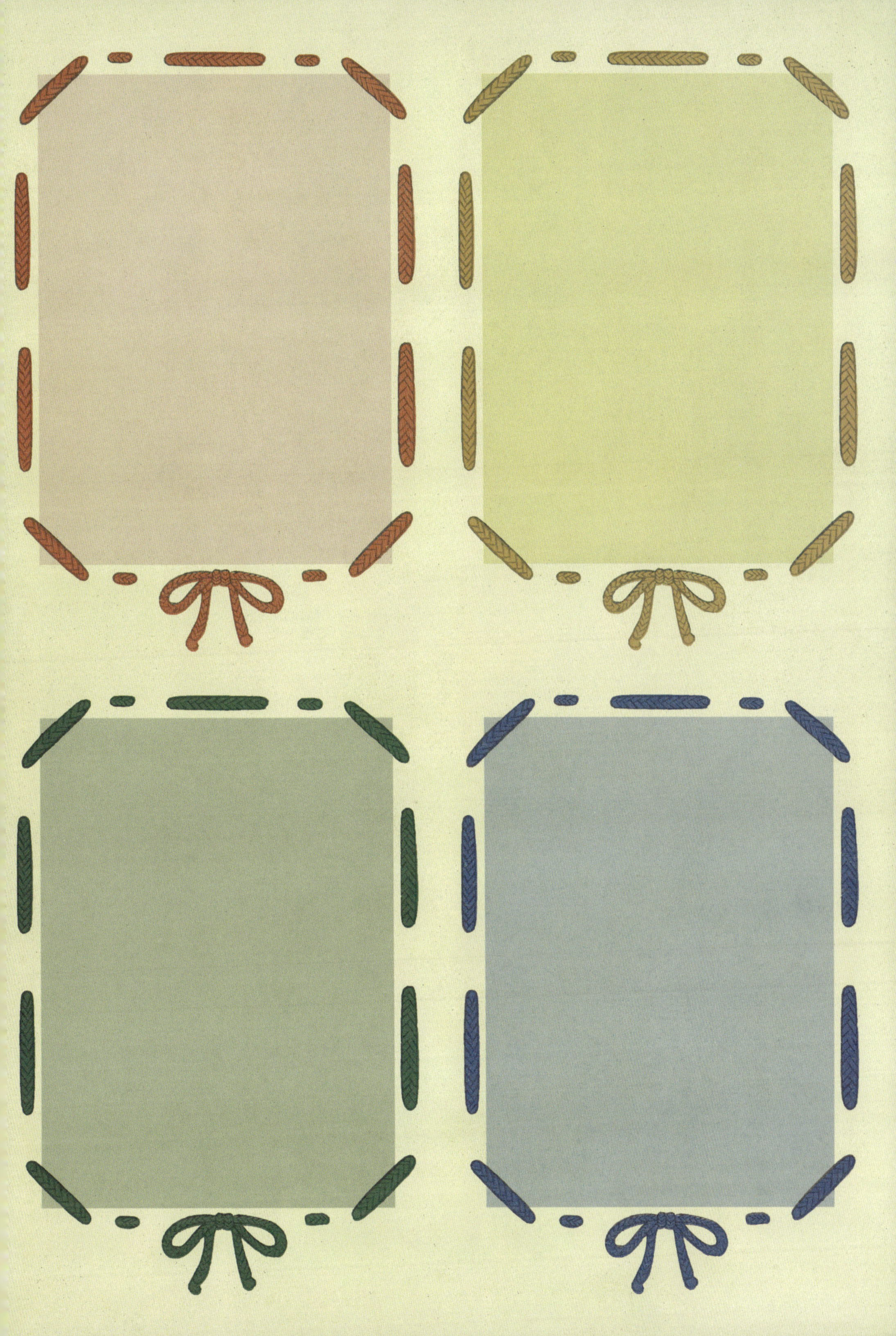

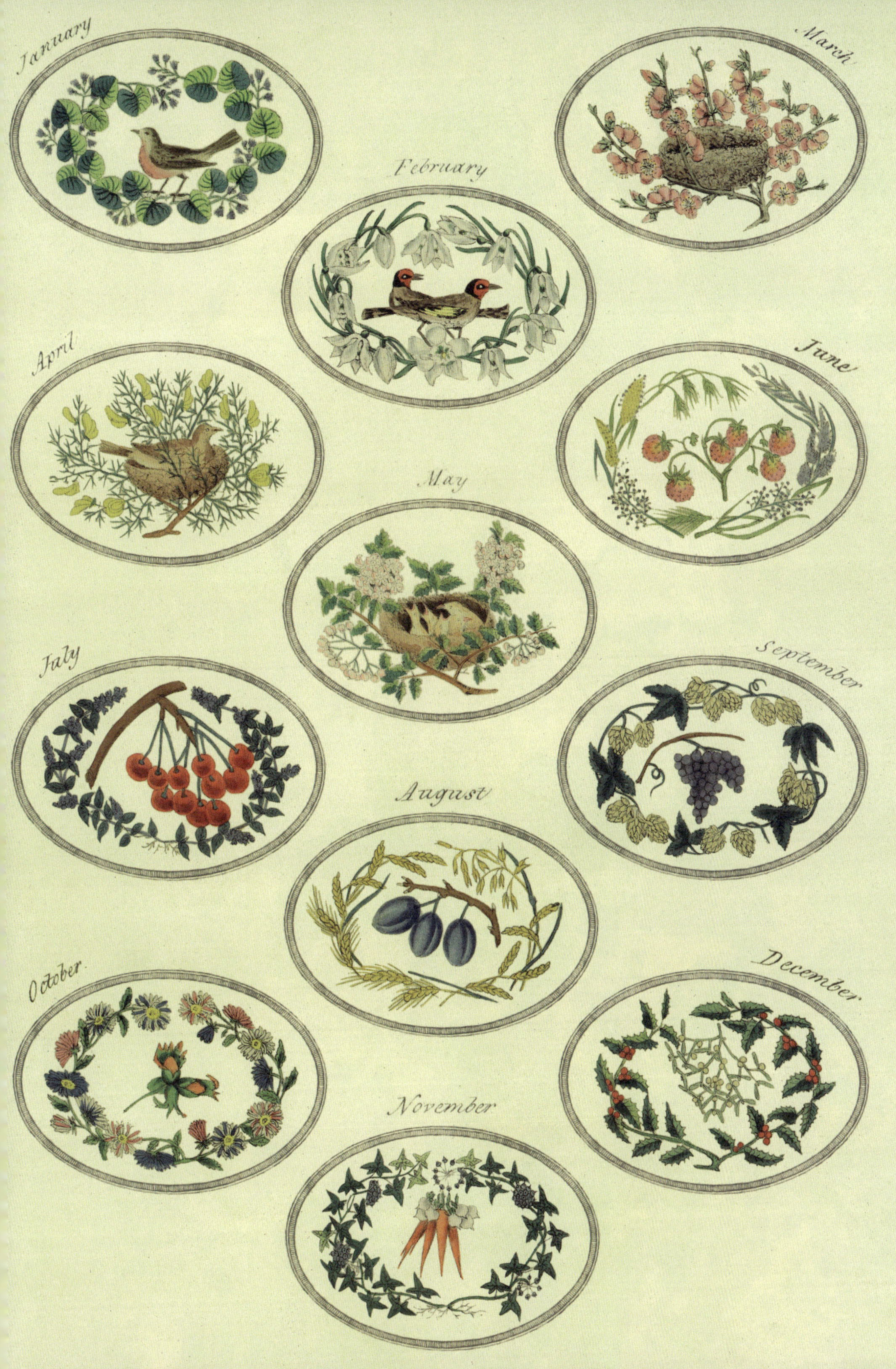

January
February
March
April
May
June
July
August
September
October
November
December

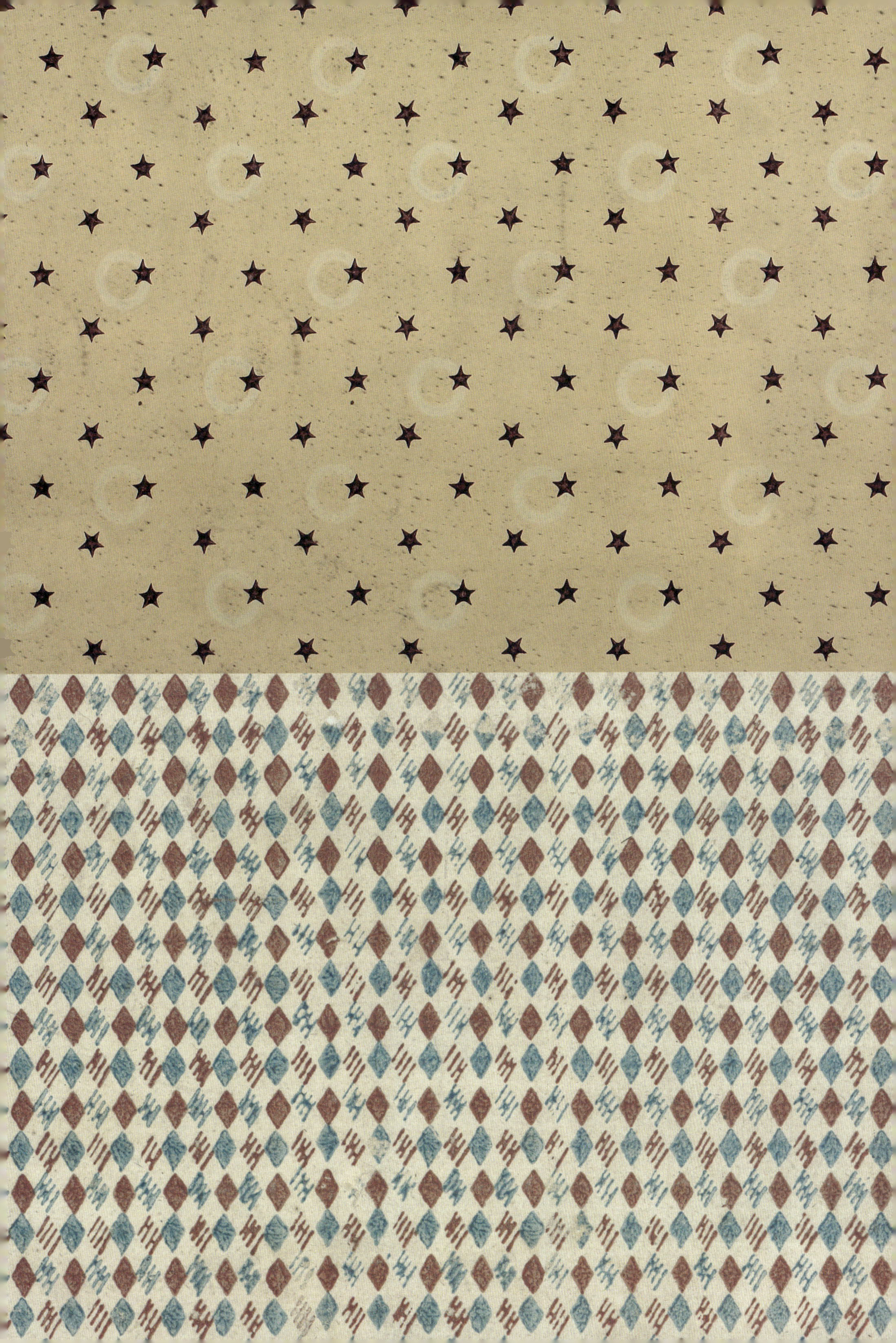

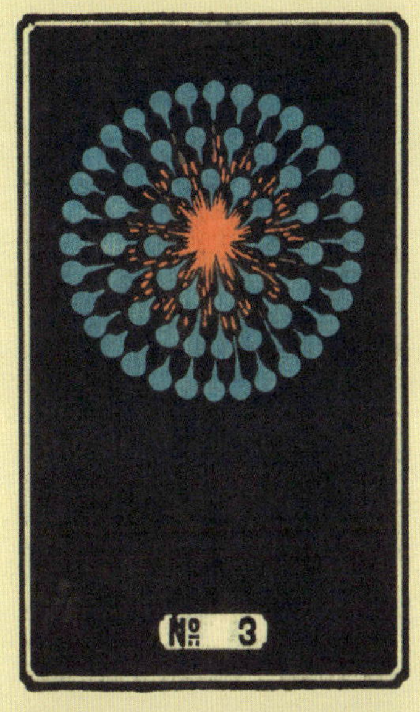

№ 3

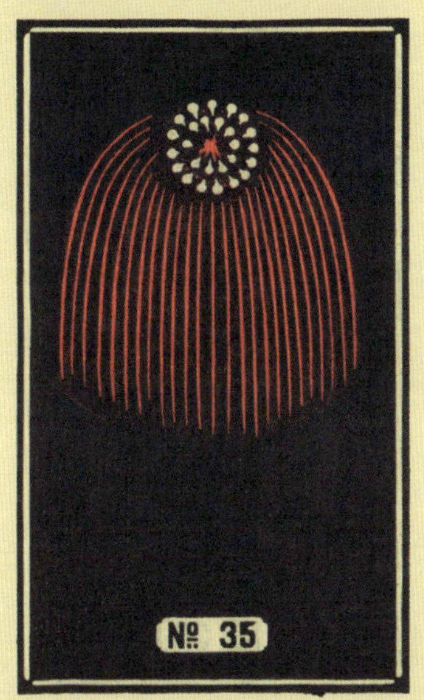

№ 35

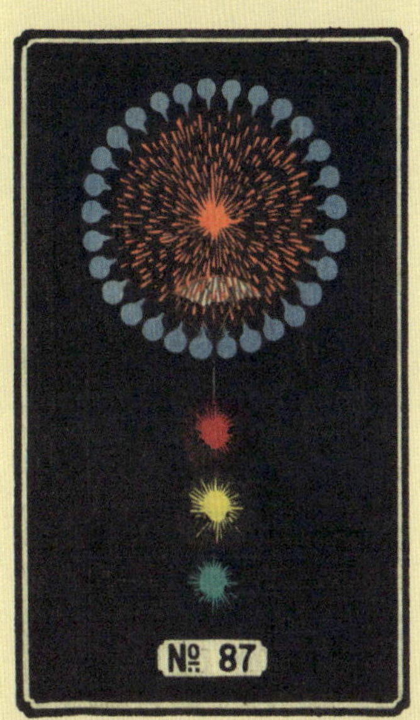

№ 87

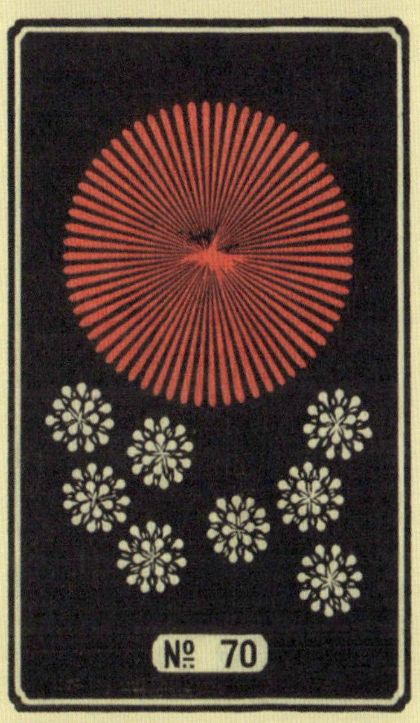

№ 70

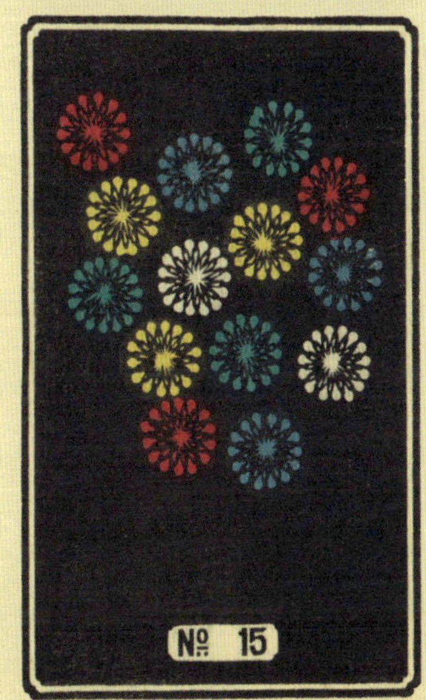

№ 15

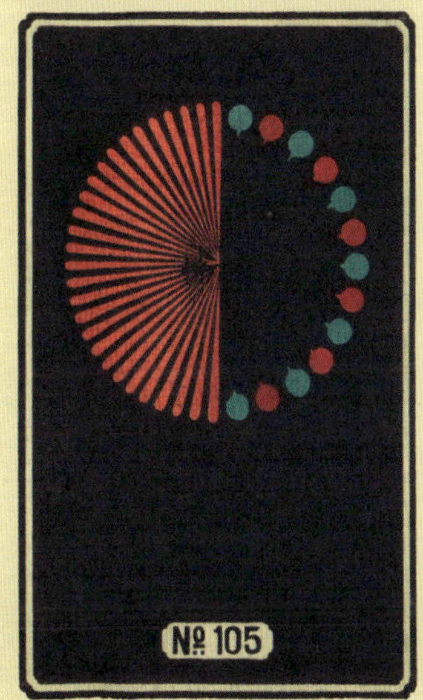

№ 105

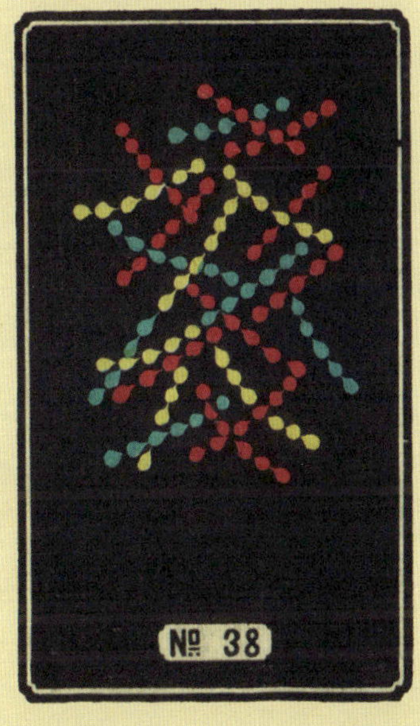

№ 38

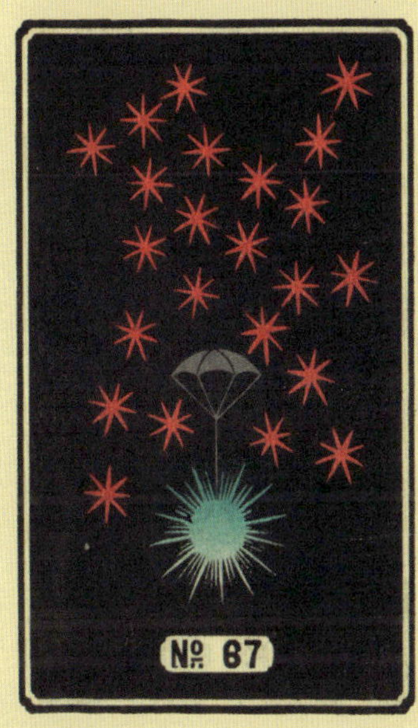

№ 67

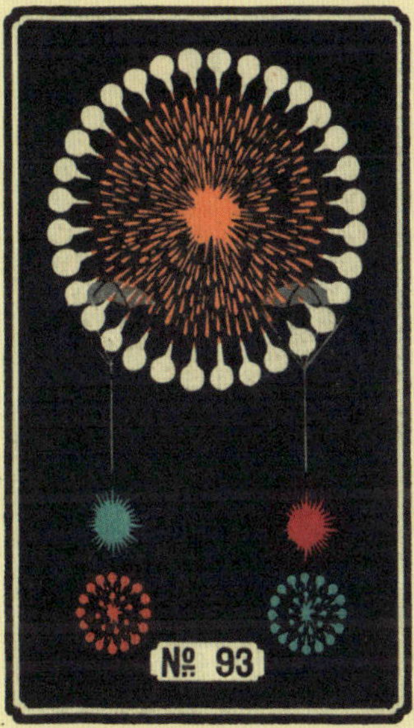

№ 93

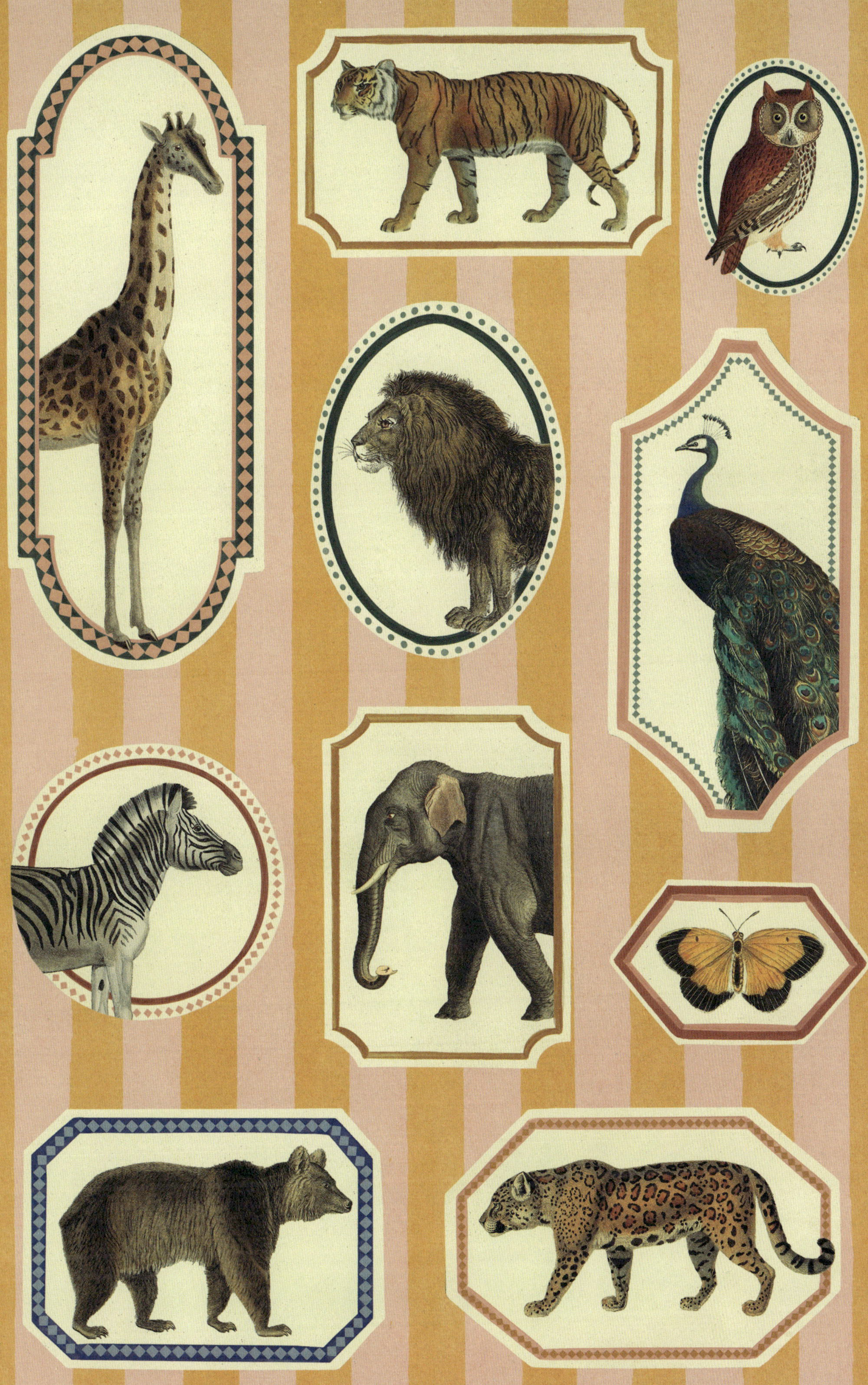

a a a a a a a a
a b b b b b c c
c d d d d e e e
e e e e e e f f f
f g g g g h h h i i
i i i i j j j k k k l l
l l m m m m m n n
n o o o o o o o p
p p p q q r r r r
r r s s s s s s
s s t t t t t t t
u u u u u u v v v w
w w x x y y y z z

Snow White.	Blackish Grey.	Berlin Blue.	Celandine Green.	Siskin Green.	Dutch Orange.	Carmine Red.
Reddish White.	Greyish Black	Verditter Blue	Mountain Green.	Sulphur Yellow.	Buff Orange.	Lake Red.
Purplish White.	Bluish Black	Greenish Blue	Leek Green.	Primrose Yellow.	Orpiment Orange.	Crimson Red.
Yellowish White.	Greenish Black	Greyish Blue.	Blackish Green.	Wax Yellow.	Brownish Orange.	Purplish Red.
Orange coloured White.	Pitch or Brownish Black	Bluish Lilac Purple.	Verdigris Green.	Lemon Yellow.	Reddish Orange.	Cochineal Red.
Greenish White.	Reddish Black	Bluish Purple.	Bluish Green.	Gamboge Yellow.	Deep Reddish Orange.	Veinous Blood Red.
Skimmed milk White.	Ink Black	Violet Purple.	Apple Green.	Kings Yellow.	Tile Red.	Brownish Purple Red.
Greyish White.	Velvet Black	Pansy Purple.	Emerald Green.	Saffron Yellow.	Hyacinth Red.	Chocolate Red.
Ash Grey.	Scotch Blue	Campanula Purple.	Grass Green	Gallstone Yellow.	Scarlet Red.	Brownish Red.
Smoke Grey.	Prussian Blue.	Imperial Purple.	Duck Green	Honey Yellow.	Vermillion Red.	Deep Orange-coloured Brown.
French Grey.	Indigo Blue	Auricula Purple.	Sap Green.	Straw Yellow.	Aurora Red.	Deep Reddish Brown.
Pearl Grey.	China Blue	Plum Purple.	Pistachio Green.	Wine Yellow.	Arterial Blood Red.	Umber Brown.
Yellowish Grey.	Azure Blue.	Red Lilac Purple.	Asparagus Green.	Sienna Yellow.	Flesh Red.	Chesnut Brown.
Bluish Grey.	Ultramarine Blue.	Lavender Purple.	Olive Green.	Ochre Yellow.	Rose Red.	Yellowish Brown.
Greenish Grey.	Flax-flower Blue.	Pale Blackish Purple.	Oil Green.	Cream Yellow.	Peach Blossom Red.	Wood Brown.

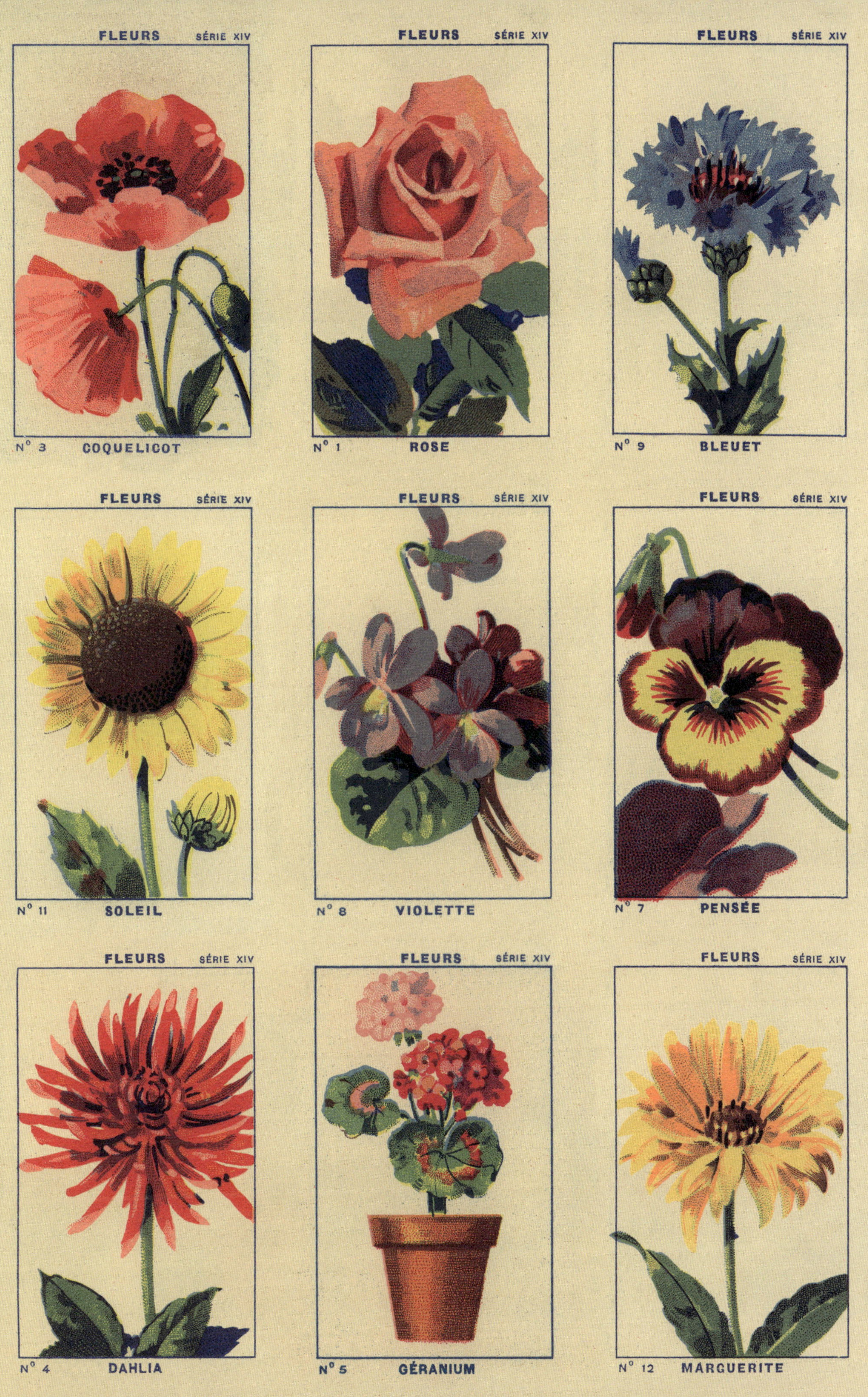

FLEURS   SÉRIE XIV
FLEURS   SÉRIE XIV
FLEURS   SÉRIE XIV
N° 3   COQUELICOT
N° 1   ROSE
N° 9   BLEUET
FLEURS   SÉRIE XIV
FLEURS   SÉRIE XIV
FLEURS   SÉRIE XIV
N° 11   SOLEIL
N° 8   VIOLETTE
N° 7   PENSÉE
FLEURS   SÉRIE XIV
FLEURS   SÉRIE XIV
FLEURS   SÉRIE XIV
N° 4   DAHLIA
N° 5   GÉRANIUM
N° 12   MARGUERITE

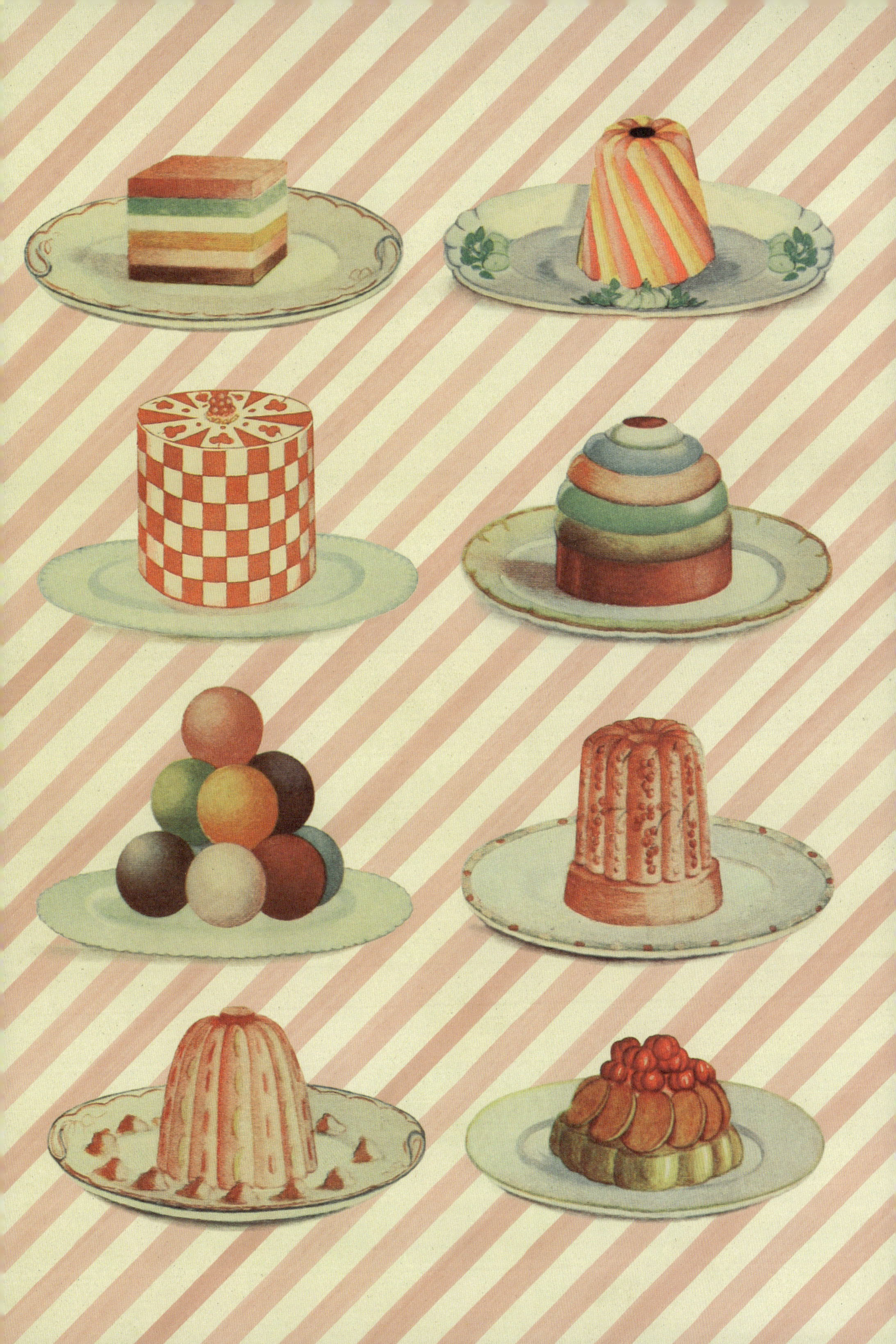

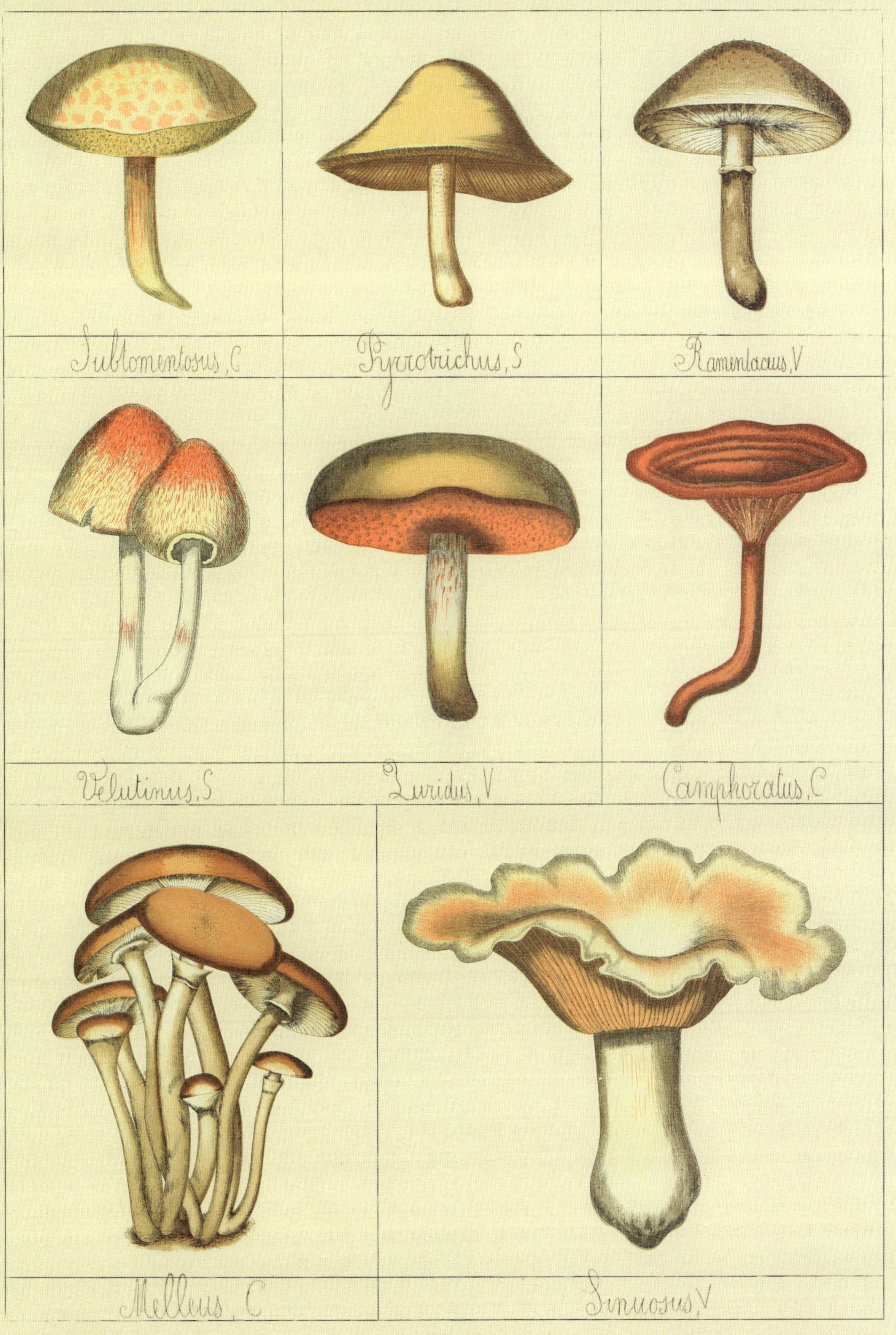

Sublomentosus, C
Pyrrotrichus, S
Ramentacus, V
Velutinus, S
Luridus, V
Camphoratus, C
Melleus, C
Sinuosus, V

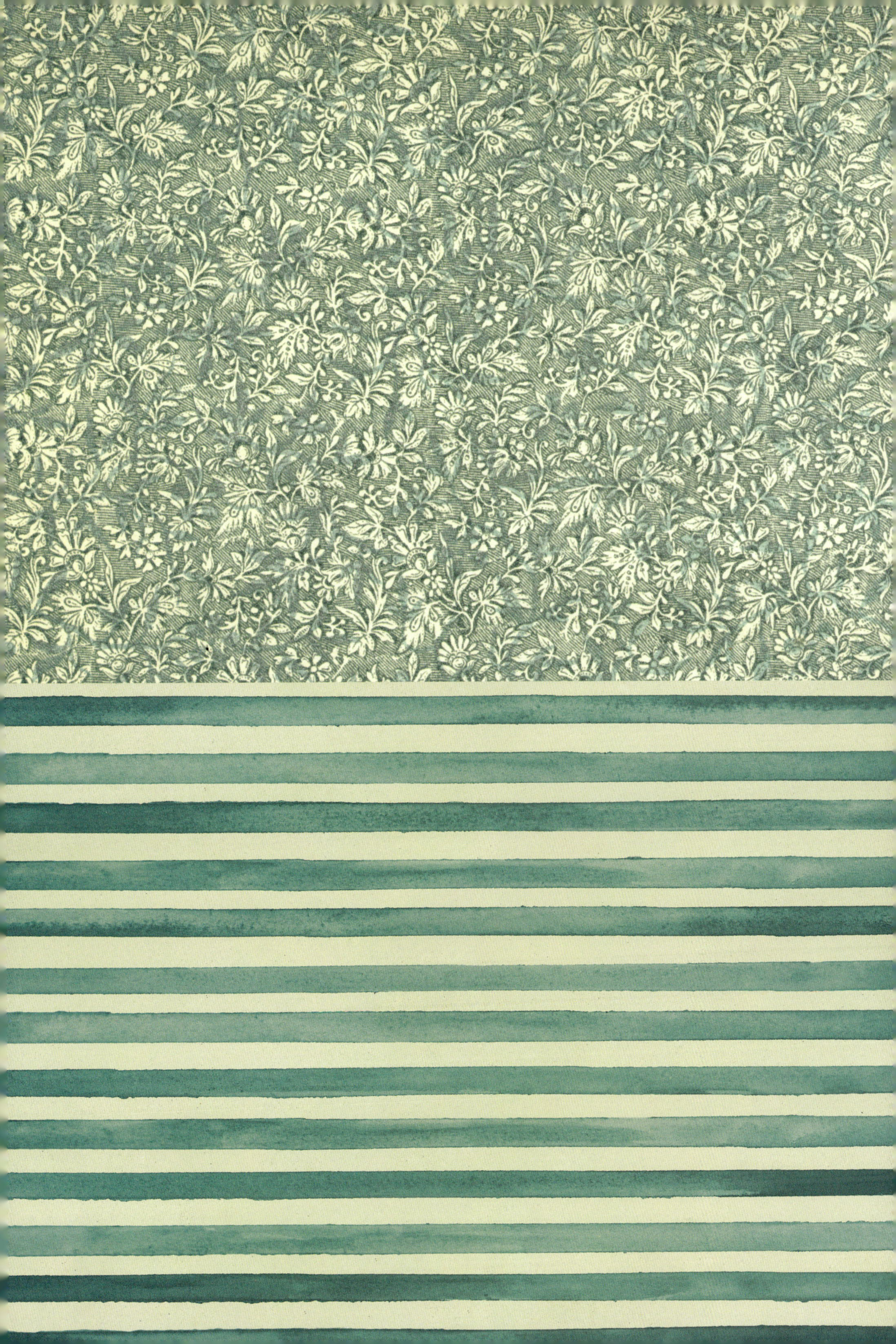

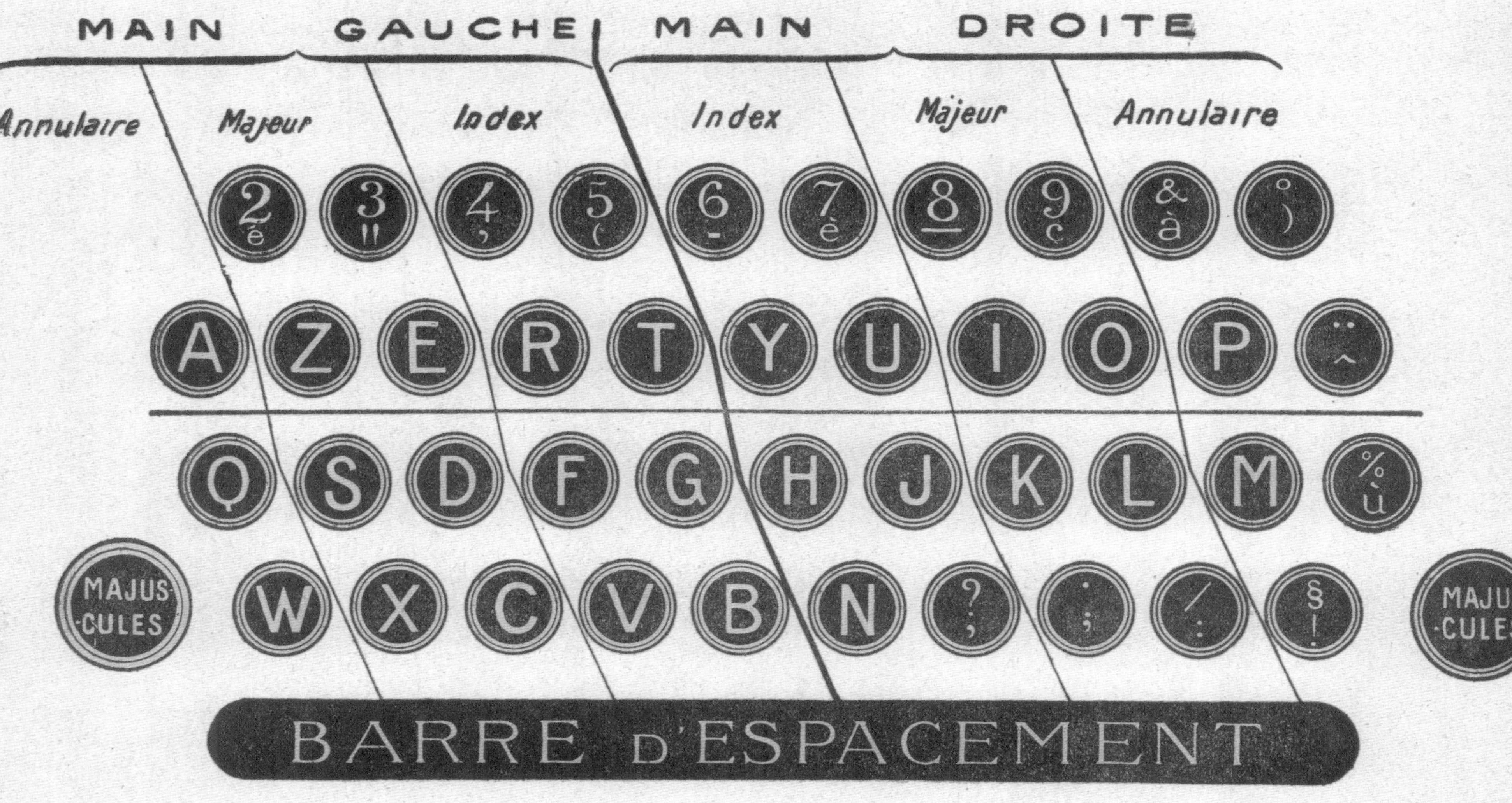

MAIN GAUCHE
MAIN DROITE
Annulaire
Majeur
Index
Index
Majeur
Annulaire
A Z E R T Y U I O P
Q S D F G H J K L M
MAJUS-CULES
W X C V B N
MAJUS-CULES
BARRE D'ESPACEMENT

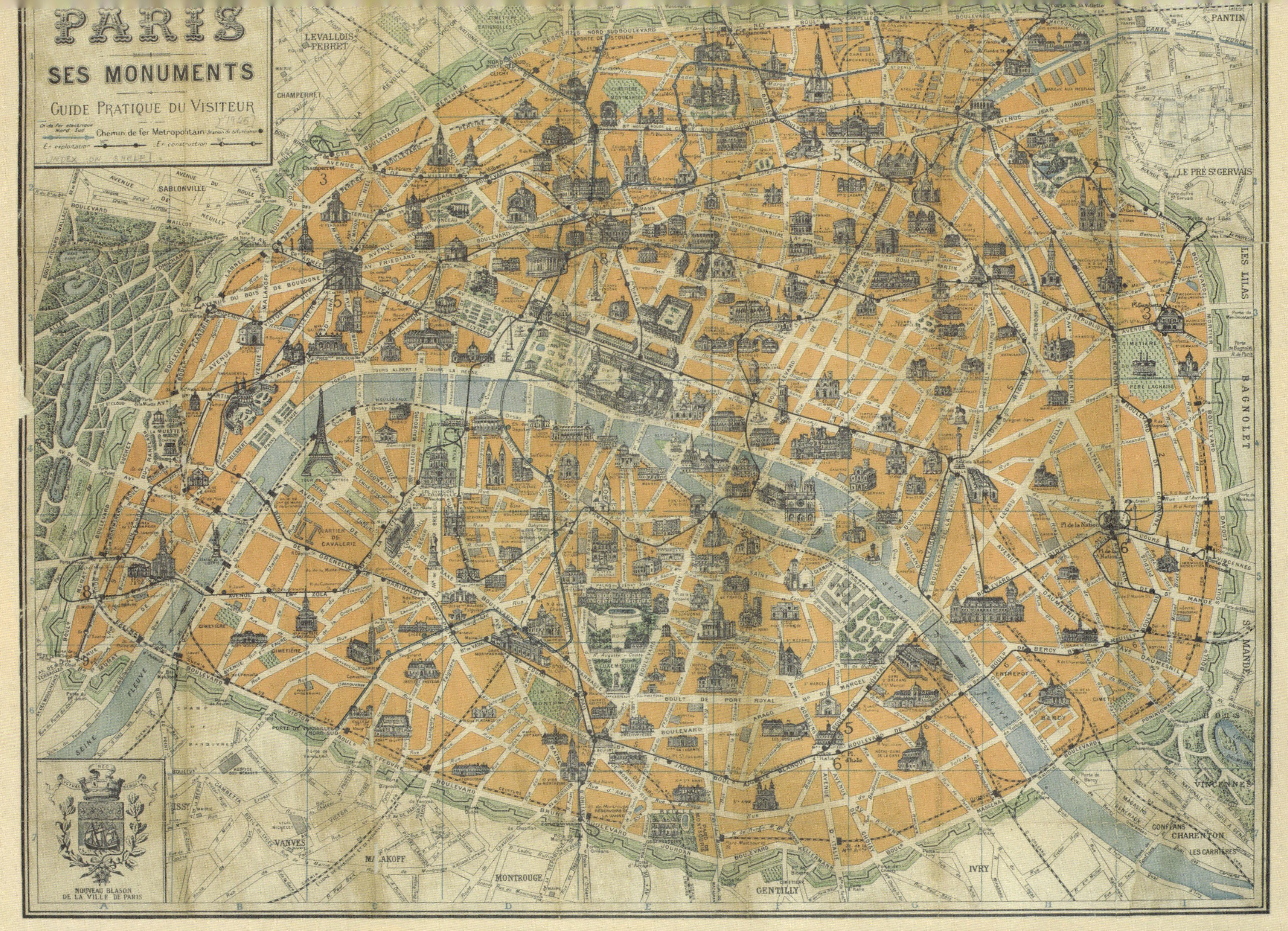

PARIS
SES MONUMENTS
GUIDE PRATIQUE DU VISITEUR
Ch. de Fer électrique Nord Sud
Chemin de fer Métropolitain
En exploitation
En construction
INDEX ON SHELF
LEVALLOIS-PERRET
CHAMPERRET
AVENUE DU ROULE
SABLONVILLE
NEUILLY
MAILLOT
BOIS DE BOULOGNE
PANTIN
LE PRÉ ST GERVAIS
LES LILAS
BAGNOLET
PÈRE LACHAISE
VOLTAIRE
VINCENNES
ST MANDÉ
BERCY
CHARENTON
CONFLANS
LES CARRIÈRES
IVRY
GENTILLY
MONTROUGE
MALAKOFF
VANVES
ISSY
SEINE
FLEUVE
QUARTIER DE CAVALERIE
BOULEVARD DE PORT ROYAL
ARAGO
NOUVEAU BLASON
DE LA VILLE DE PARIS

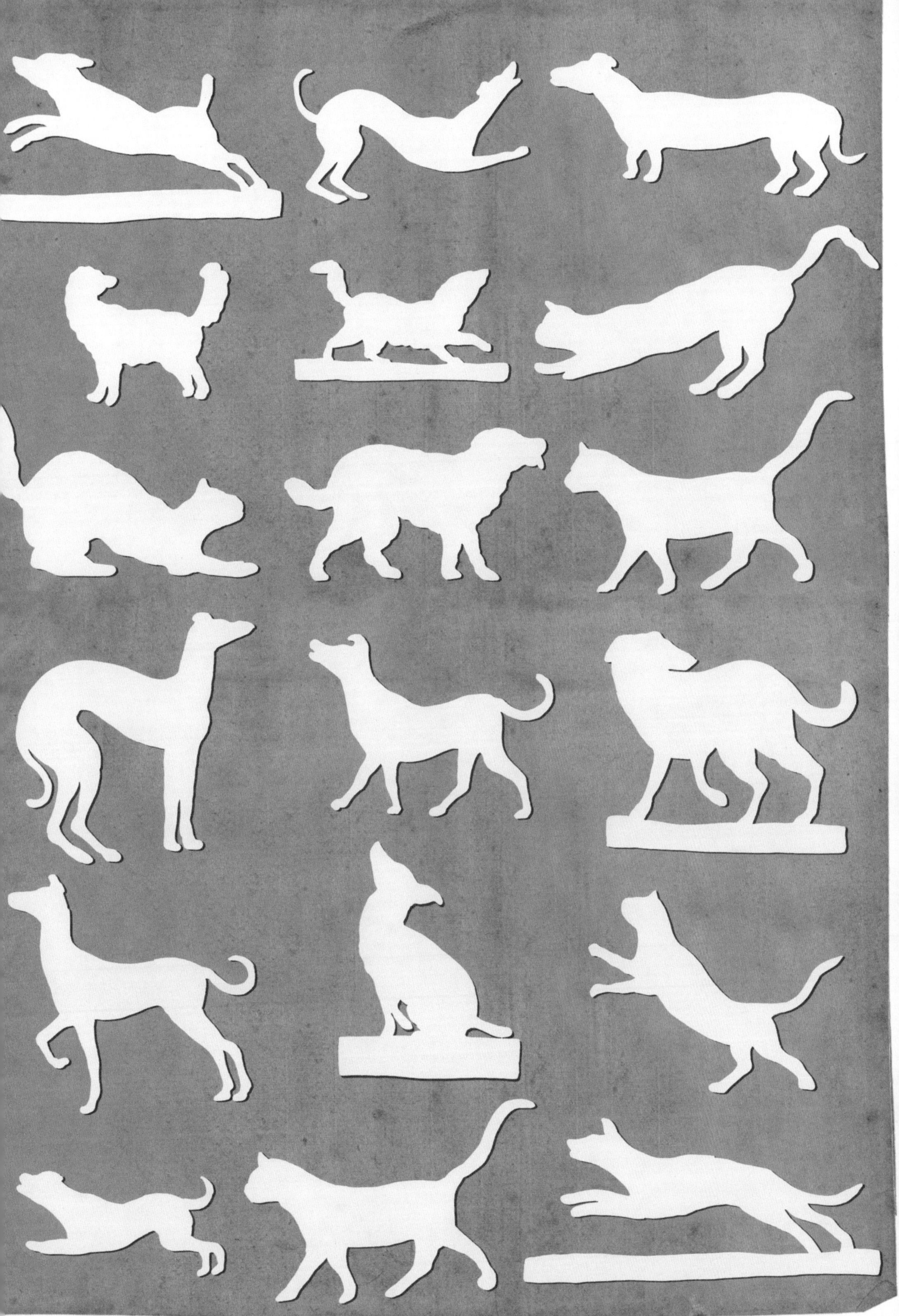

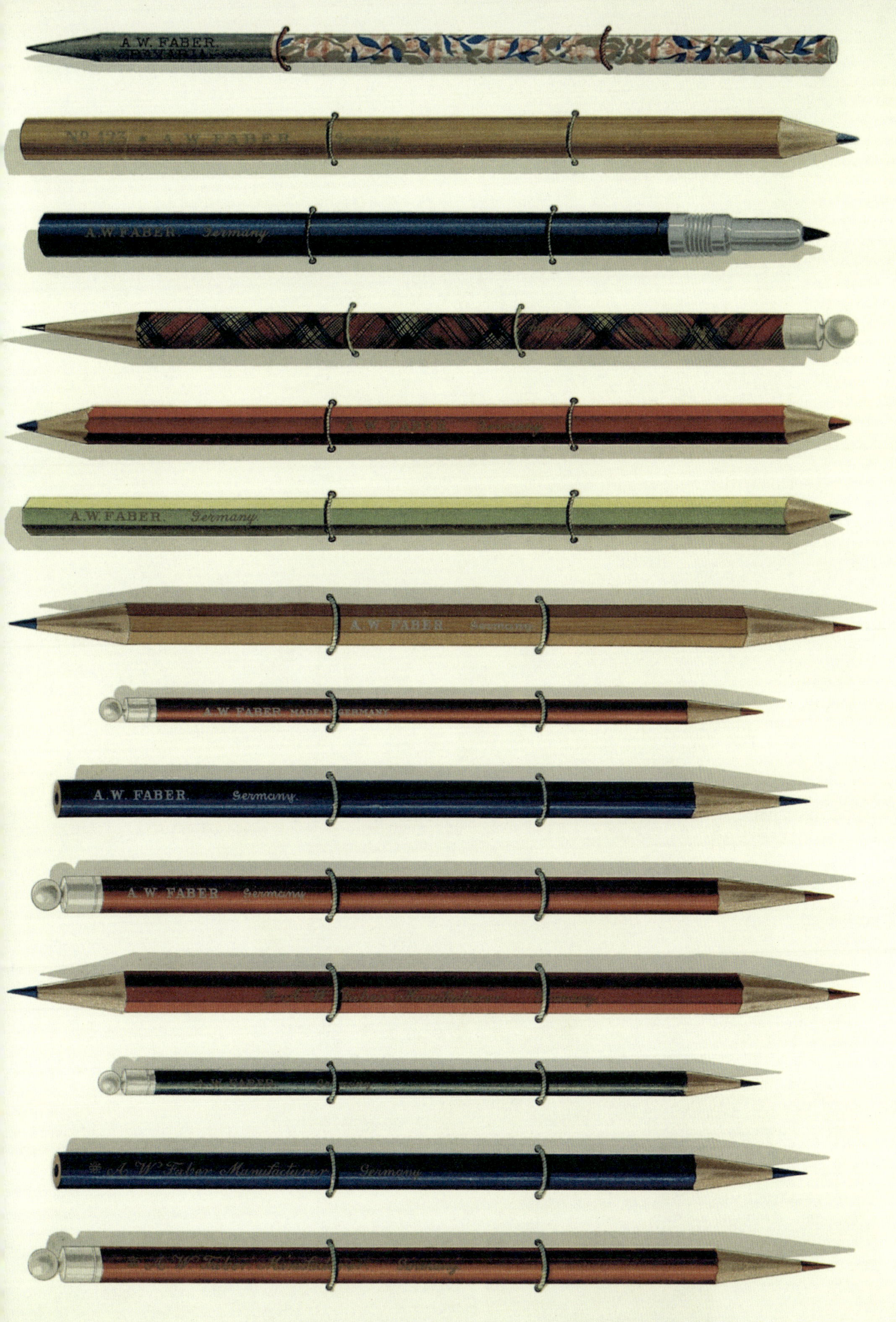

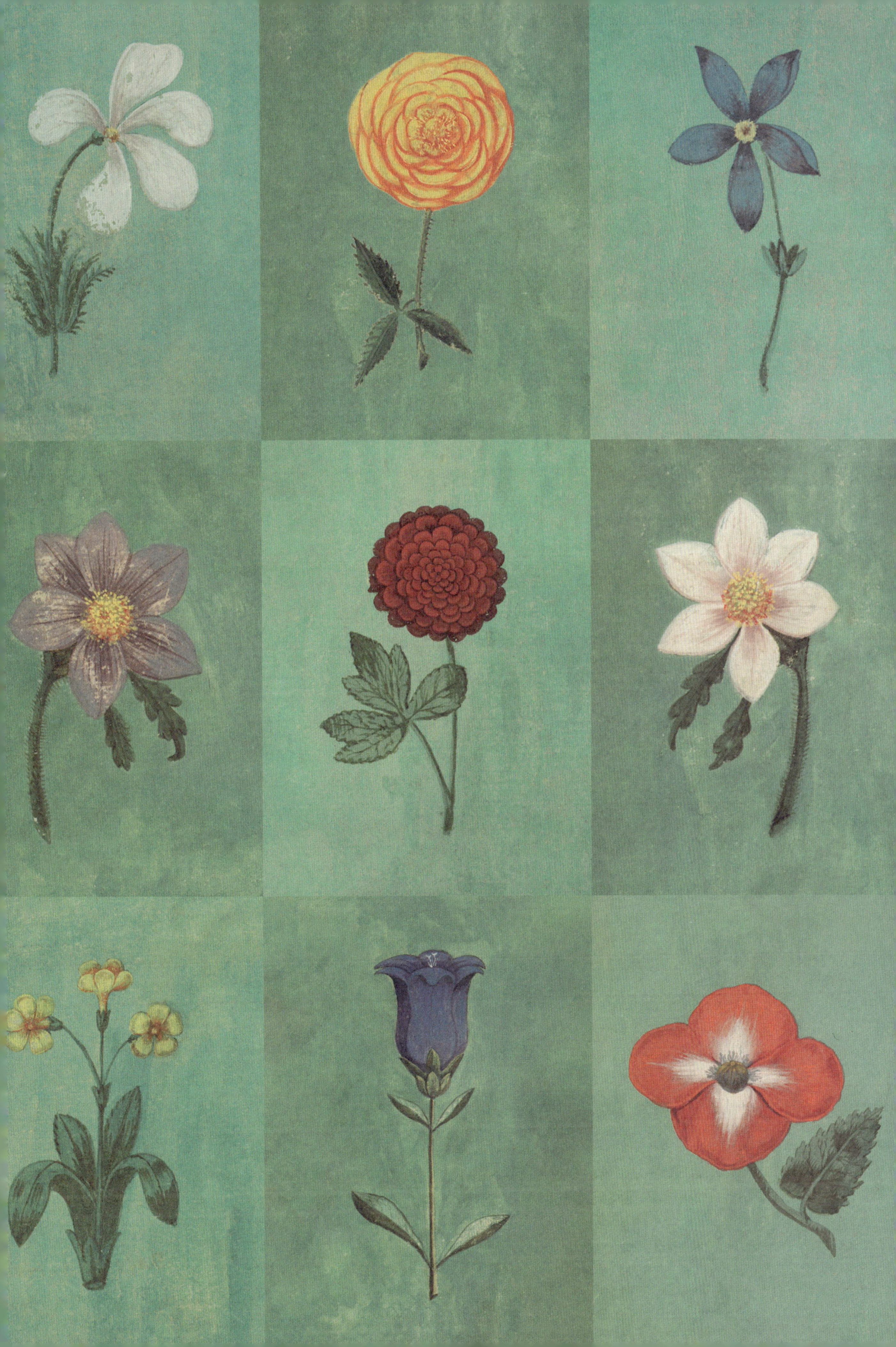

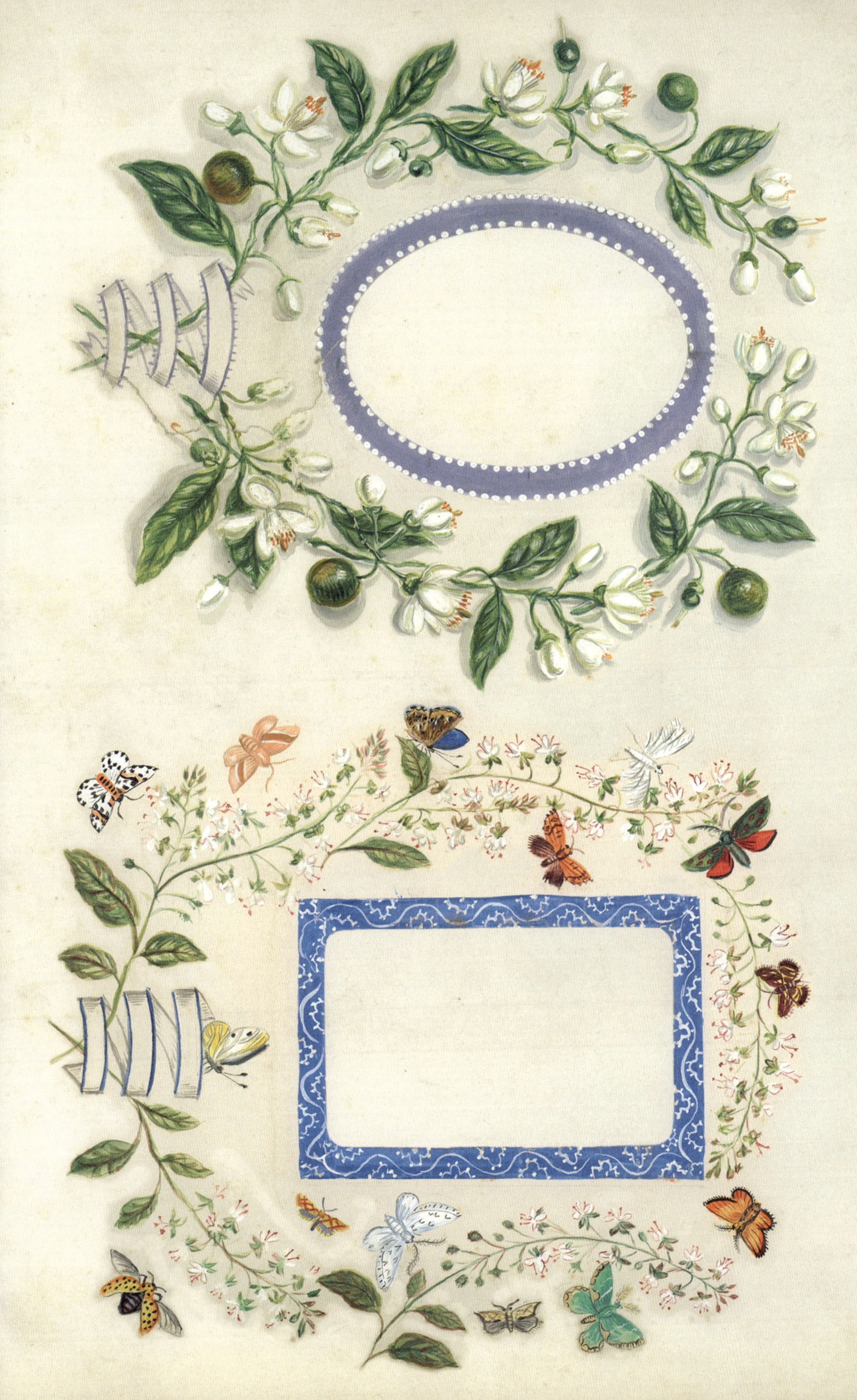

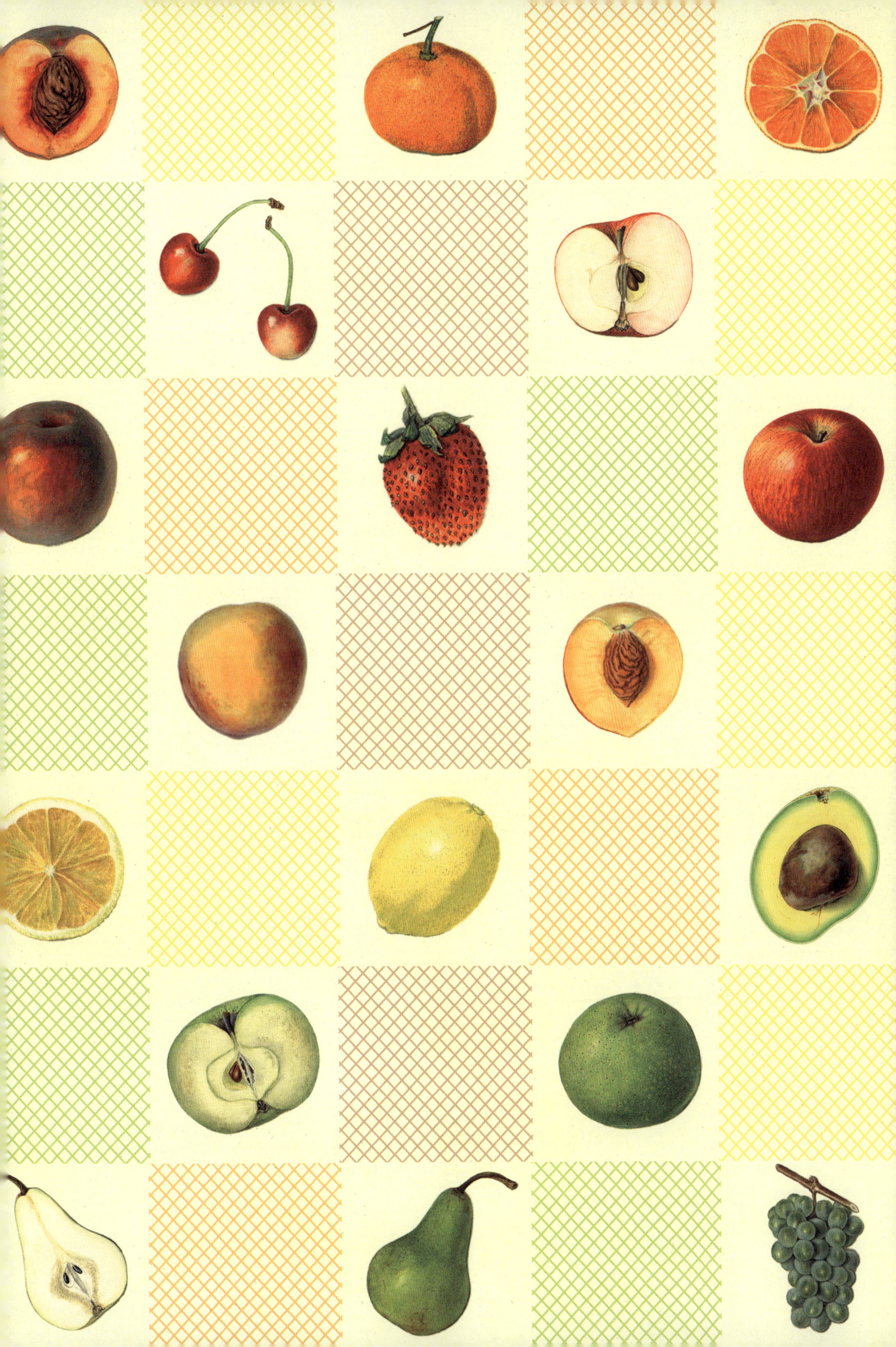

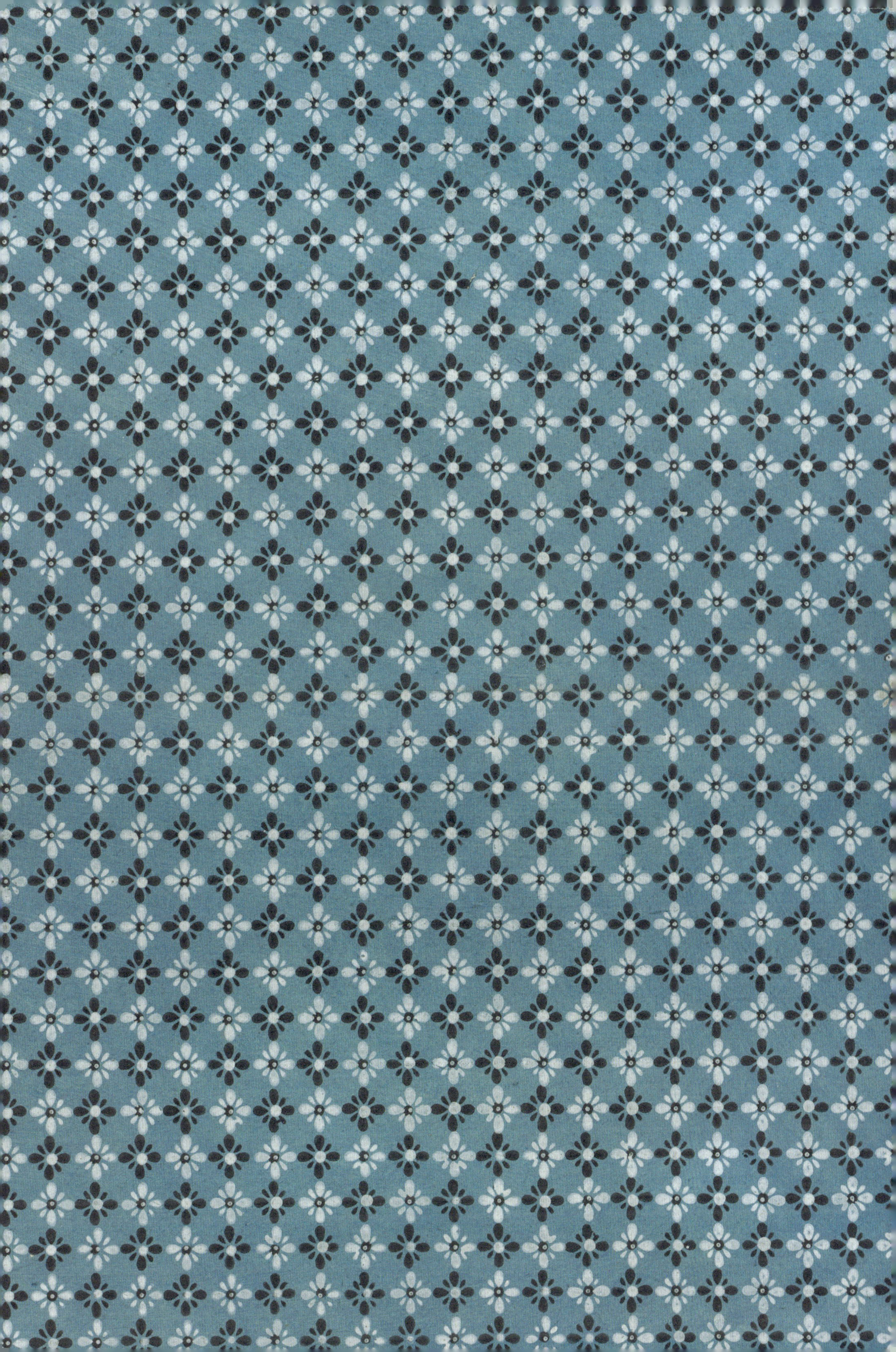

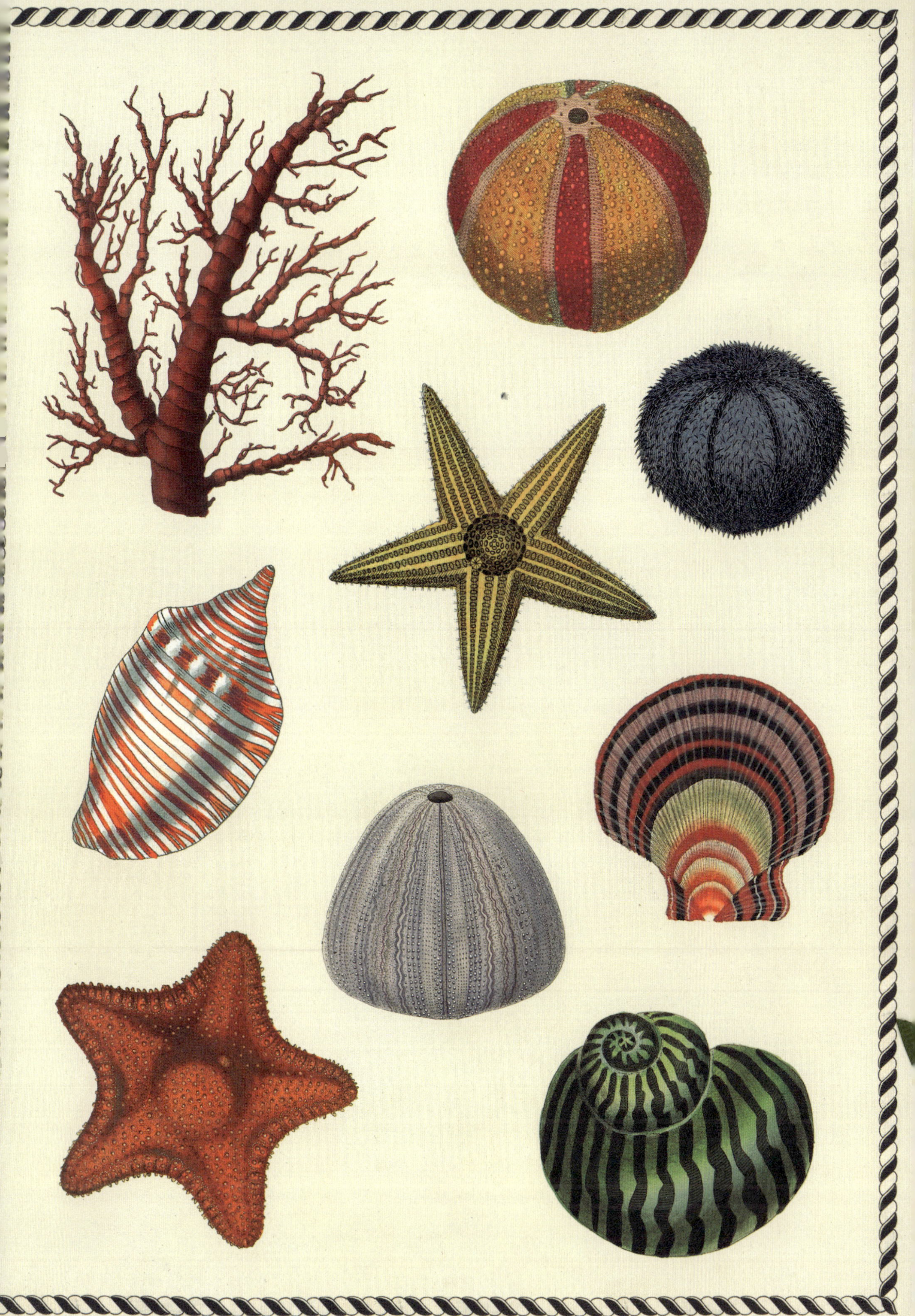

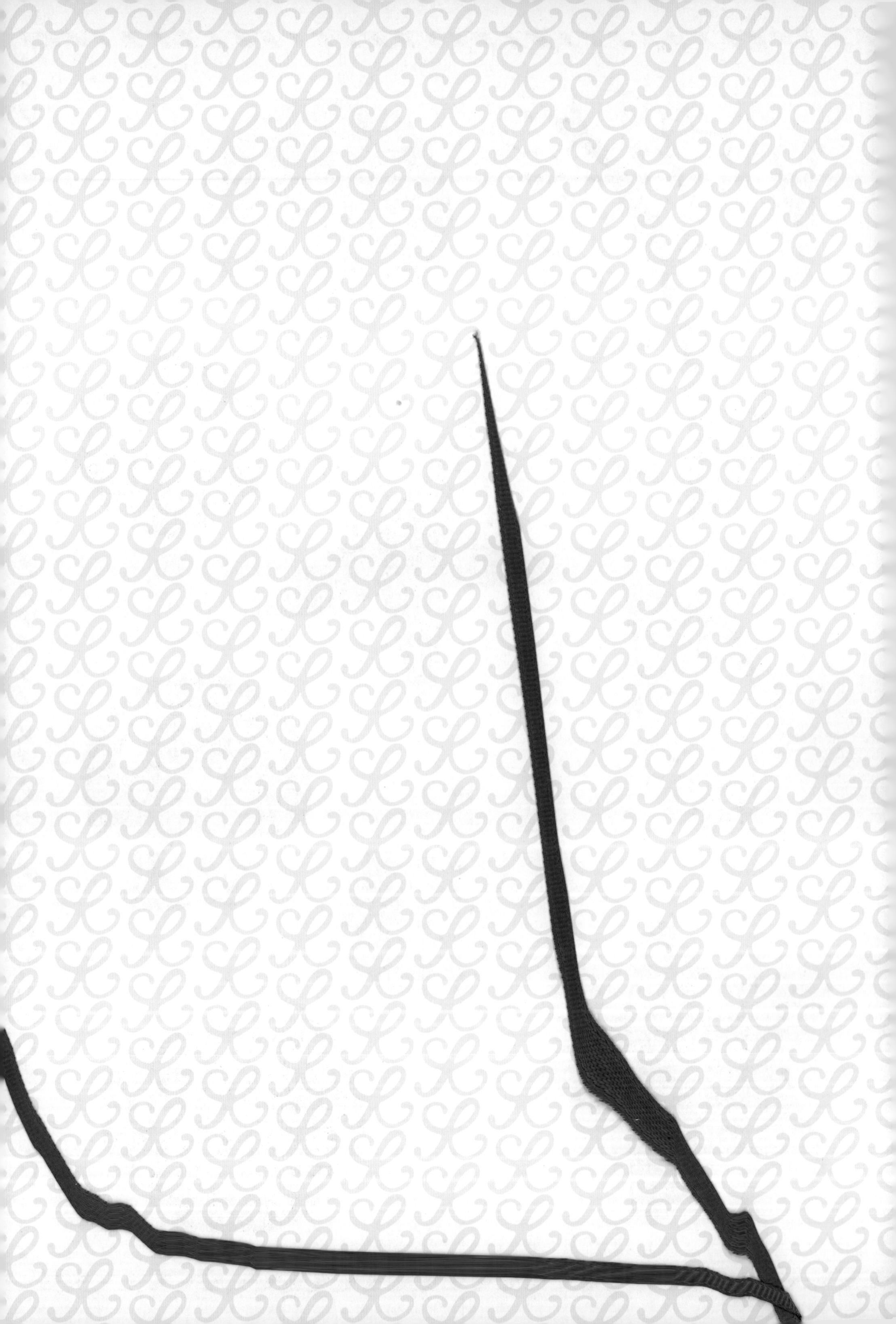

A B C D E
F G H I J K
L M N O P
Q R S T U
V W X Y Z

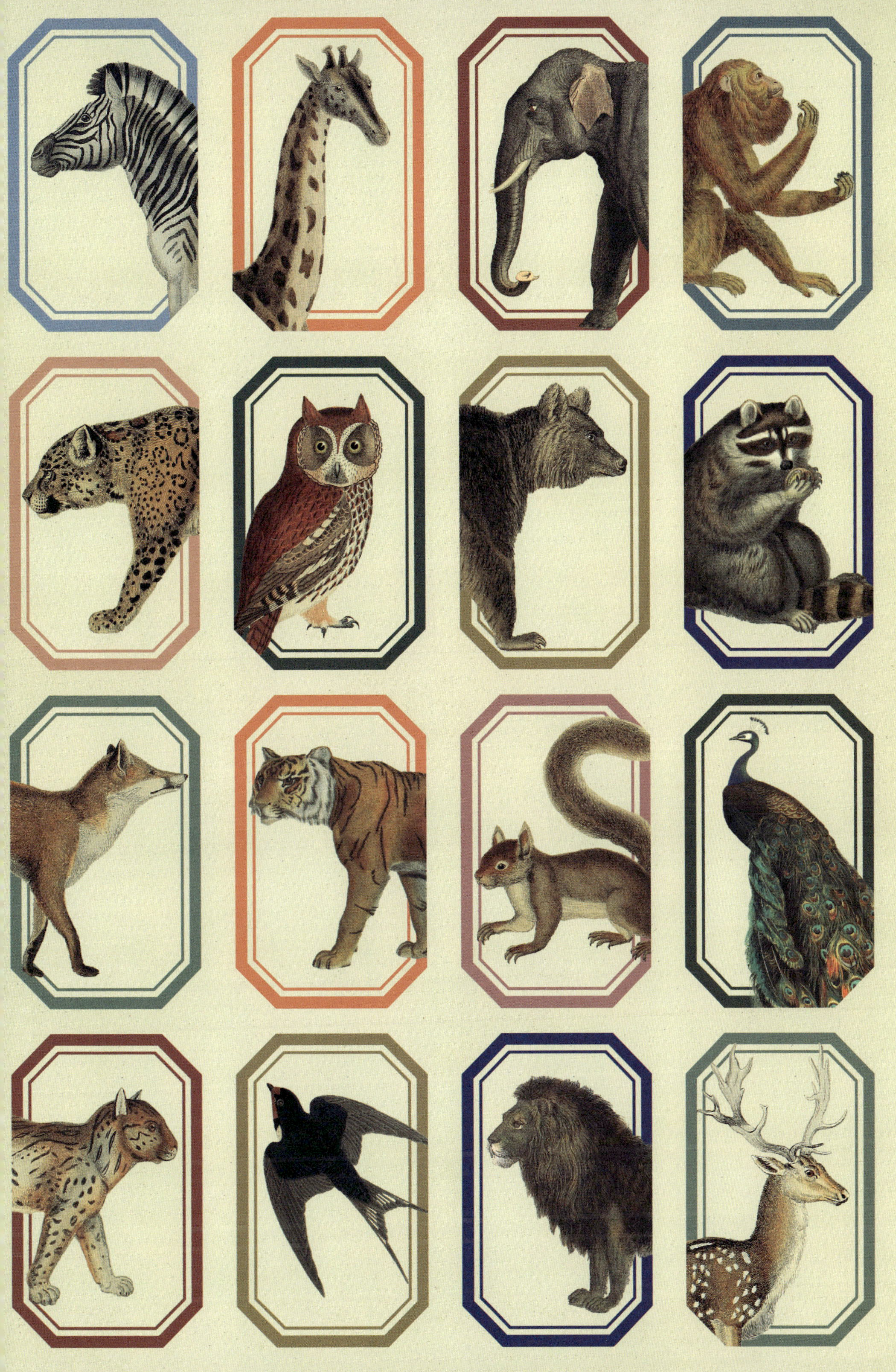

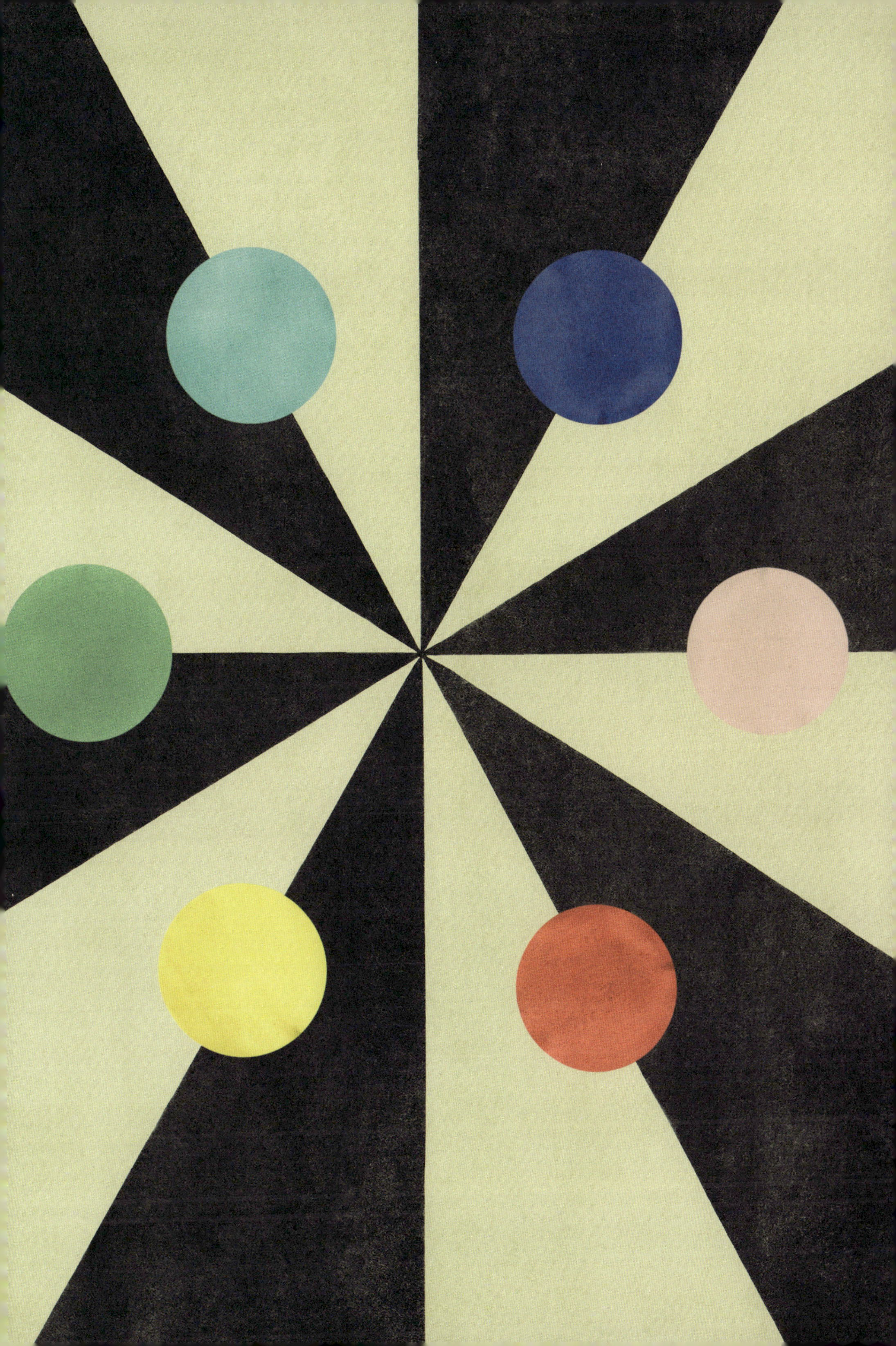

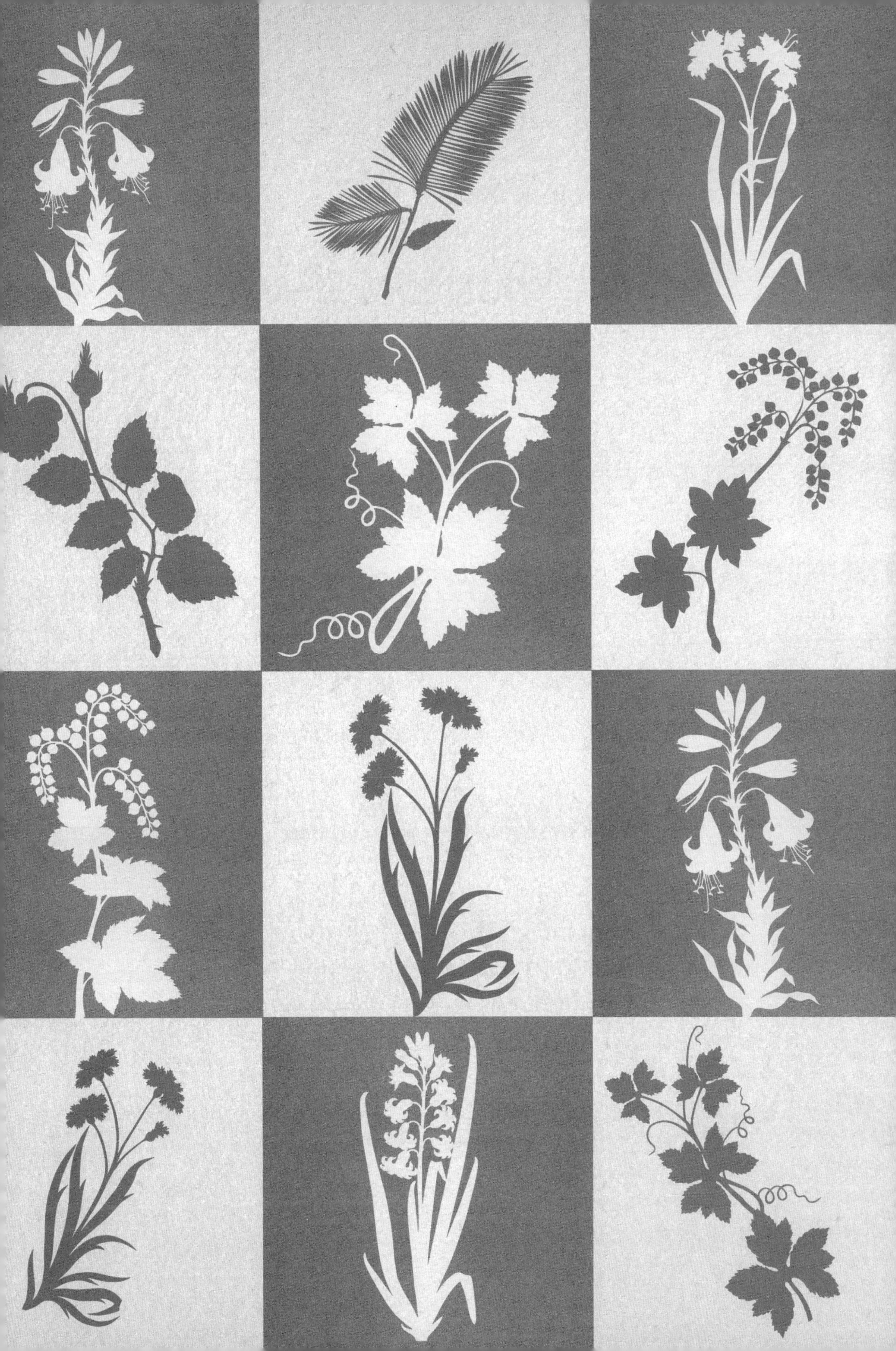

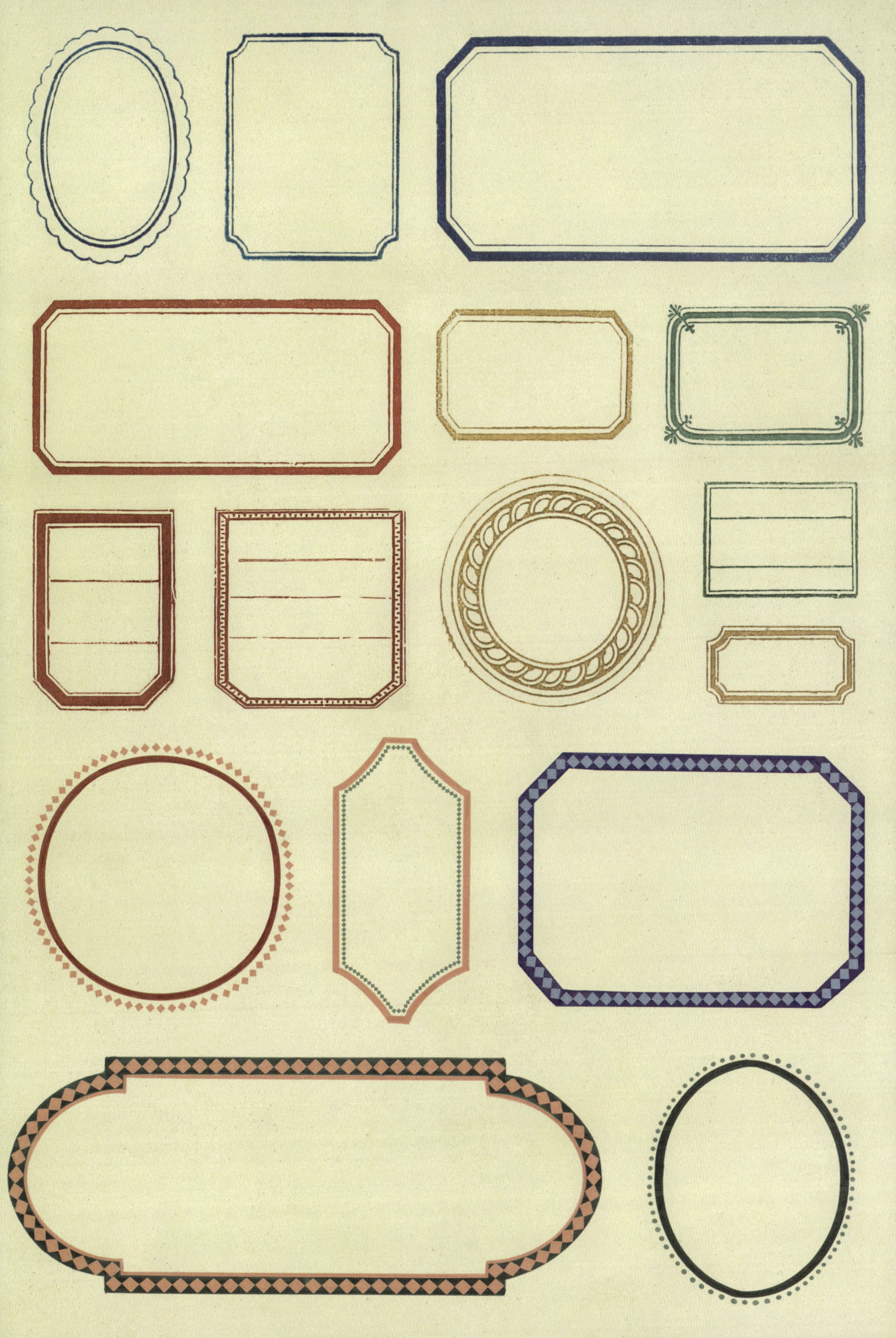

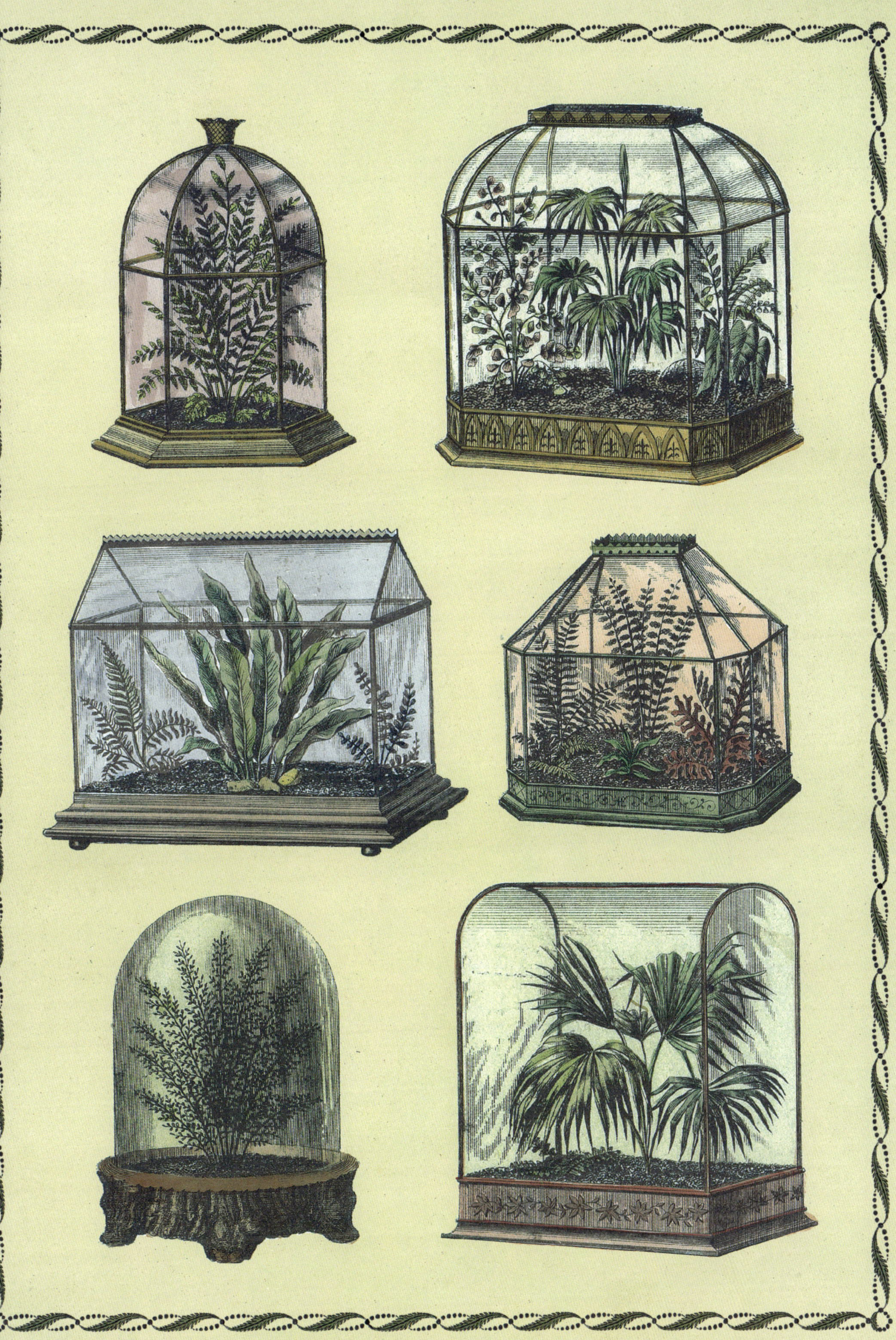

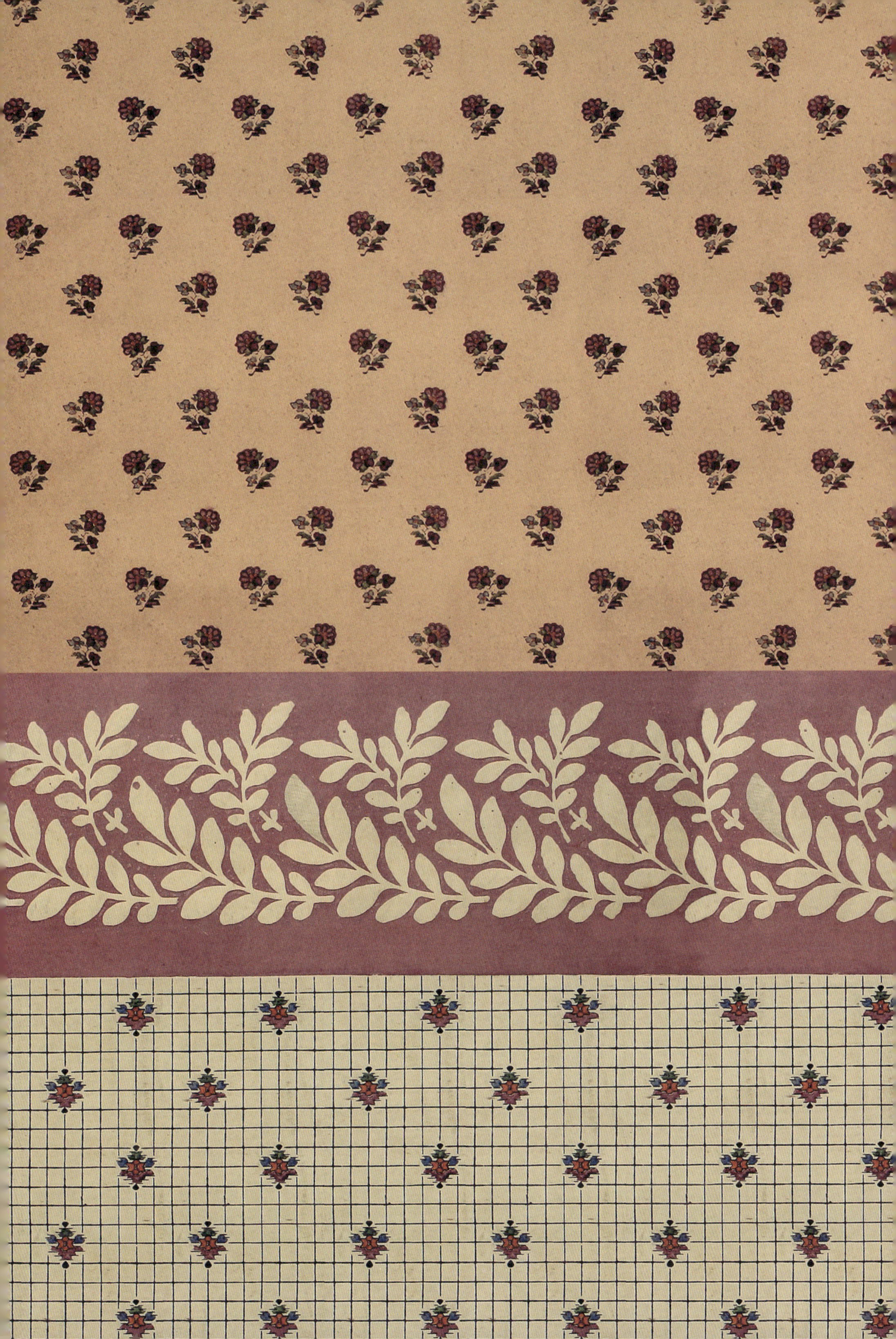

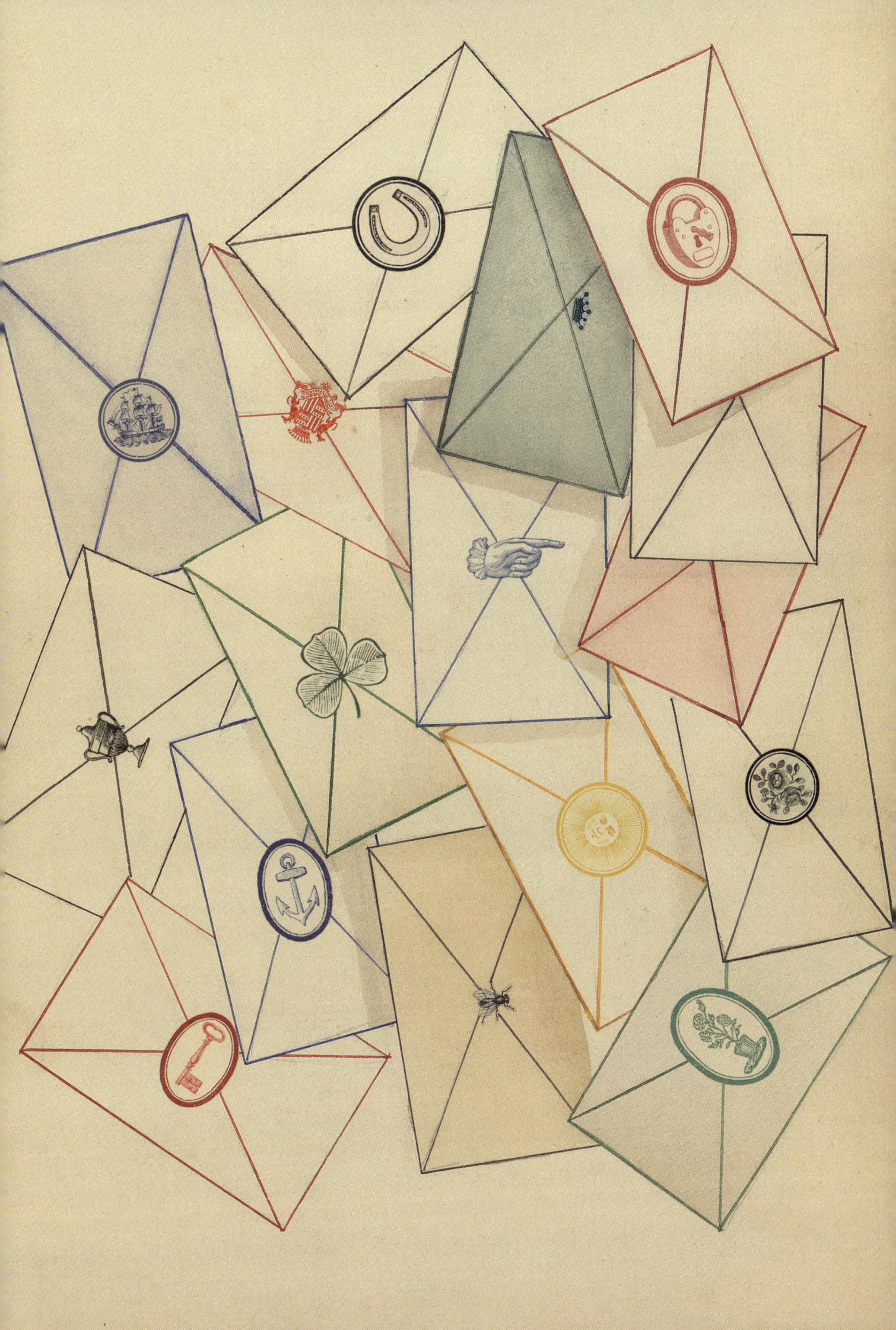

Je t'aime

ÉTOILE ★

SOLEIL

FLEURS

MON CHÉRI

LA BELLA VITA

moi et toi

CIAO

JOIE DE VIVRE

C'EST LA VIE

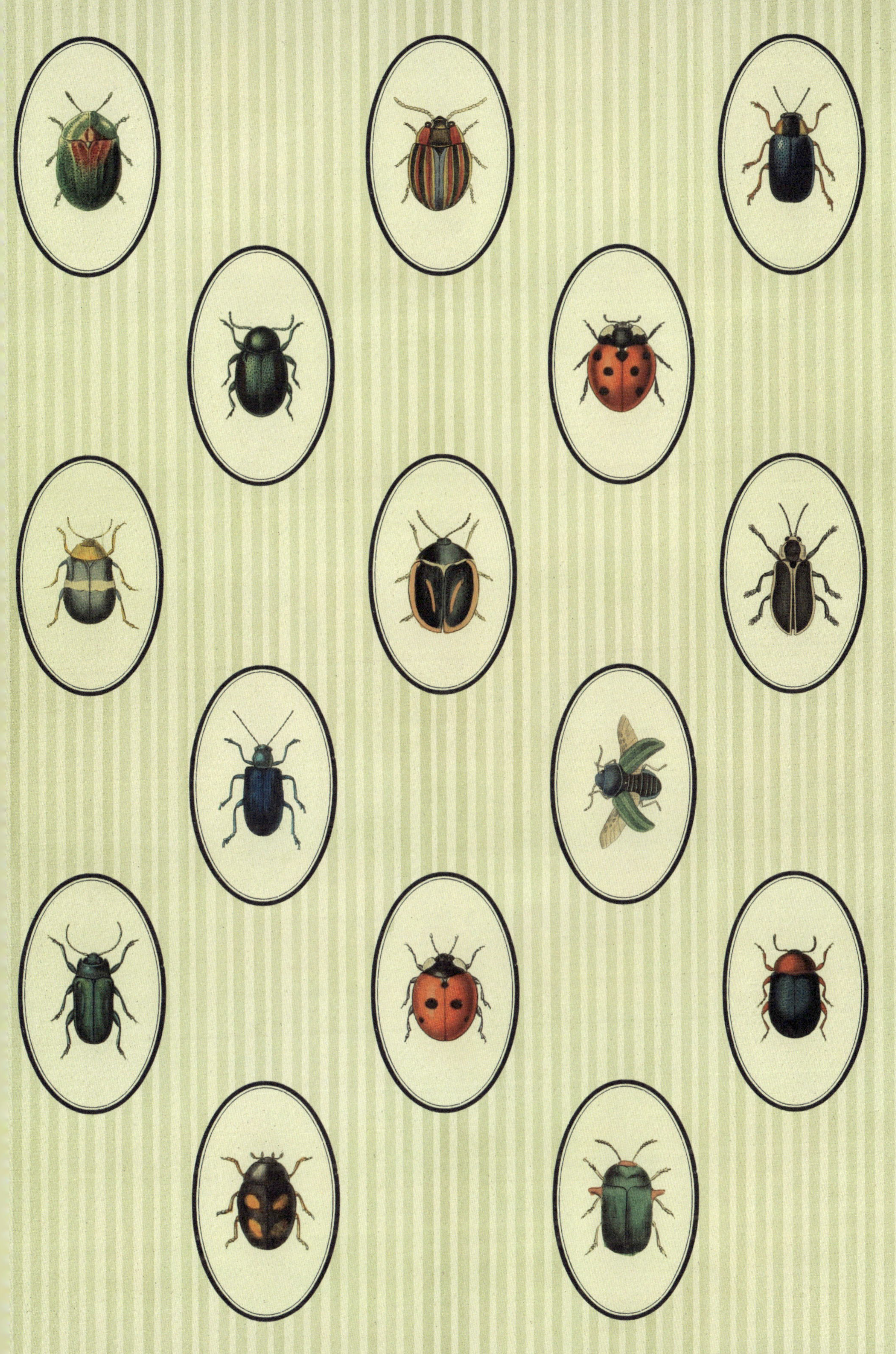

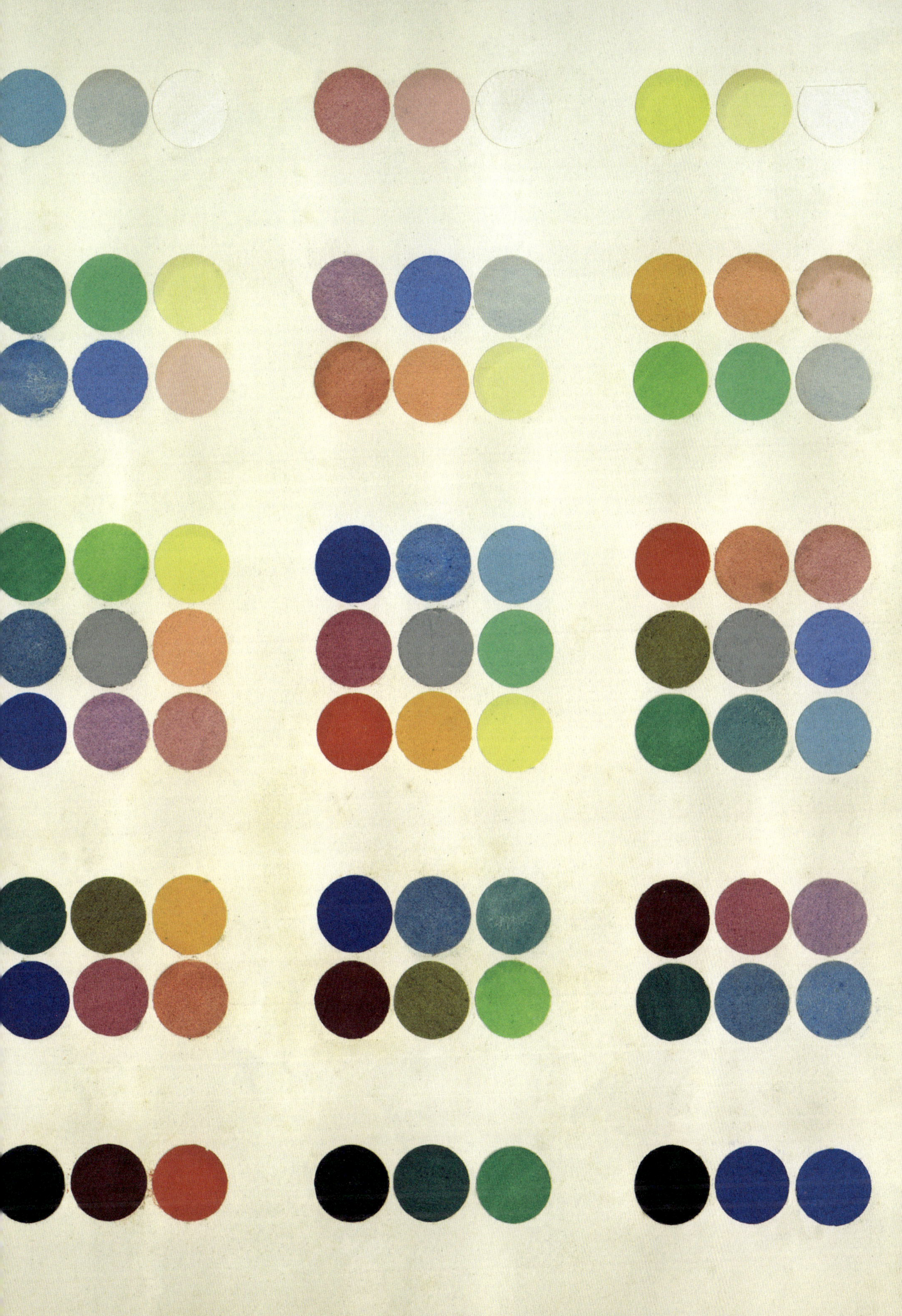

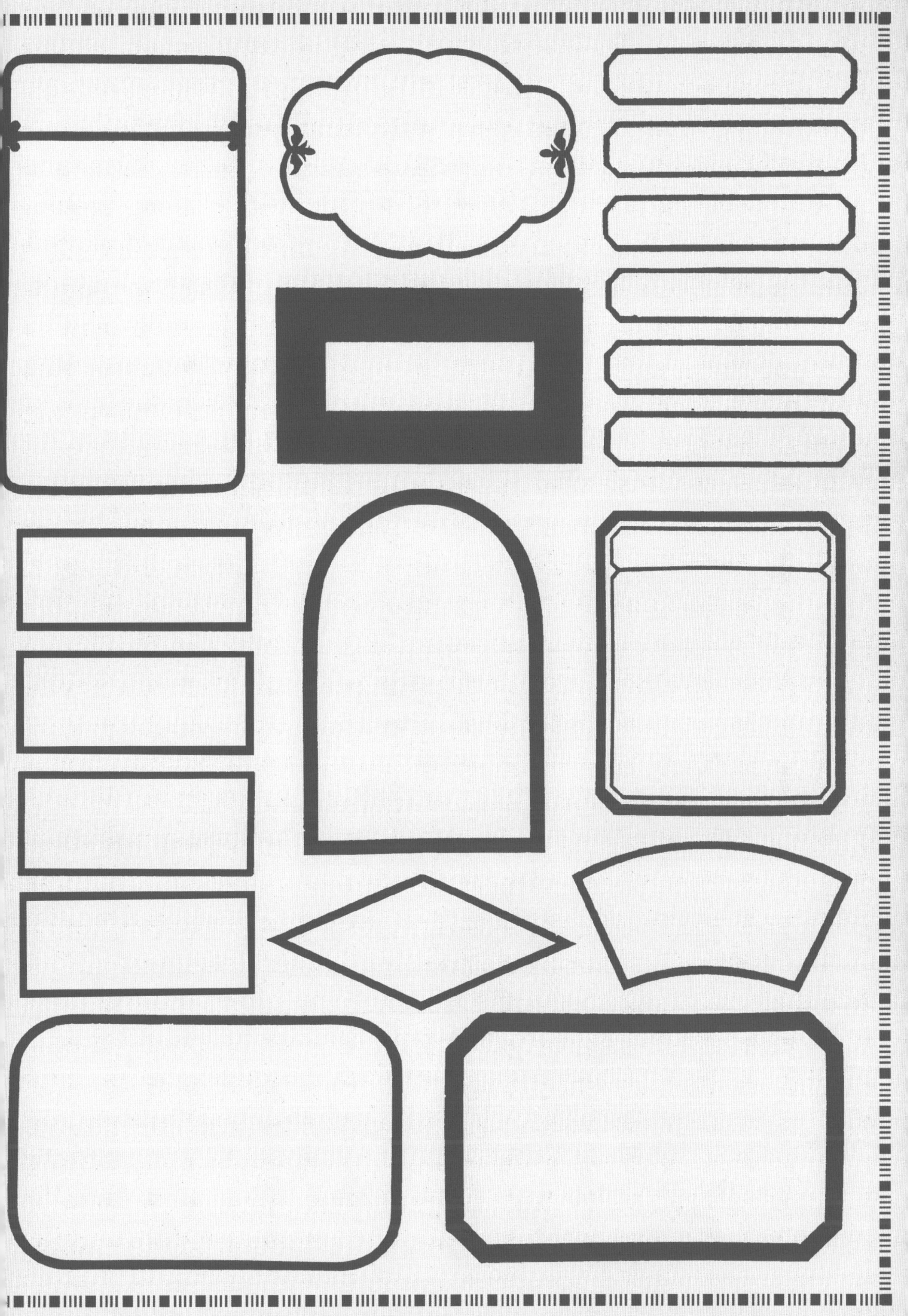

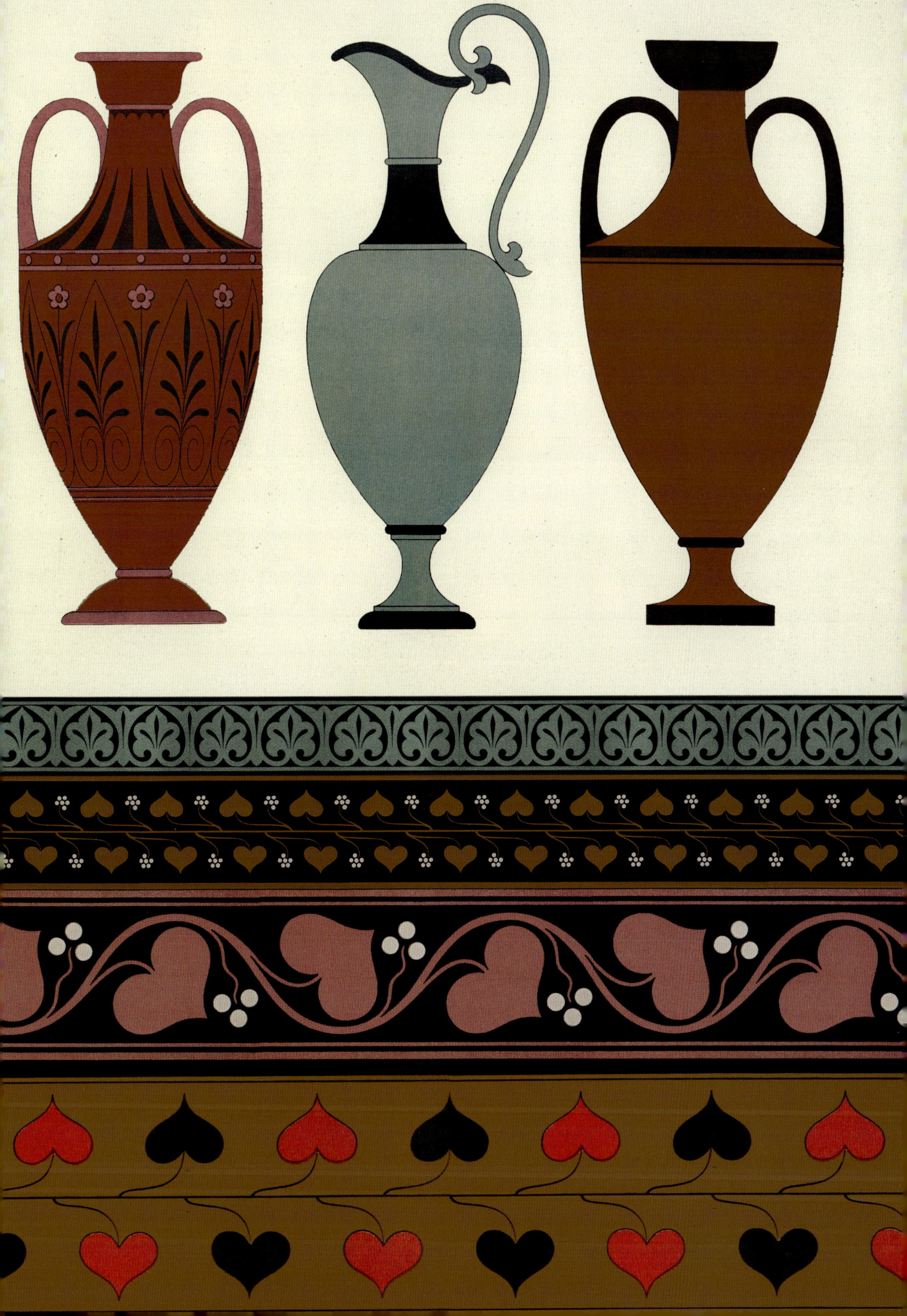

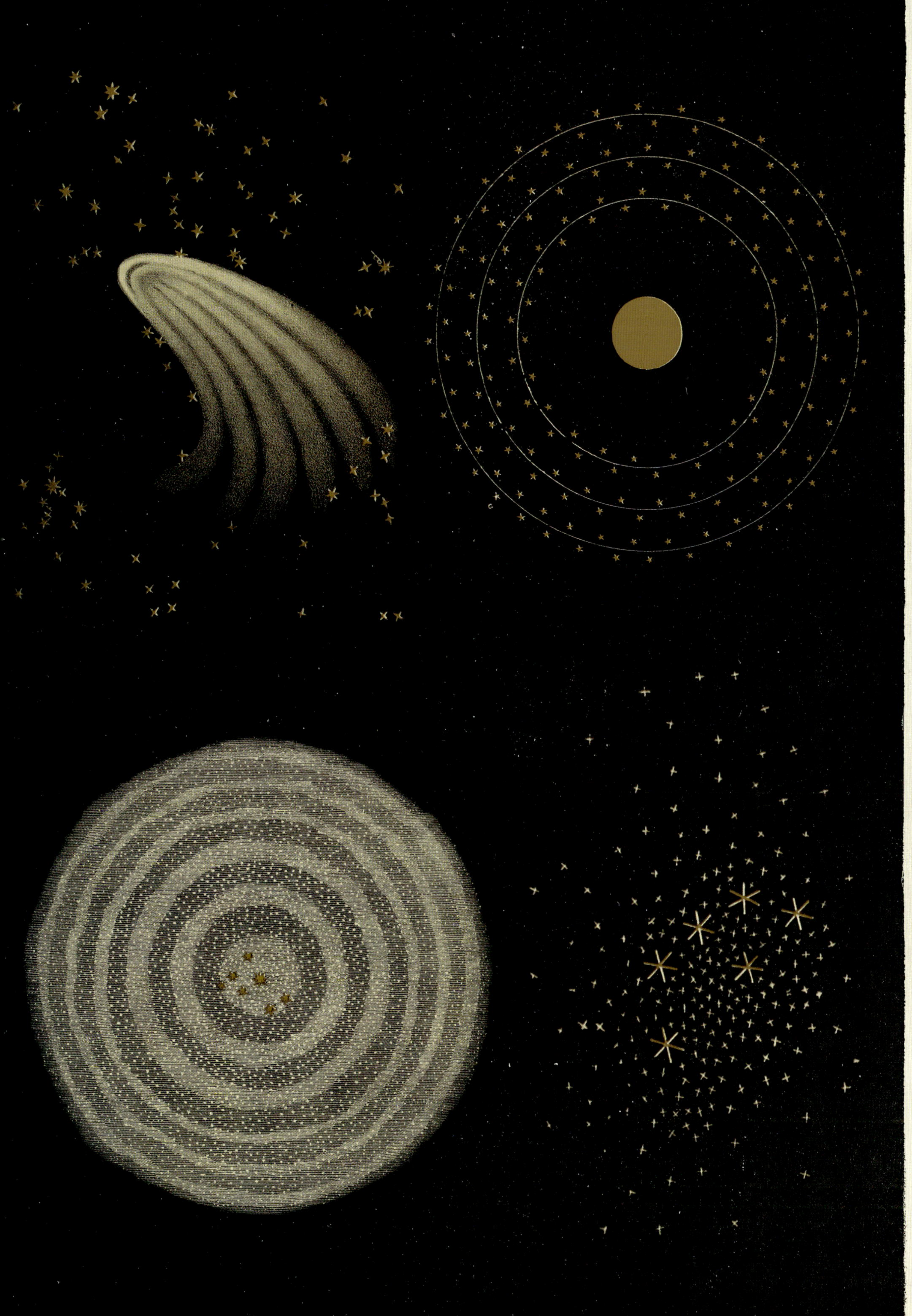

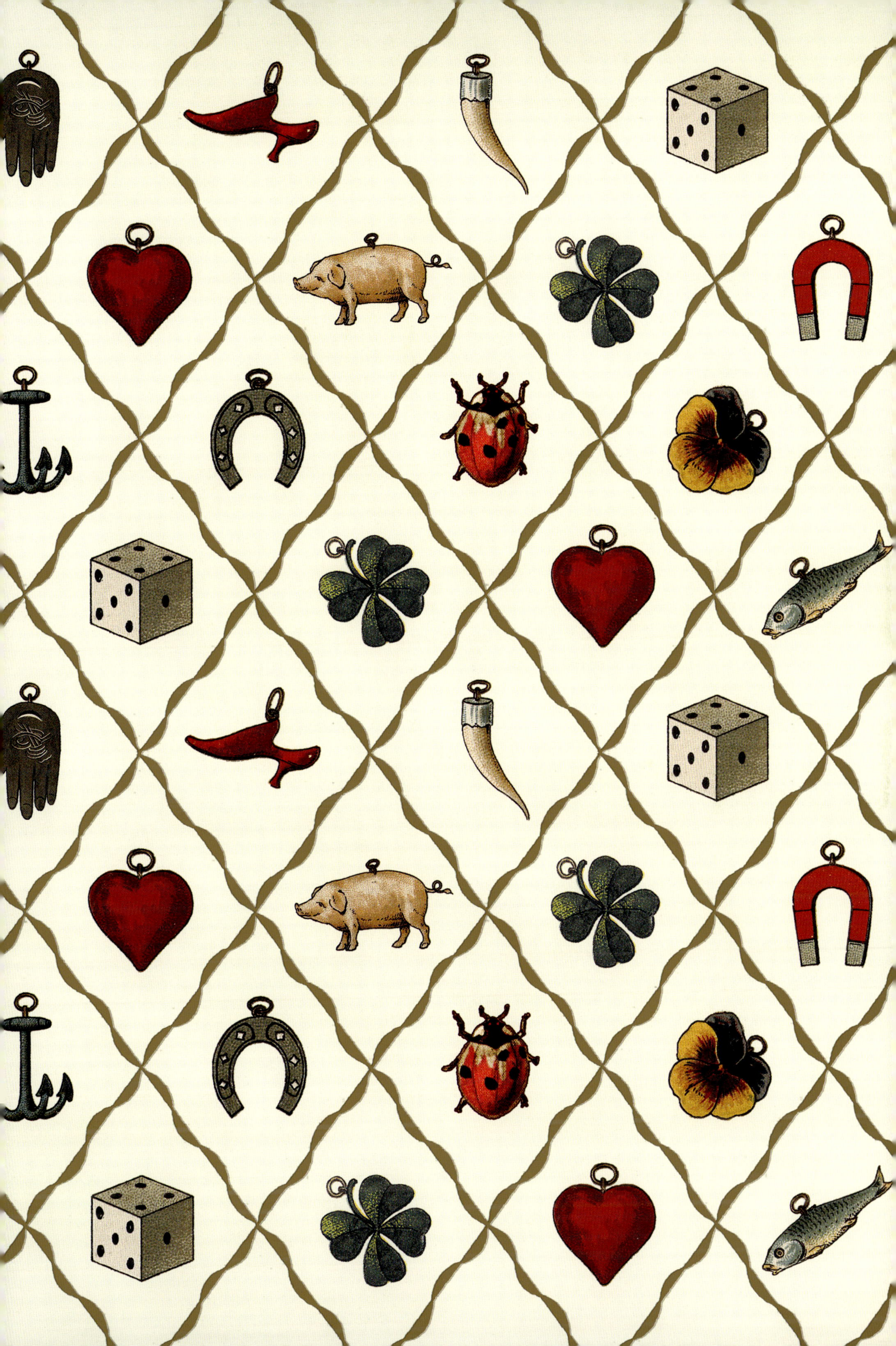

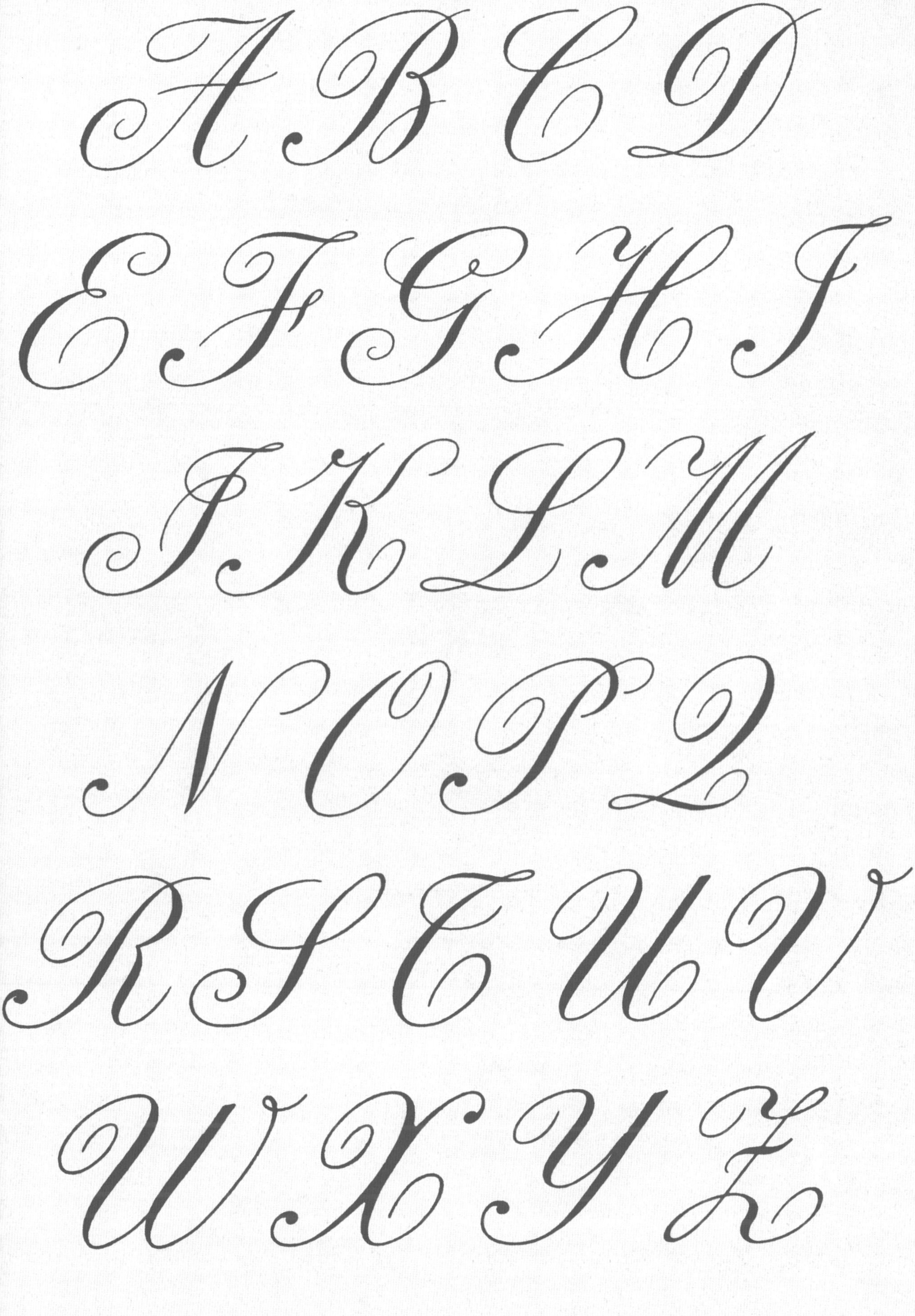

A B C D

E F G H I

J K L M

N O P Q

R S T U V

W X Y Z

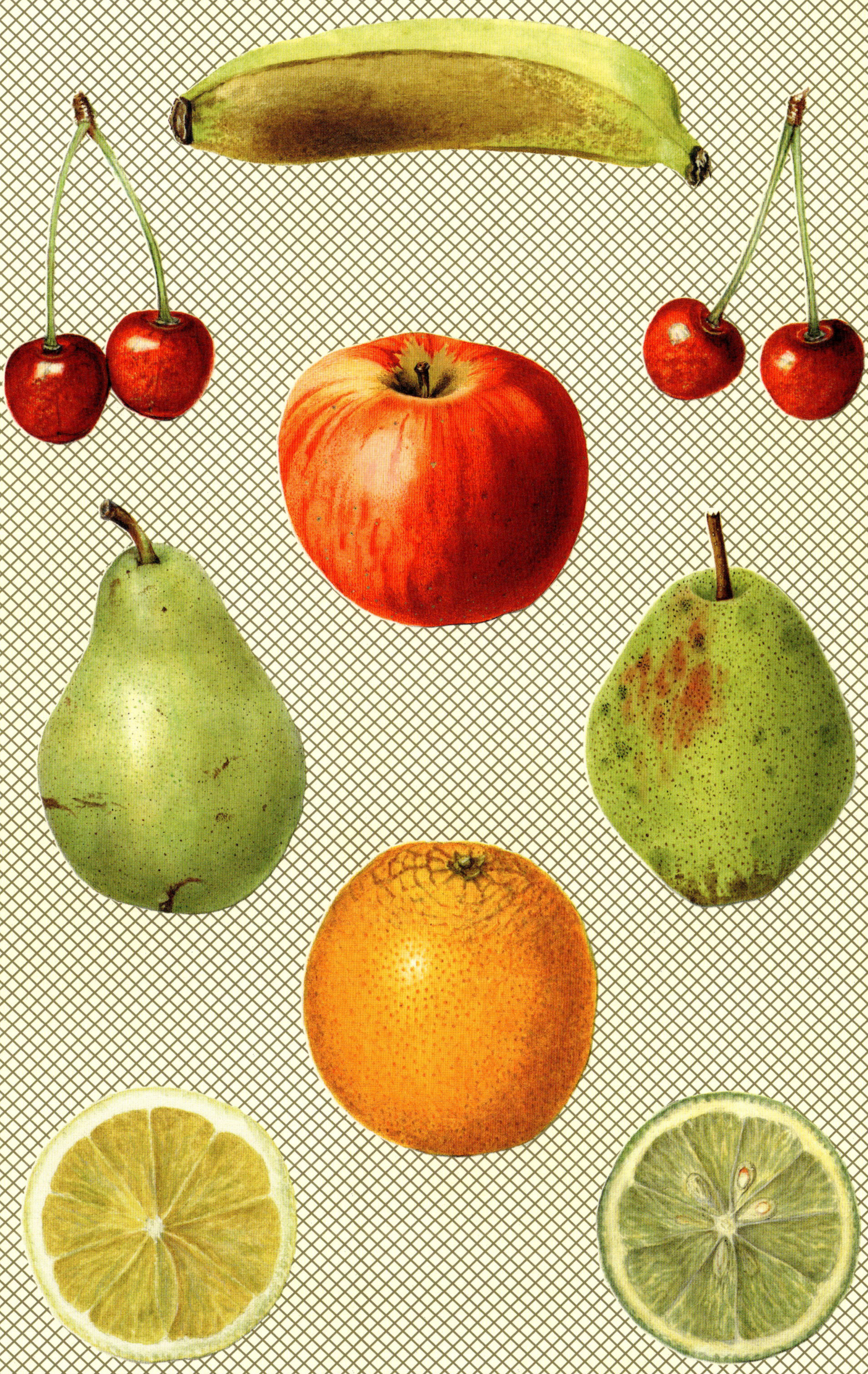

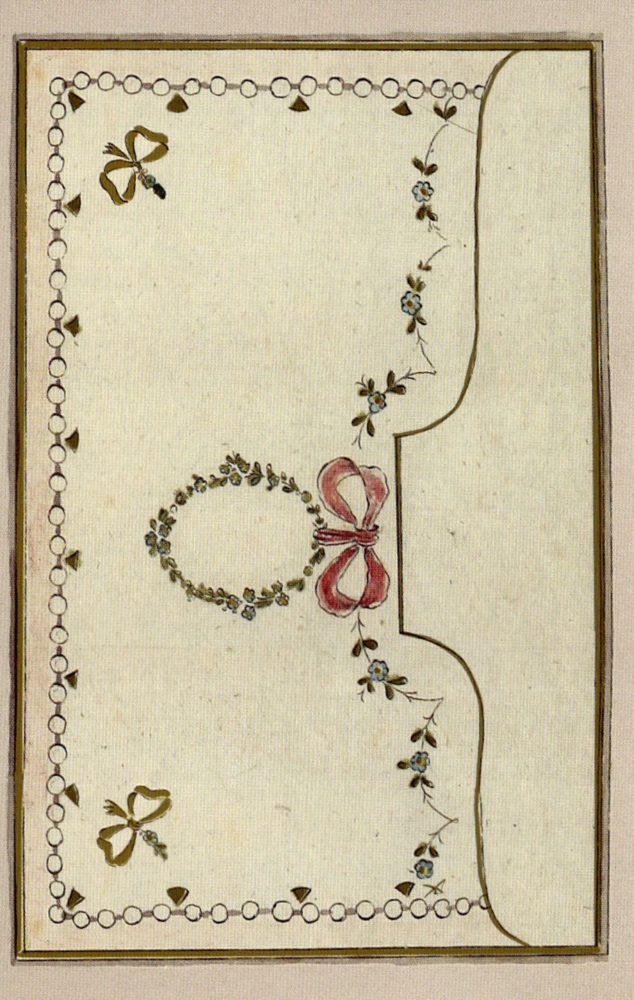
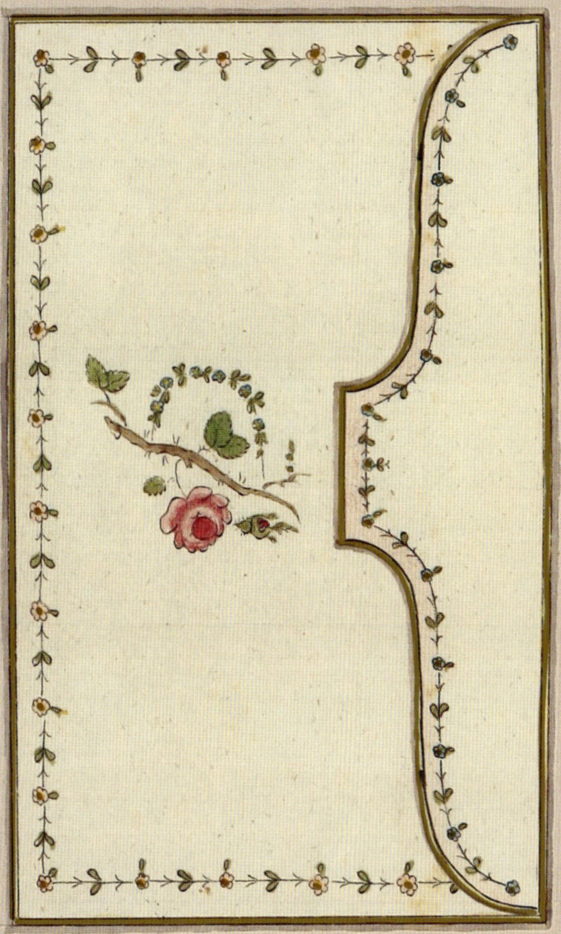
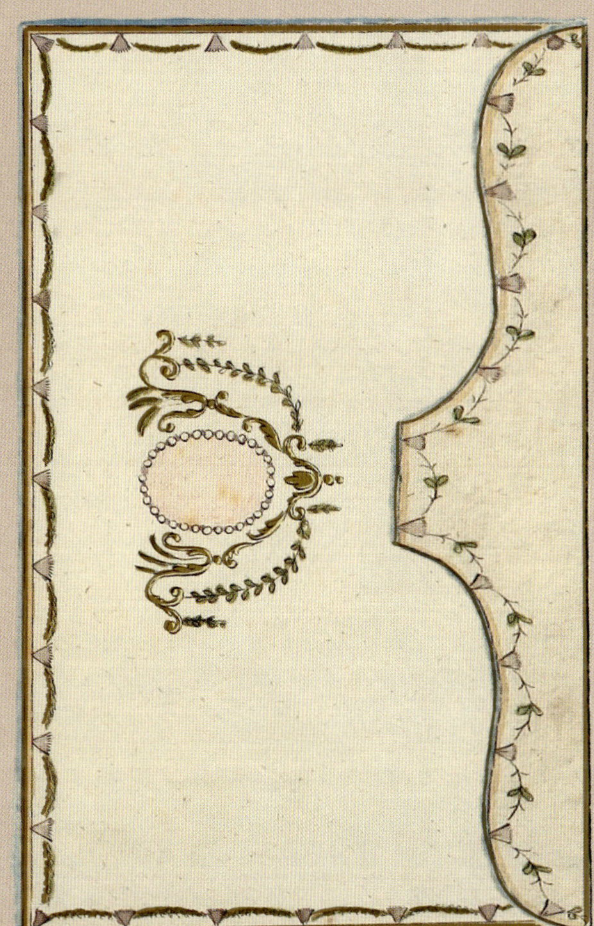
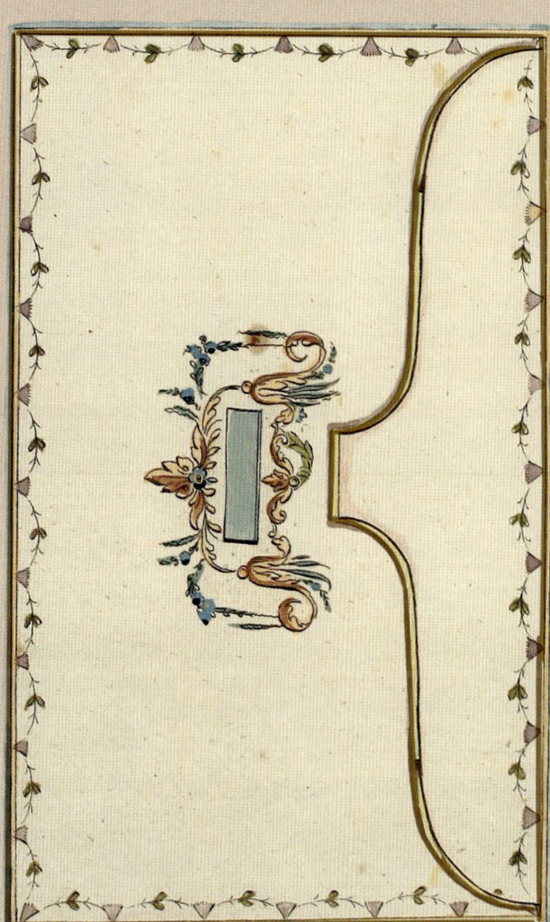

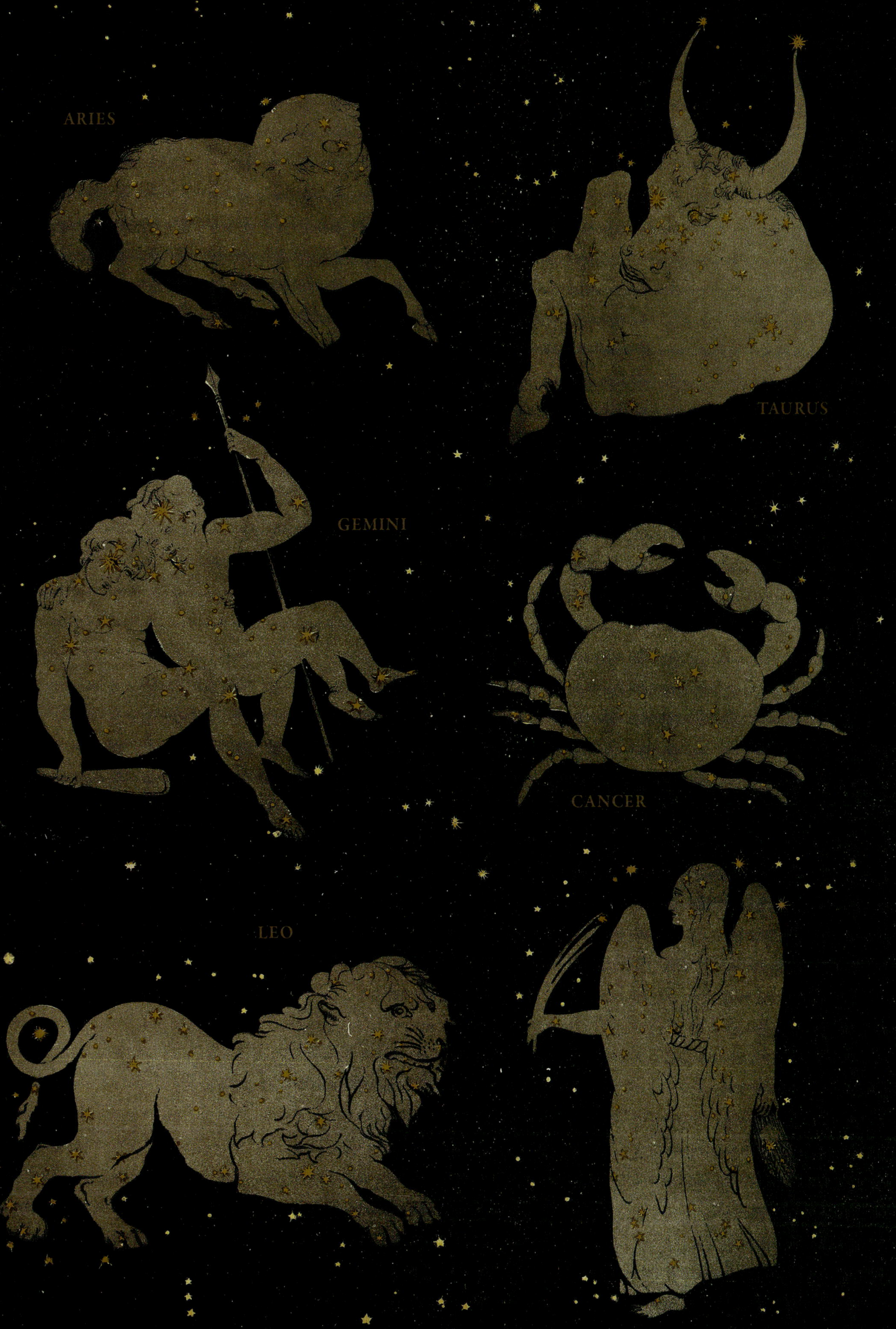

ARIES
TAURUS
GEMINI
CANCER
LEO

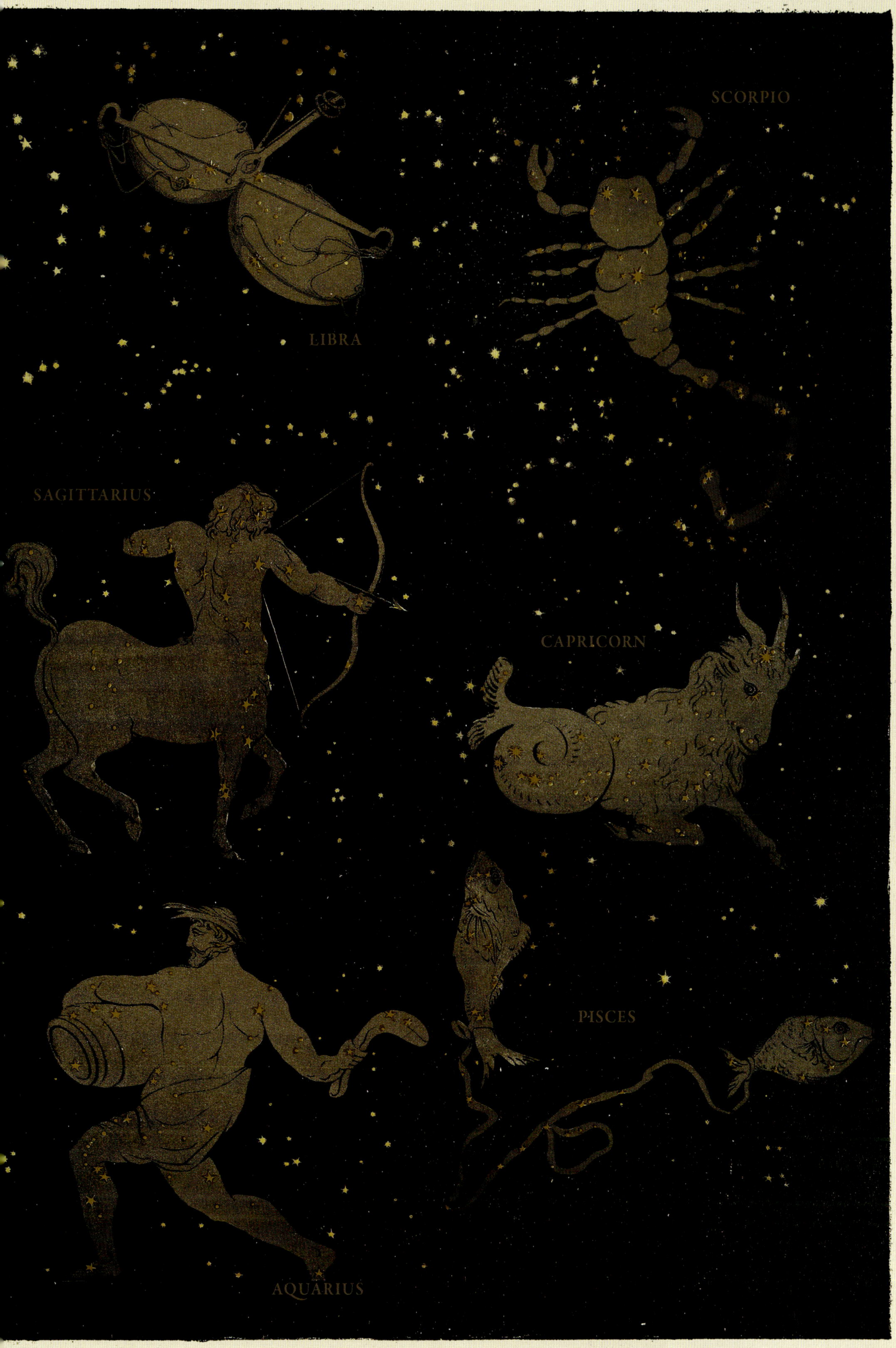

SCORPIO
LIBRA
SAGITTARIUS
CAPRICORN
PISCES
AQUARIUS

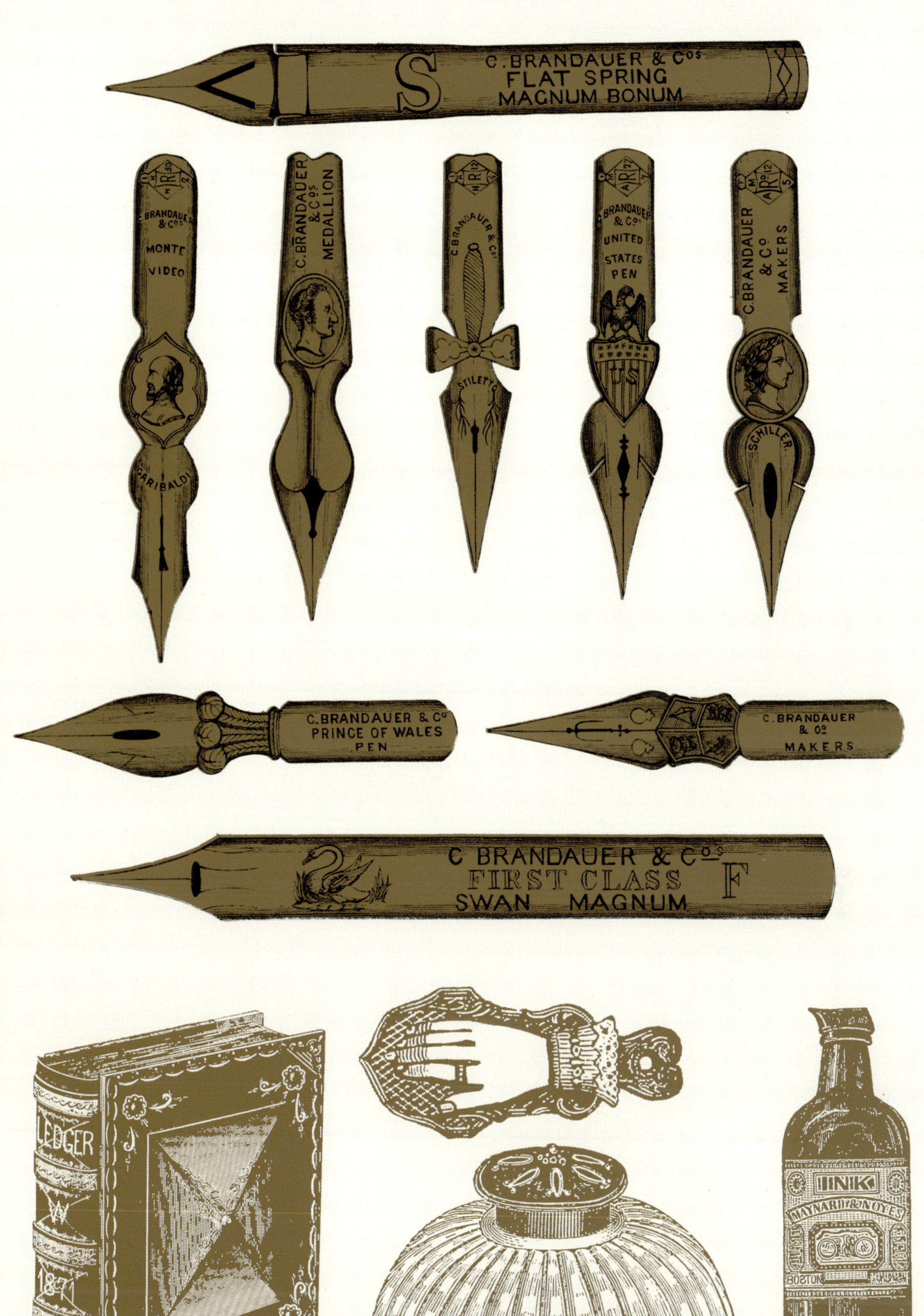

C. BRANDAUER & Cos
FLAT SPRING
MAGNUM BONUM
S
BRANDAUER & Cos
MONTE
VIDEO
GARIBALDI
C. BRANDAUER & Cos
MEDALLION
C. BRANDAUER & Co
STILETTO
C. BRANDAUER & Cos
UNITED
STATES
PEN
U.S.
C. BRANDAUER & Co
MAKERS
SCHILLER
C. BRANDAUER & Co
PRINCE OF WALES
PEN
C. BRANDAUER & Co
MAKERS
C. BRANDAUER & Cos
FIRST CLASS
SWAN MAGNUM
F
LEDGER
DA & CO.
INK
MAYNARD & NOYES
BOSTON

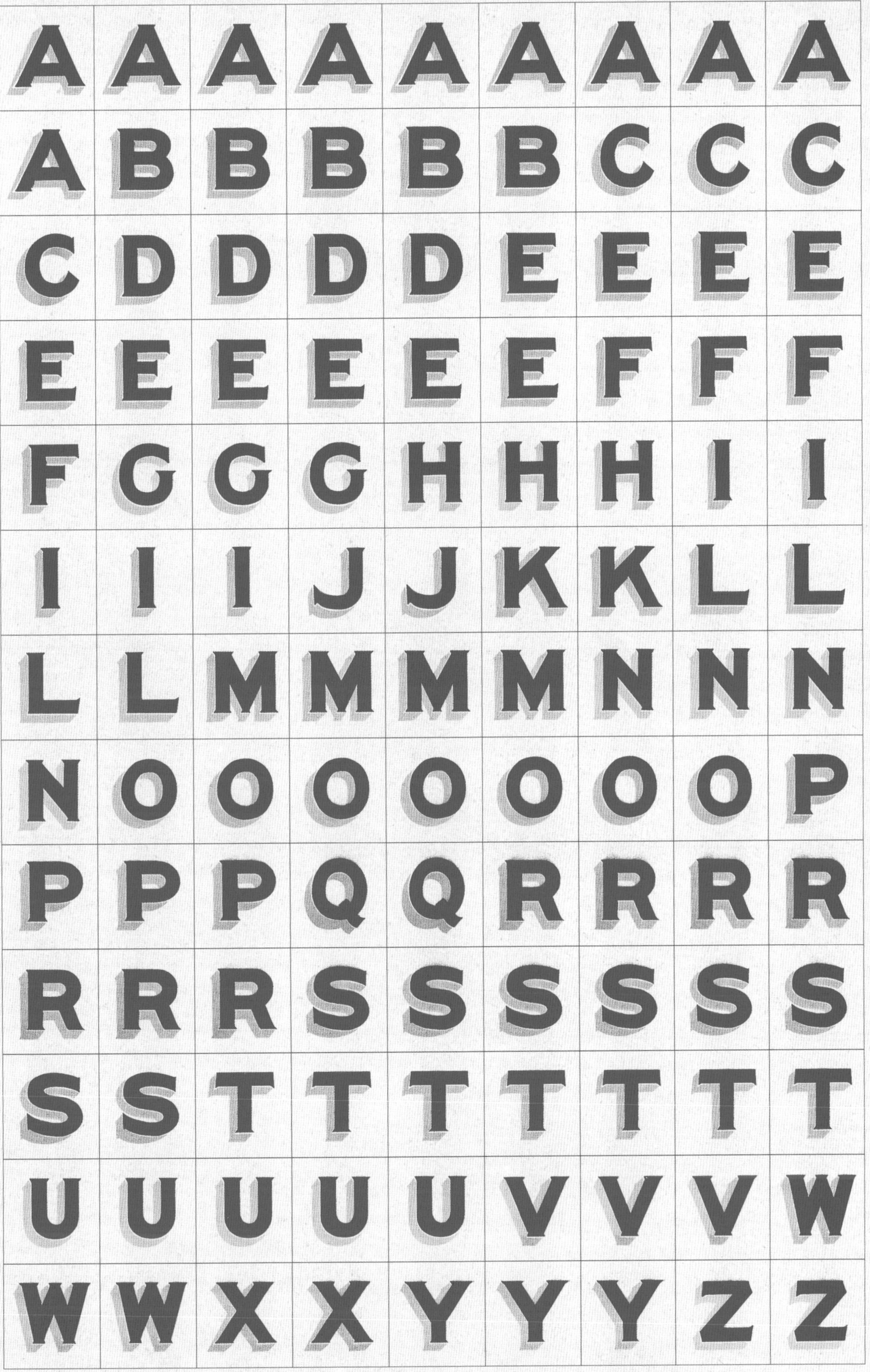

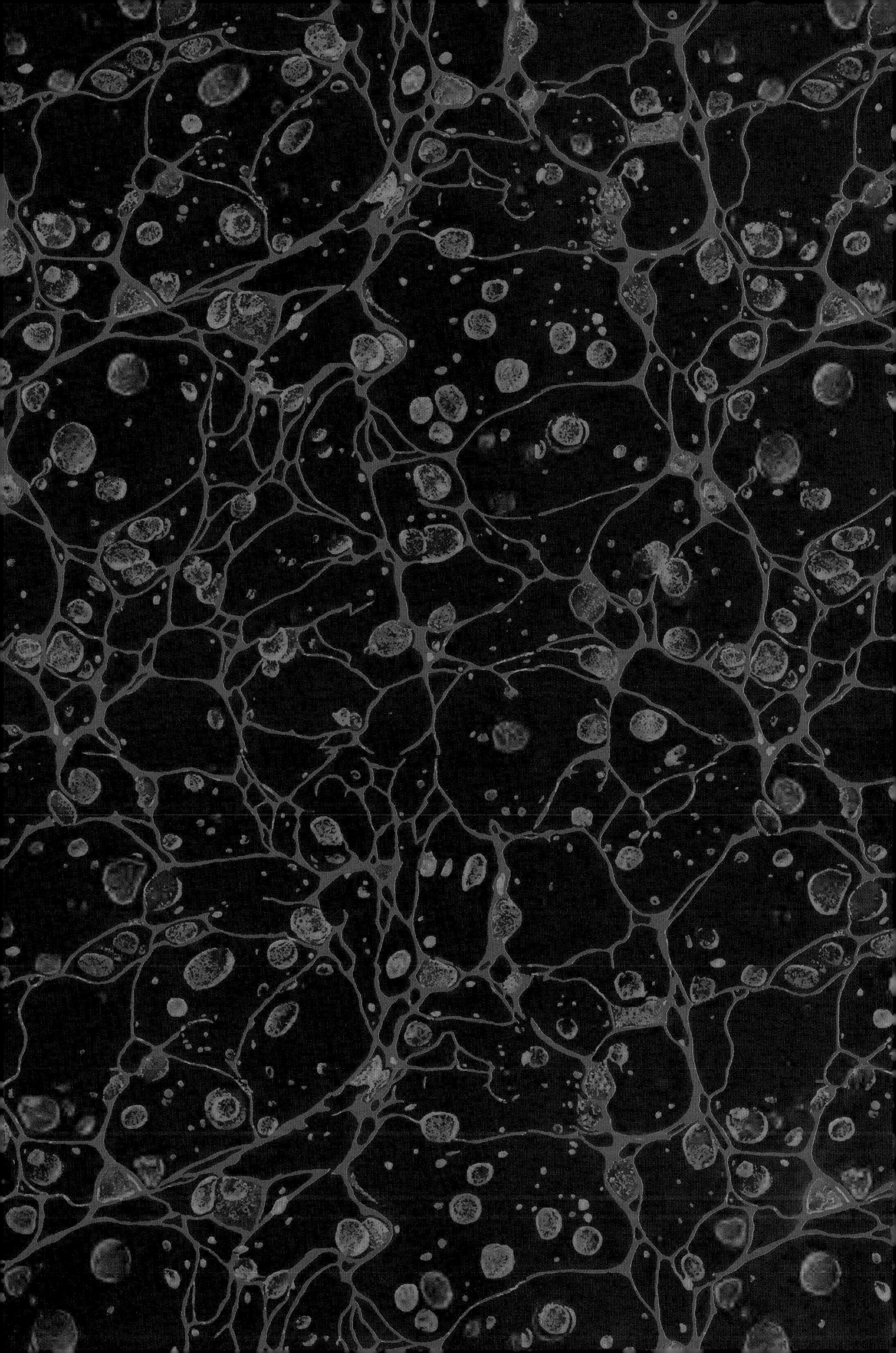

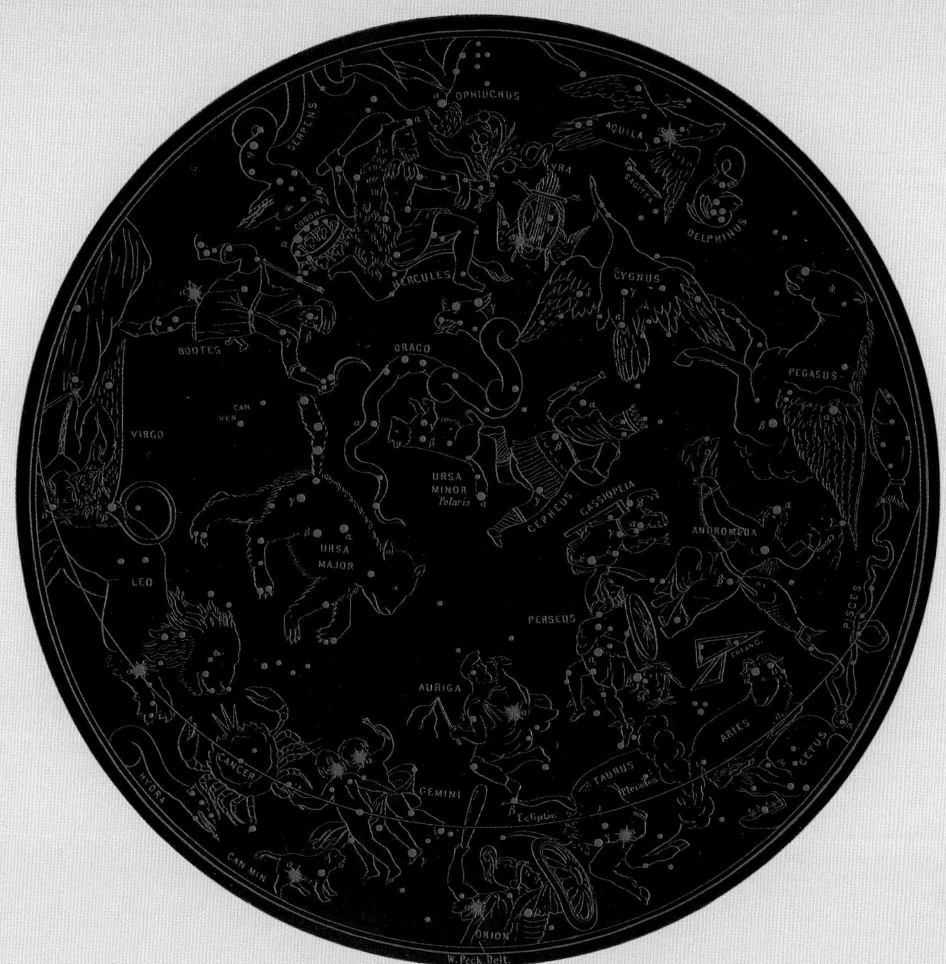

NORTHERN HEMISPHERE.

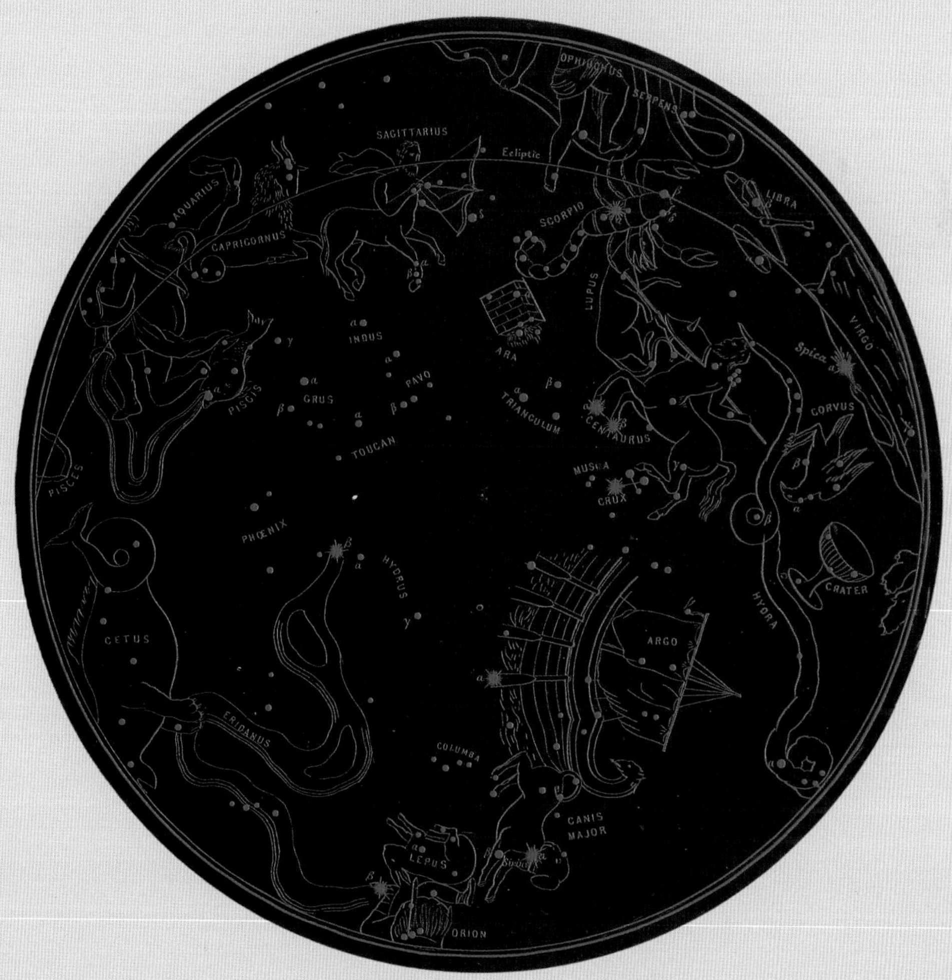

SOUTHERN HEMISPHERE.

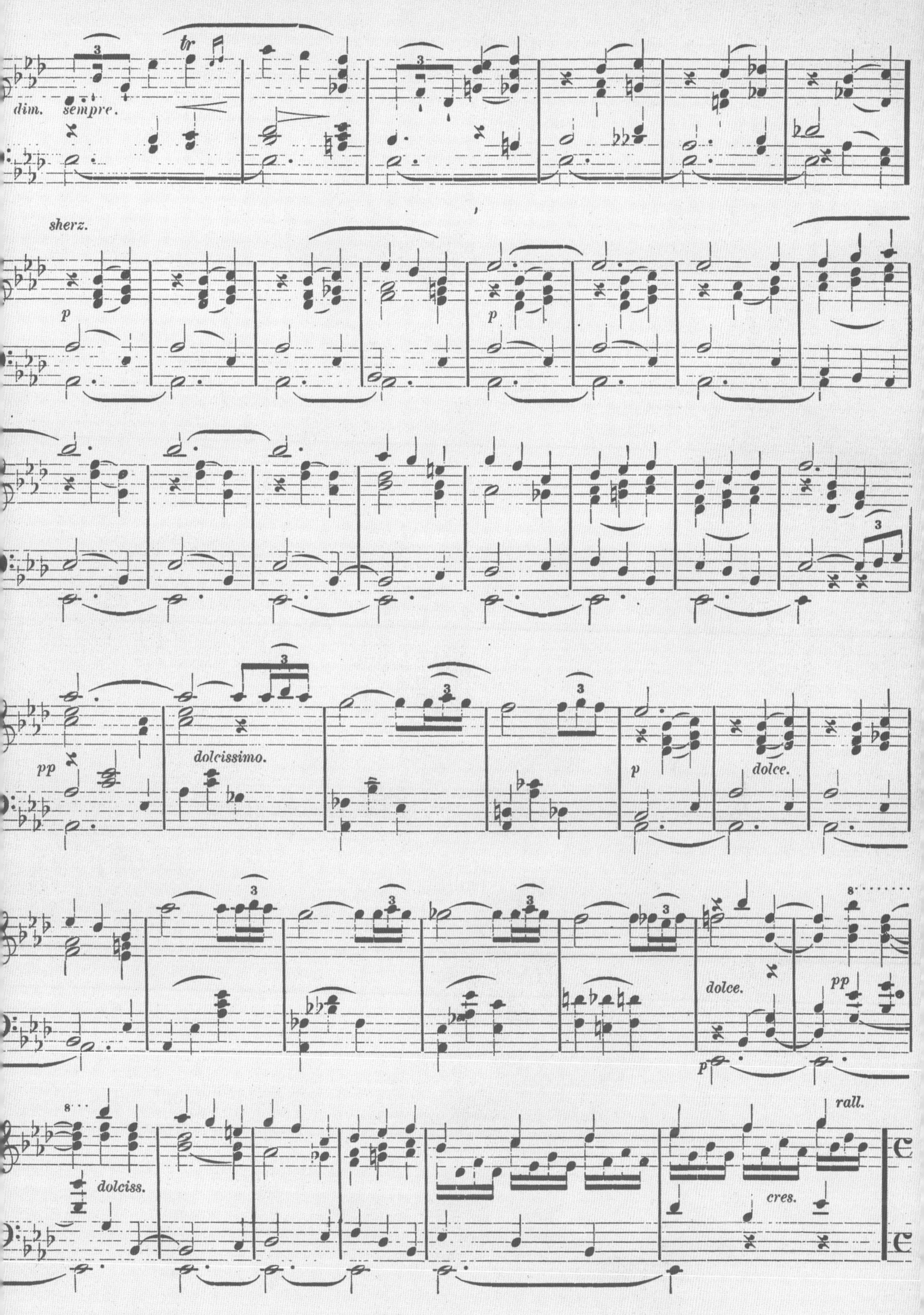

dim. sempre.
sherz.
p
pp
dolcissimo.
p
dolce.
dolce.
pp
dolciss.
cres.
rall.
tr
3
p
3
8
8

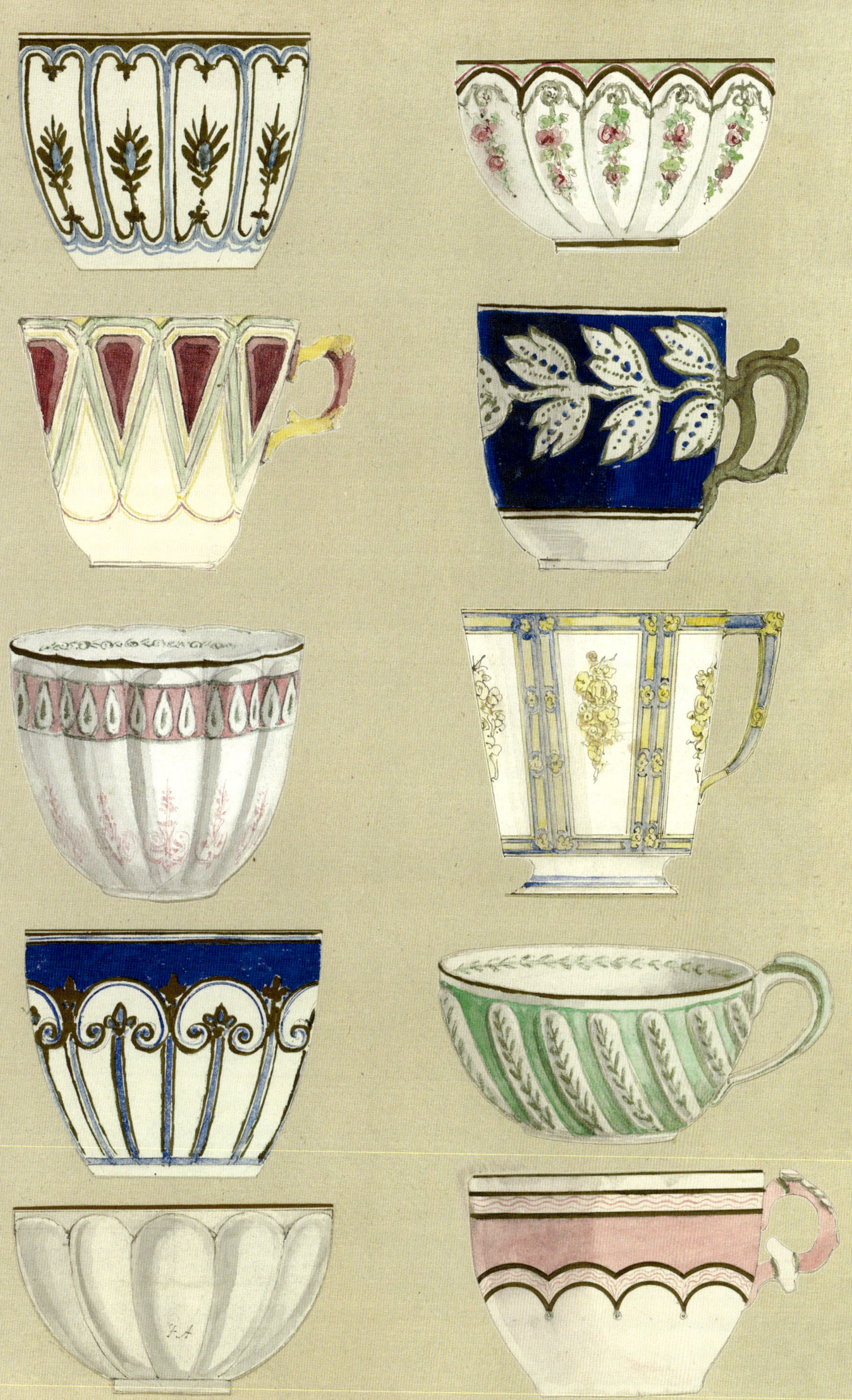

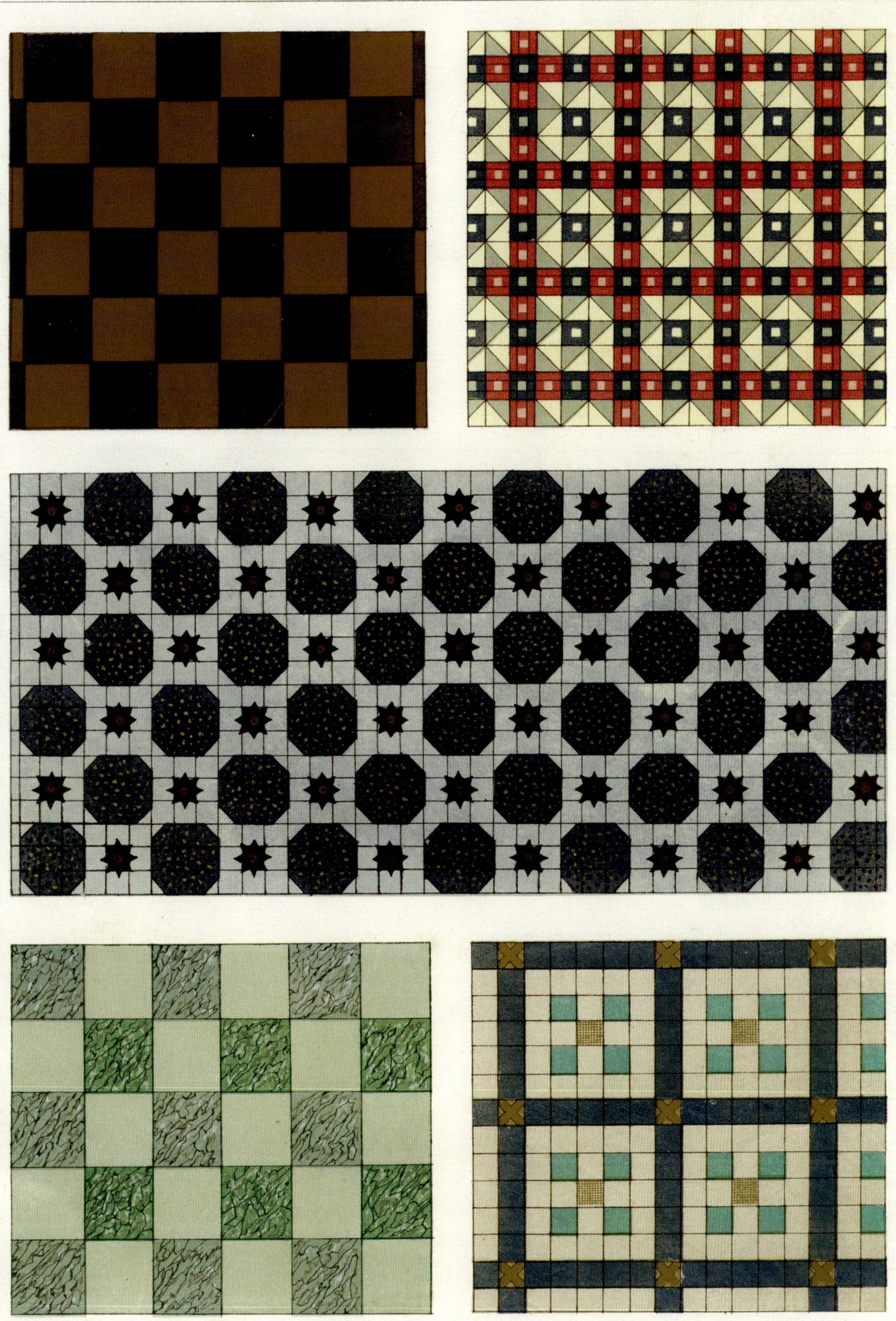

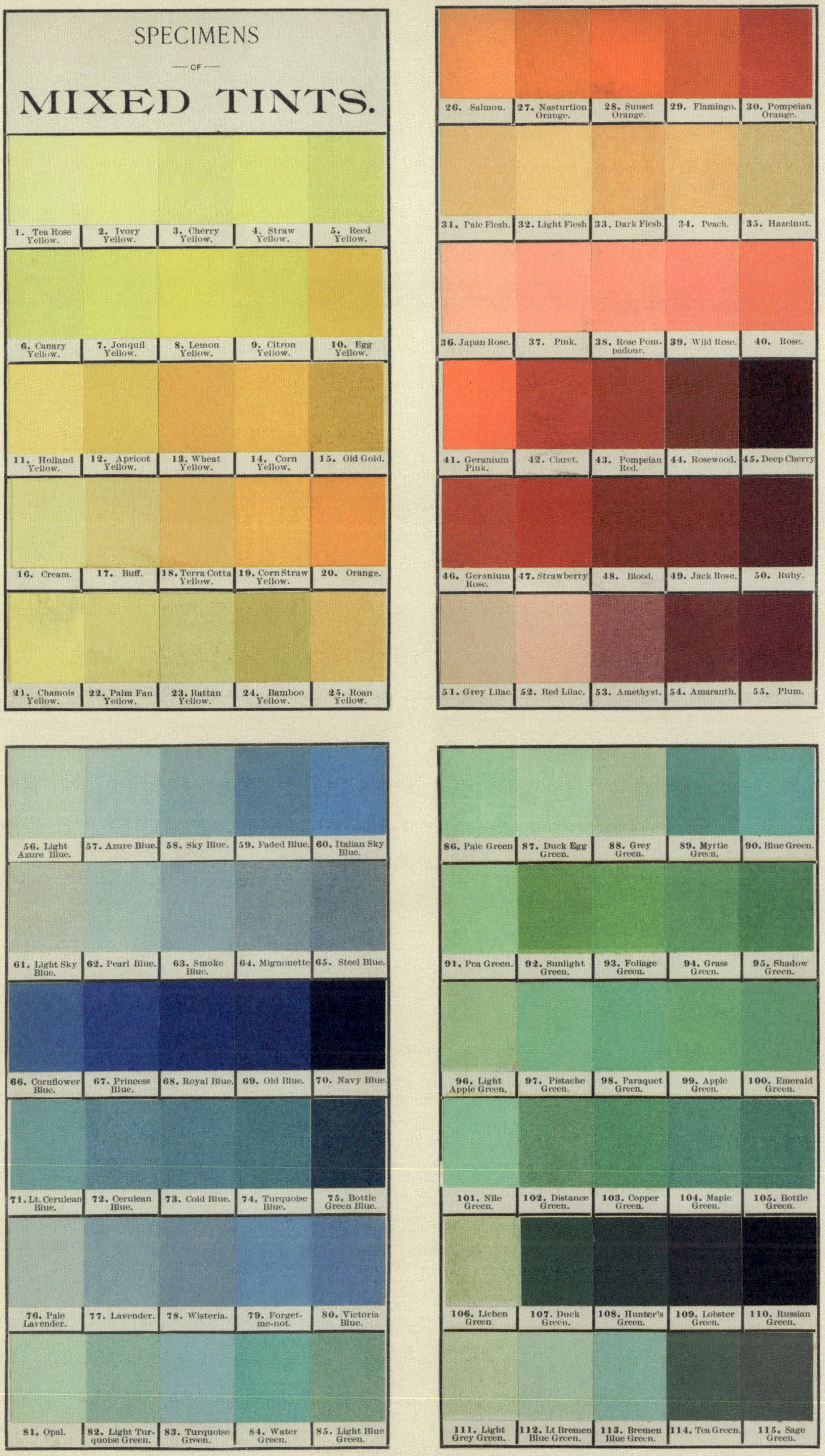

SPECIMENS

— OF —

MIXED TINTS.

1. Tea Rose Yellow.
2. Ivory Yellow.
3. Cherry Yellow.
4. Straw Yellow.
5. Reed Yellow.
6. Canary Yellow.
7. Jonquil Yellow.
8. Lemon Yellow.
9. Citron Yellow.
10. Egg Yellow.
11. Holland Yellow.
12. Apricot Yellow.
13. Wheat Yellow.
14. Corn Yellow.
15. Old Gold.
16. Cream.
17. Buff.
18. Terra Cotta Yellow.
19. Corn Straw Yellow.
20. Orange.
21. Chamois Yellow.
22. Palm Fan Yellow.
23. Rattan Yellow.
24. Bamboo Yellow.
25. Roan Yellow.

26. Salmon.
27. Nasturtion Orange.
28. Sunset Orange.
29. Flamingo.
30. Pompeian Orange.
31. Pale Flesh.
32. Light Flesh.
33. Dark Flesh.
34. Peach.
35. Hazelnut.
36. Japan Rose.
37. Pink.
38. Rose Pompadour.
39. Wild Rose.
40. Rose.
41. Geranium Pink.
42. Claret.
43. Pompeian Red.
44. Rosewood.
45. Deep Cherry.
46. Geranium Rose.
47. Strawberry.
48. Blood.
49. Jack Rose.
50. Ruby.
51. Grey Lilac.
52. Red Lilac.
53. Amethyst.
54. Amaranth.
55. Plum.

56. Light Azure Blue.
57. Azure Blue.
58. Sky Blue.
59. Faded Blue.
60. Italian Sky Blue.
61. Light Sky Blue.
62. Pearl Blue.
63. Smoke Blue.
64. Mignonette.
65. Steel Blue.
66. Cornflower Blue.
67. Princess Blue.
68. Royal Blue.
69. Old Blue.
70. Navy Blue.
71. Lt. Cerulean Blue.
72. Cerulean Blue.
73. Cold Blue.
74. Turquoise Blue.
75. Bottle Green Blue.
76. Pale Lavender.
77. Lavender.
78. Wisteria.
79. Forget-me-not.
80. Victoria Blue.
81. Opal.
82. Light Turquoise Green.
83. Turquoise Green.
84. Water Green.
85. Light Blue Green.

86. Pale Green.
87. Duck Egg Green.
88. Grey Green.
89. Myrtle Green.
90. Blue Green.
91. Pea Green.
92. Sunlight Green.
93. Foliage Green.
94. Grass Green.
95. Shadow Green.
96. Light Apple Green.
97. Pistache Green.
98. Paraquet Green.
99. Apple Green.
100. Emerald Green.
101. Nile Green.
102. Distance Green.
103. Copper Green.
104. Maple Green.
105. Bottle Green.
106. Lichen Green.
107. Duck Green.
108. Hunter's Green.
109. Lobster Green.
110. Russian Green.
111. Light Grey Green.
112. Lt Bremen Blue Green.
113. Bremen Blue Green.
114. Tea Green.
115. Sage Green.

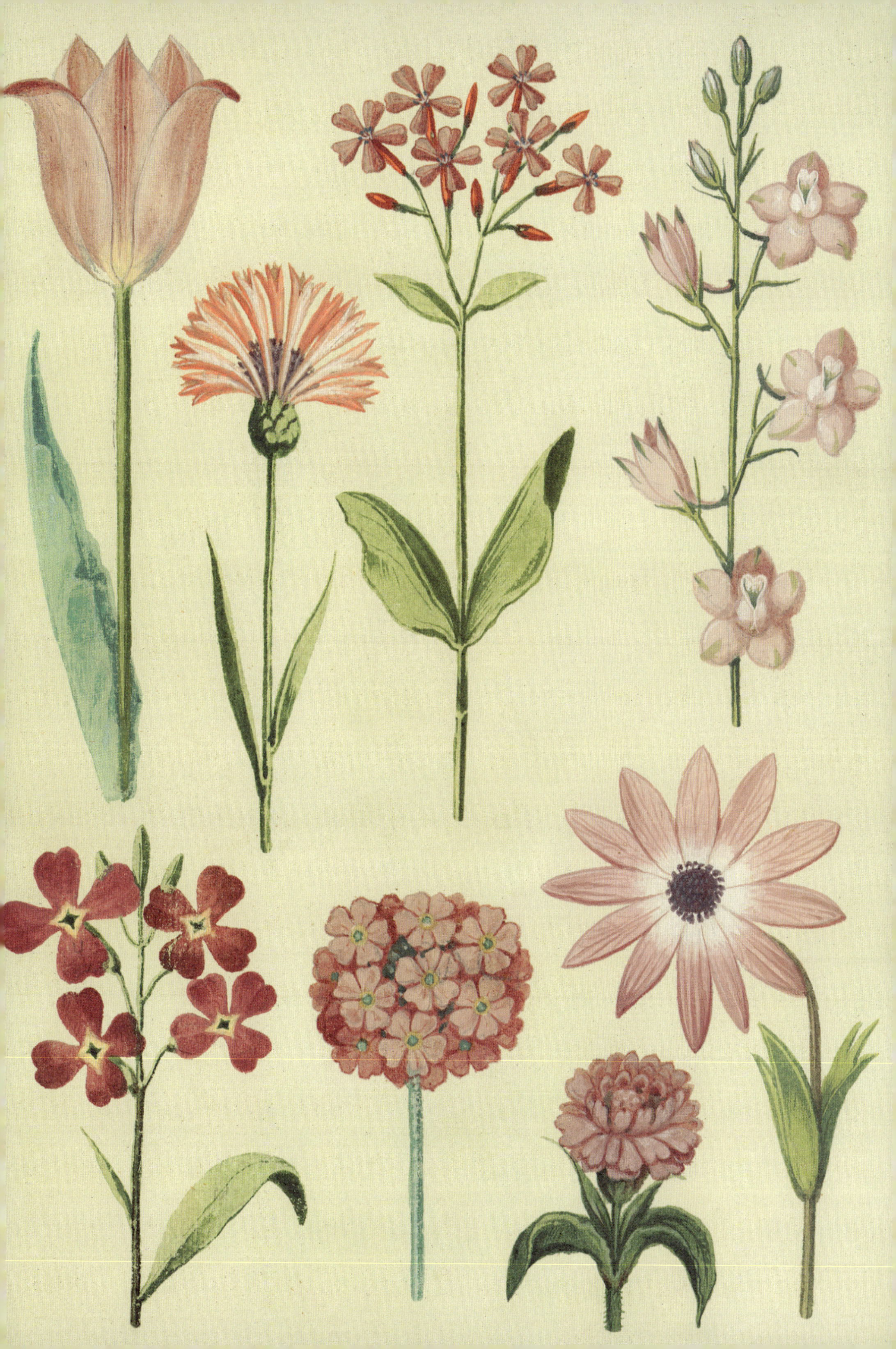

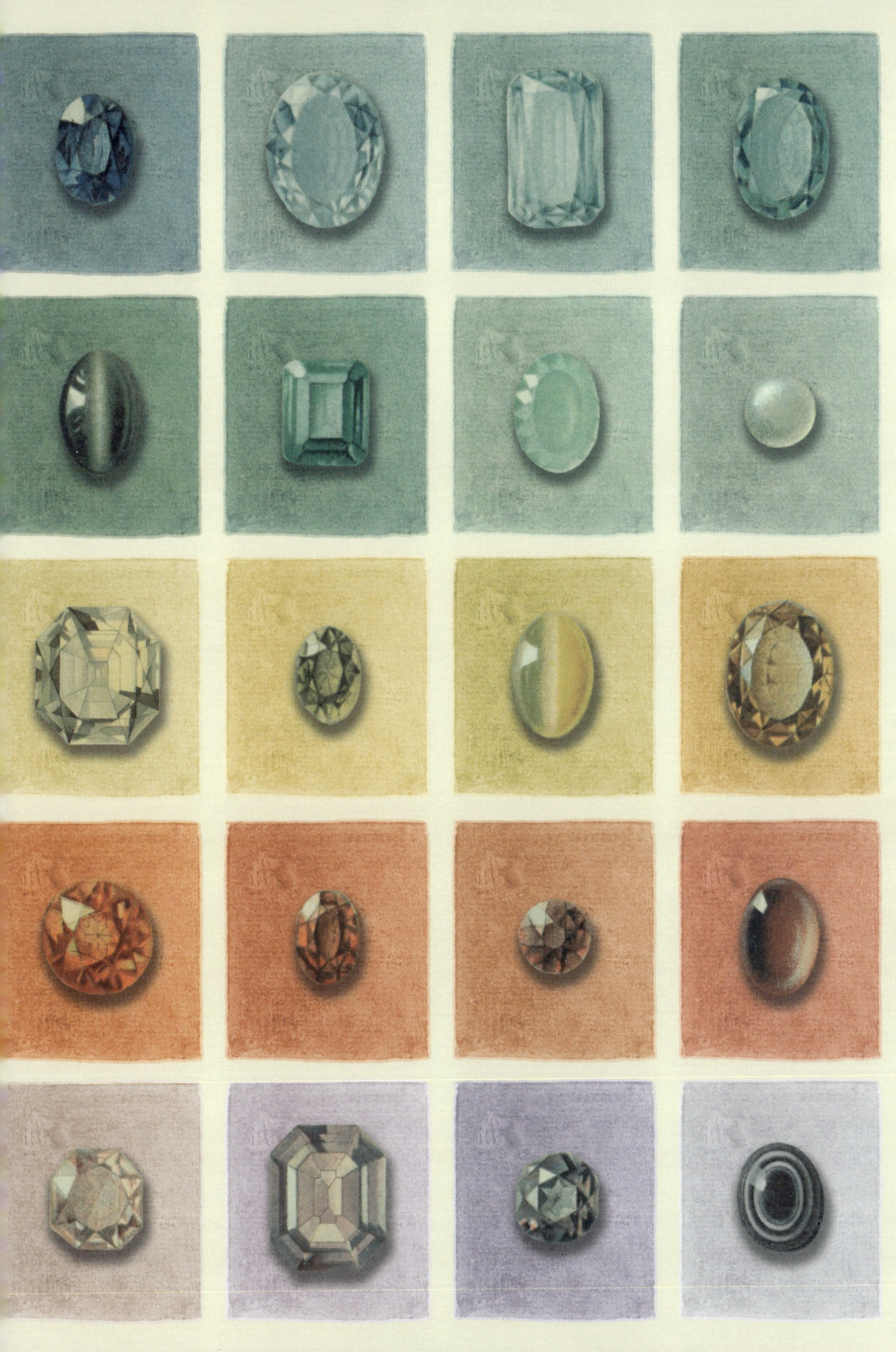

Knowledge is power,

Knowledge is power,

Knowledge is power,

Knowledge is power,

Knowledge is power,

Endeavour to do well,

Endeavour to do well,

Endeavour to do well,

Endeavour to do well,

Endeavour to do well,

Endeavour to do well,

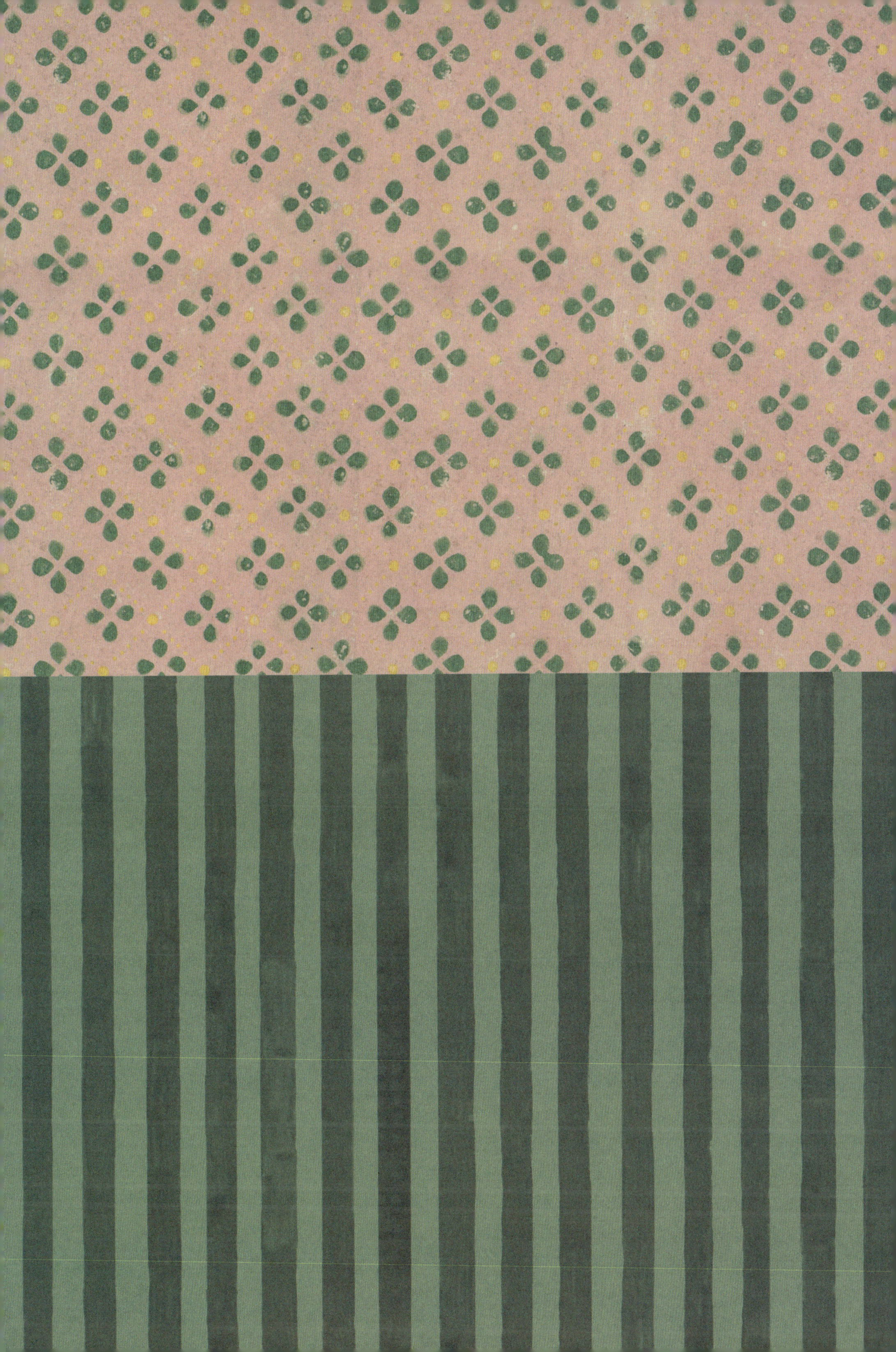

A.	a.	*a.*	N.	n.	*n.*
B.	b.	*b.*	O.	o.	*o.*
C.	c.	*c.*	P.	p.	*p.*
D.	d.	*d.*	Q.	q.	*q.*
E.	e.	*e.*	R.	r.	*r.*
F.	f.	*f.*	S.	s.	*s.*
G.	g.	*g.*	T.	t.	*t.*
H.	h.	*h.*	U.	u.	*u.*
I.	i.	*i.*	V.	v.	*v.*
J.	j.	*j.*	W.	w.	*w.*
K.	k.	*k.*	X.	x.	*x.*
L.	l.	*l.*	Y.	y.	*y.*
M.	m.	*m.*	Z.	z.	*z.*

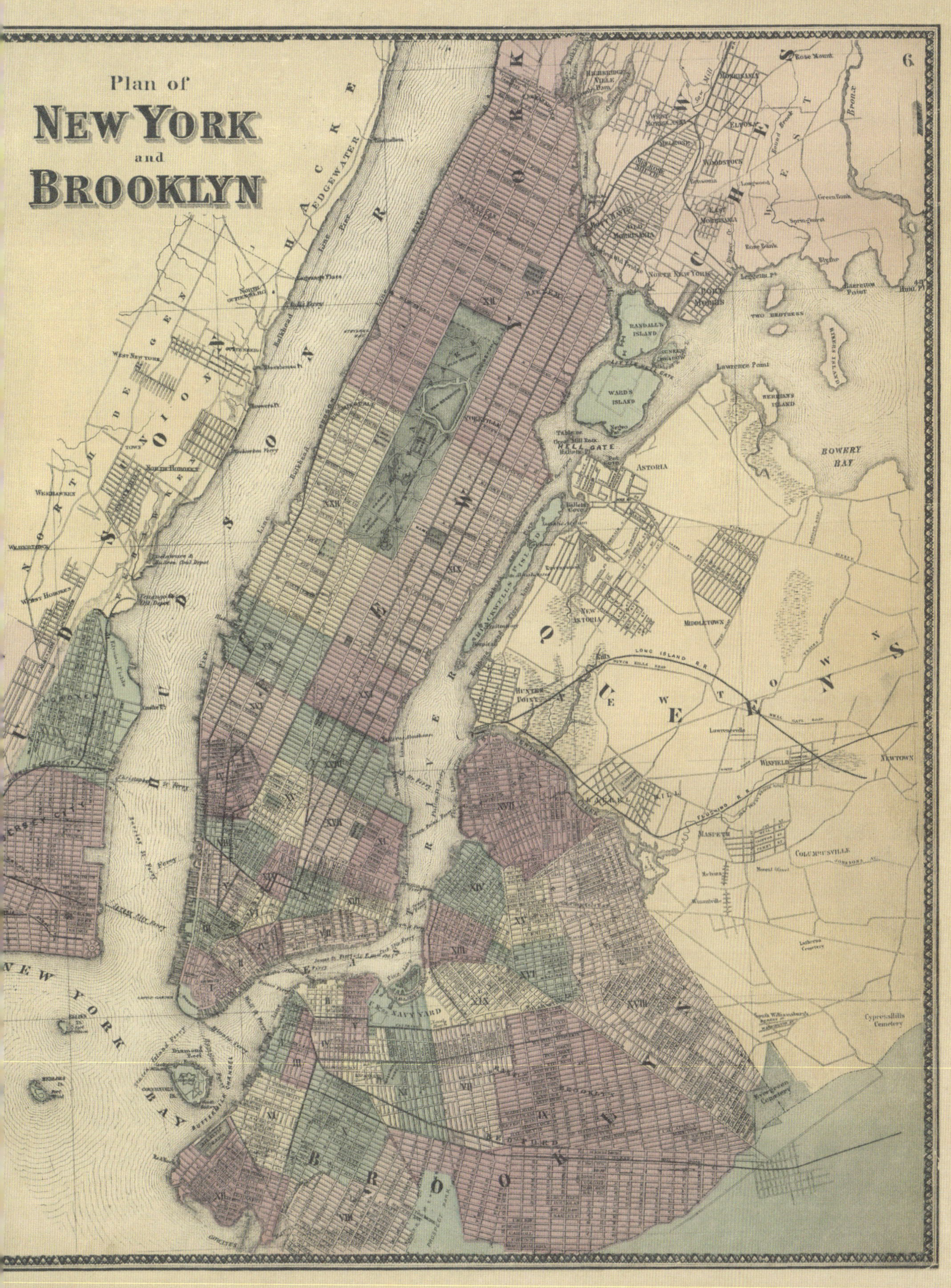
Plan of
NEW YORK
and
BROOKLYN
6

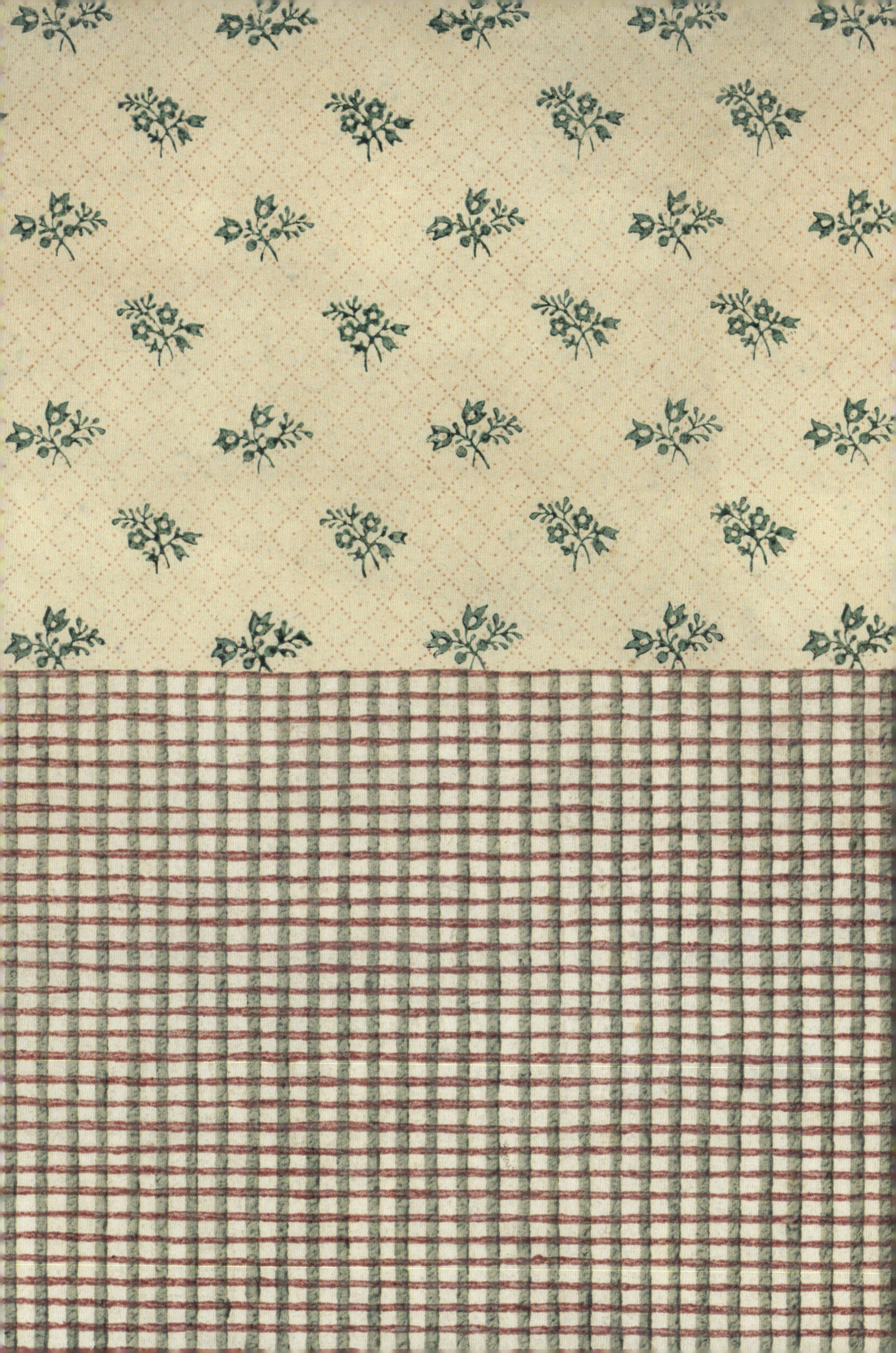

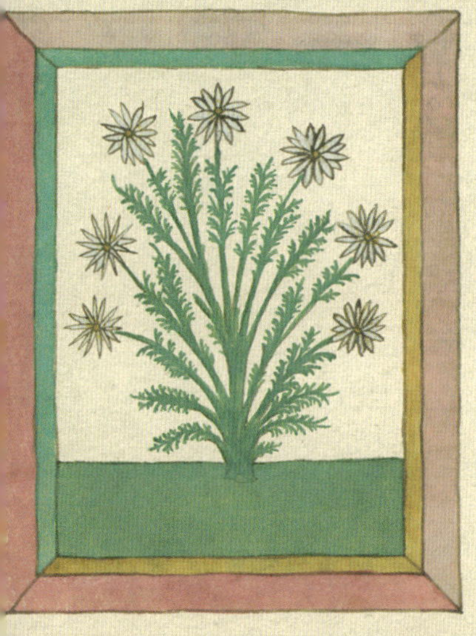
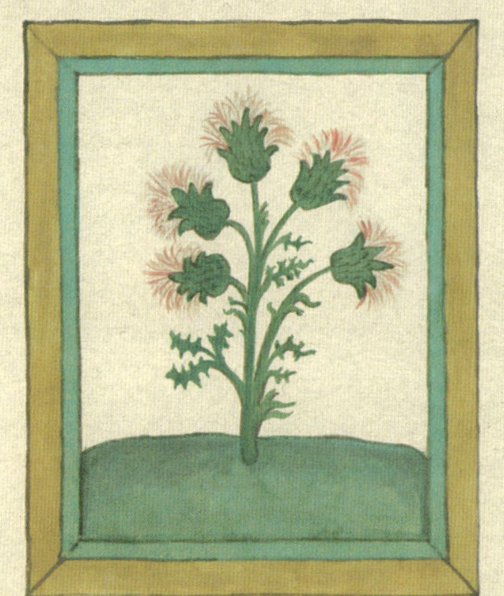
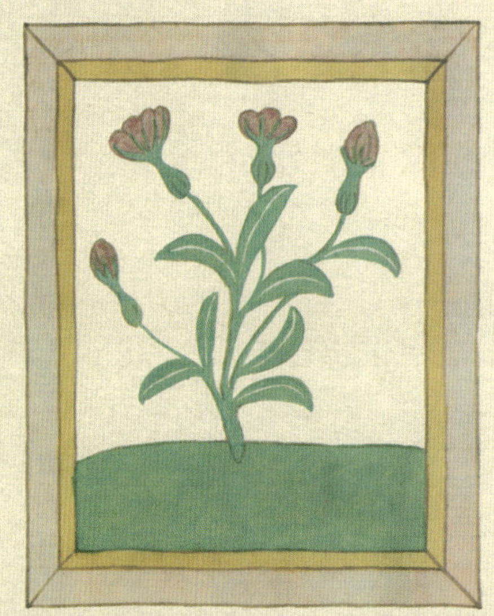
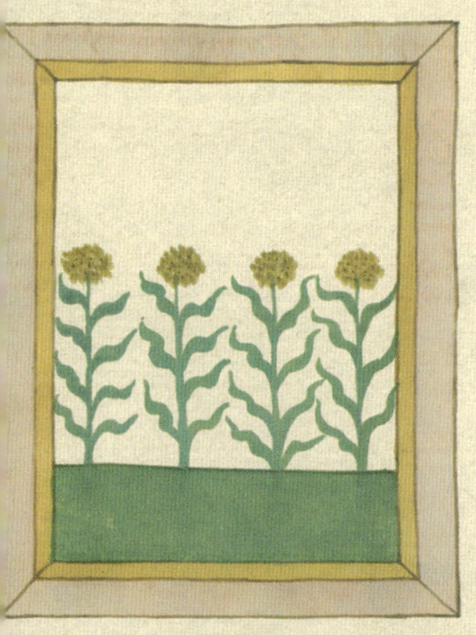
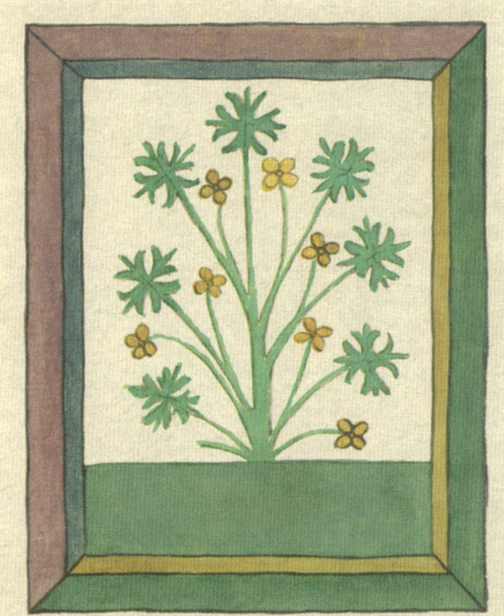
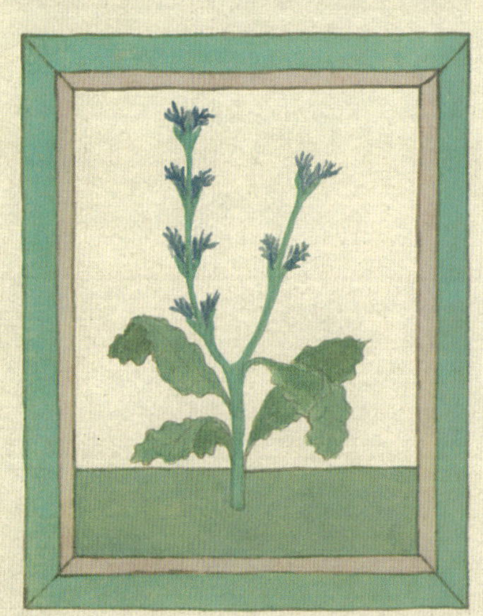
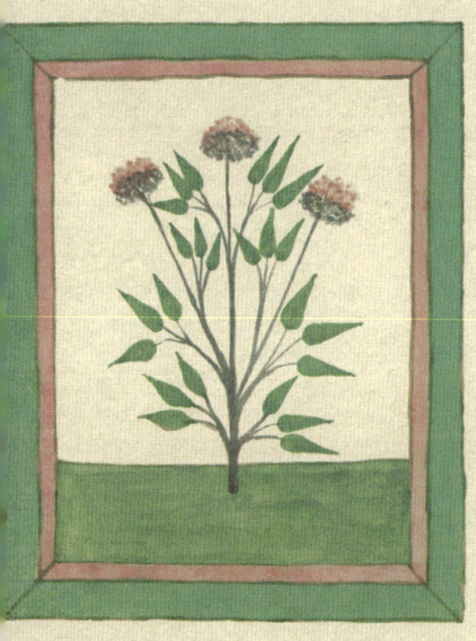
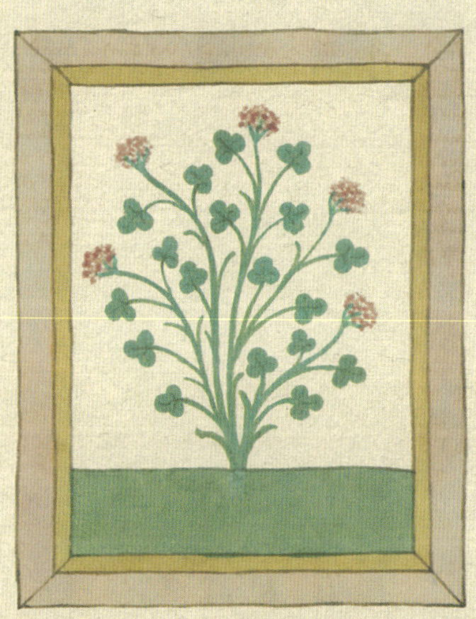
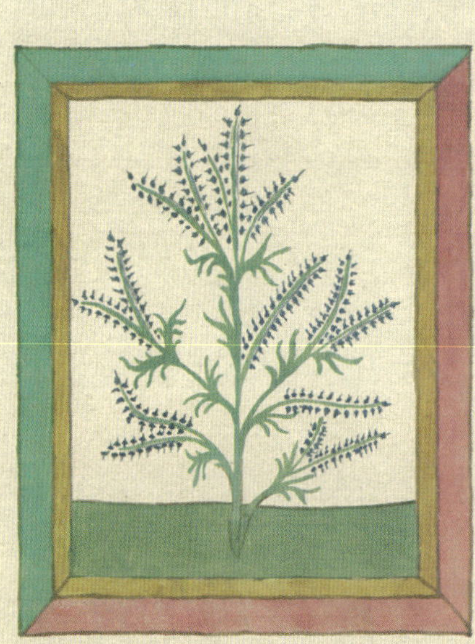

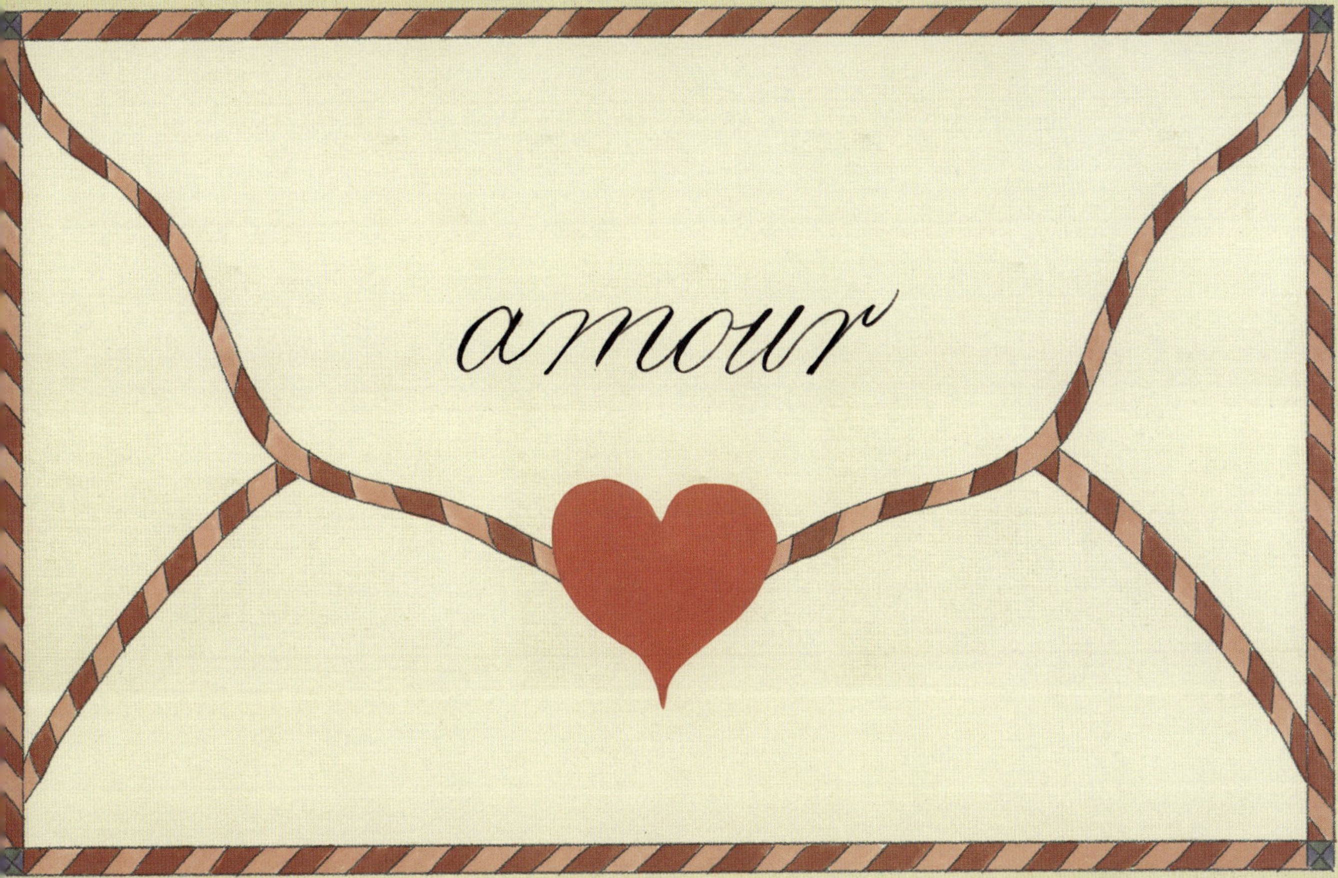

amour

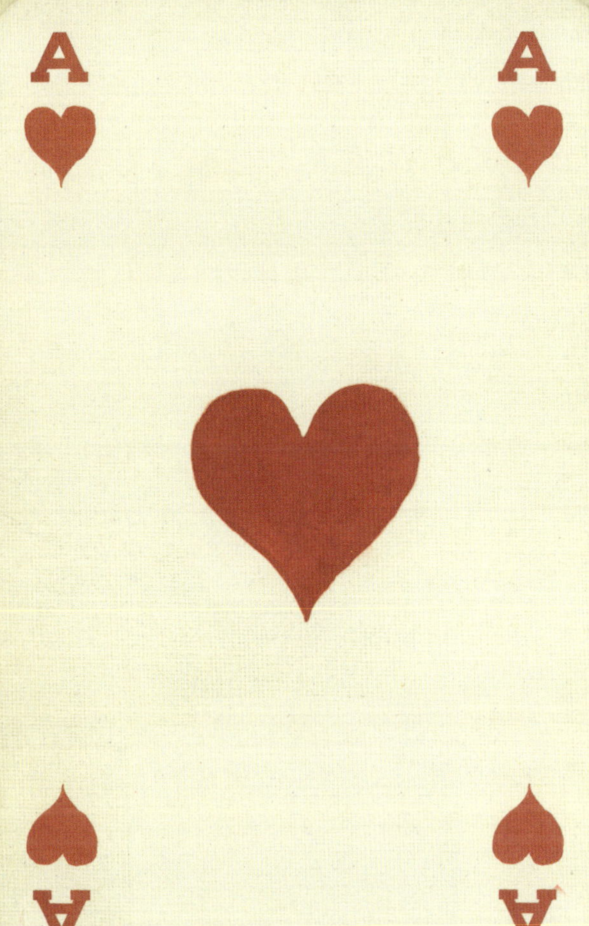

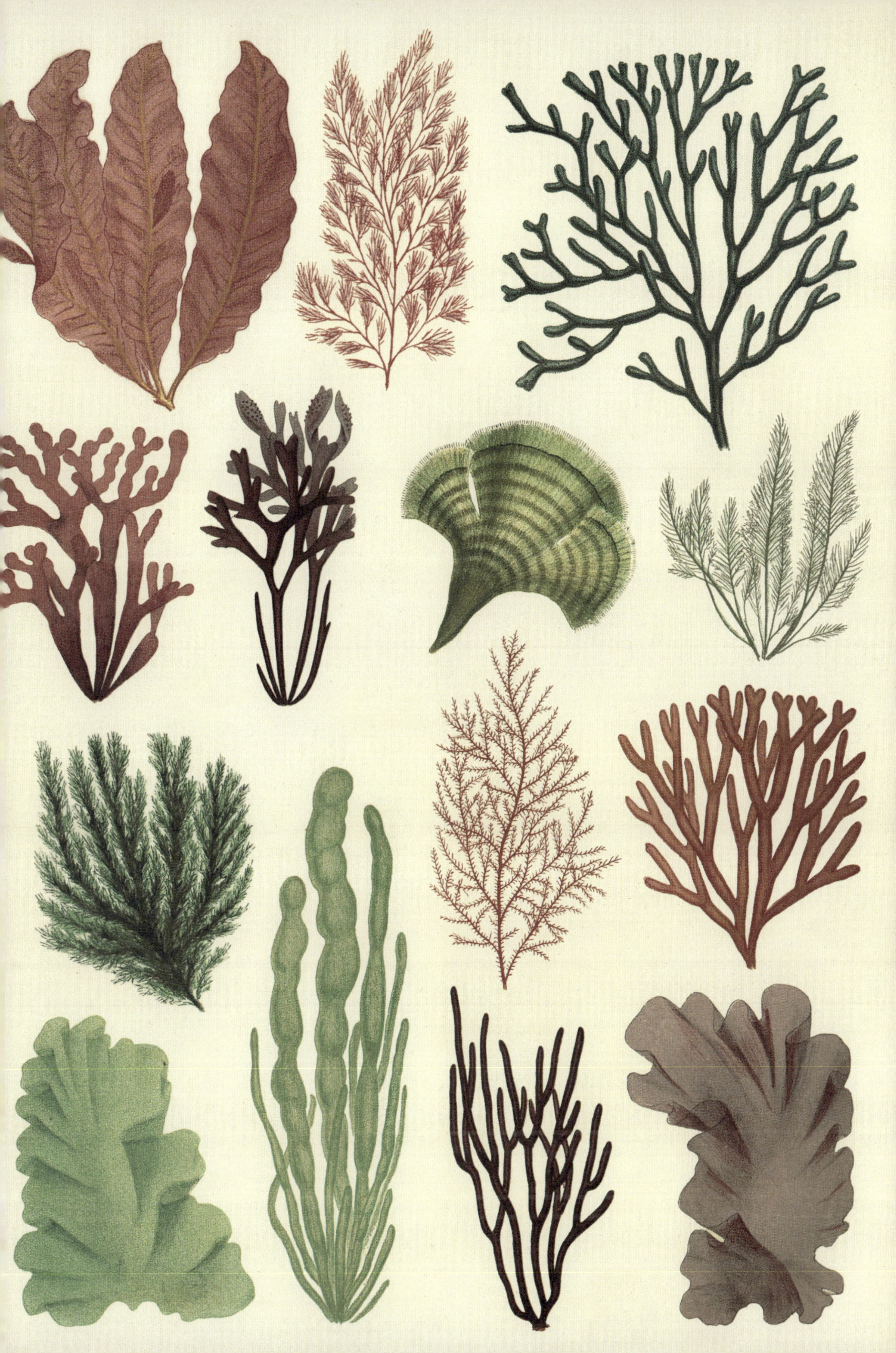

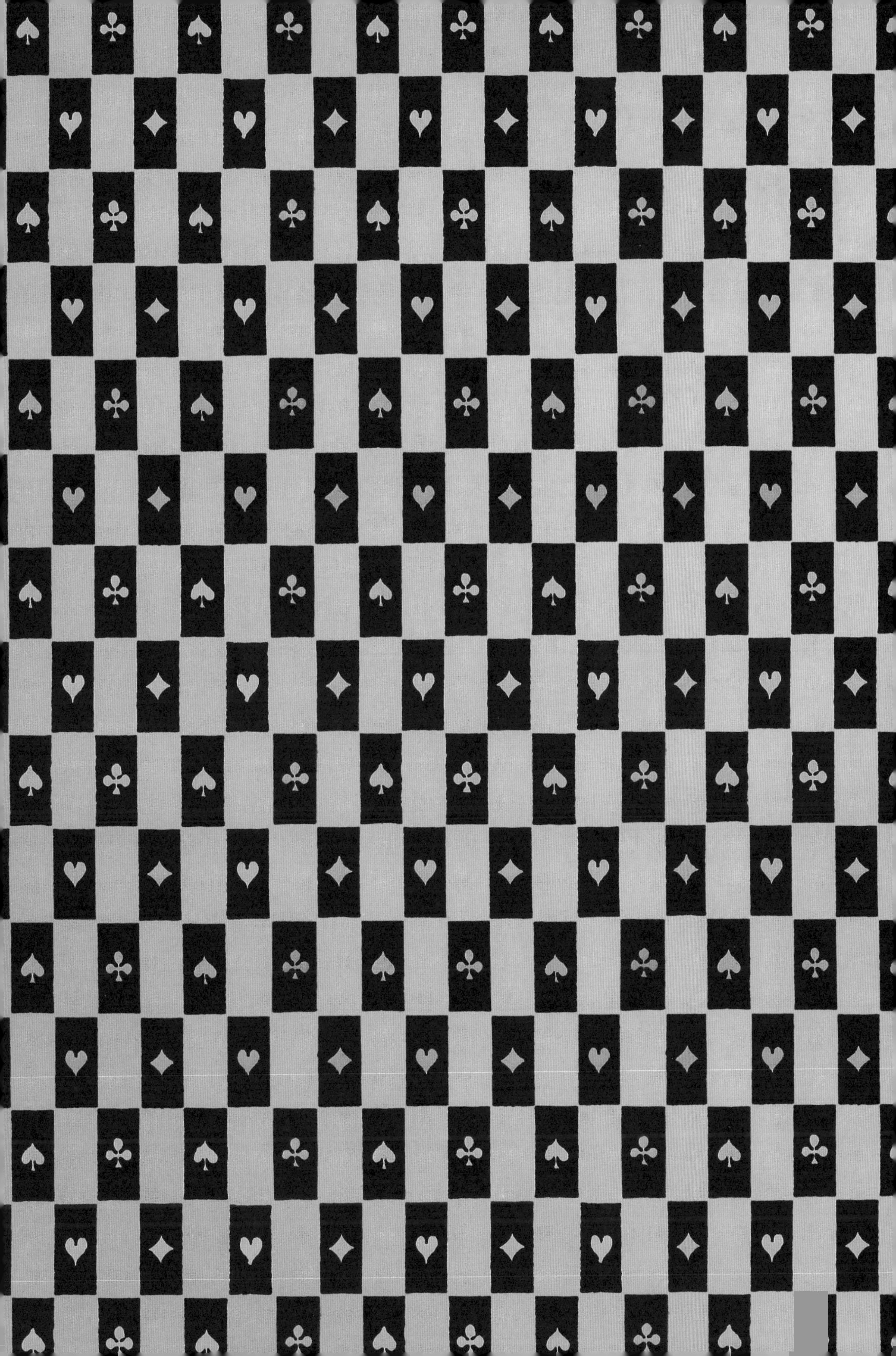

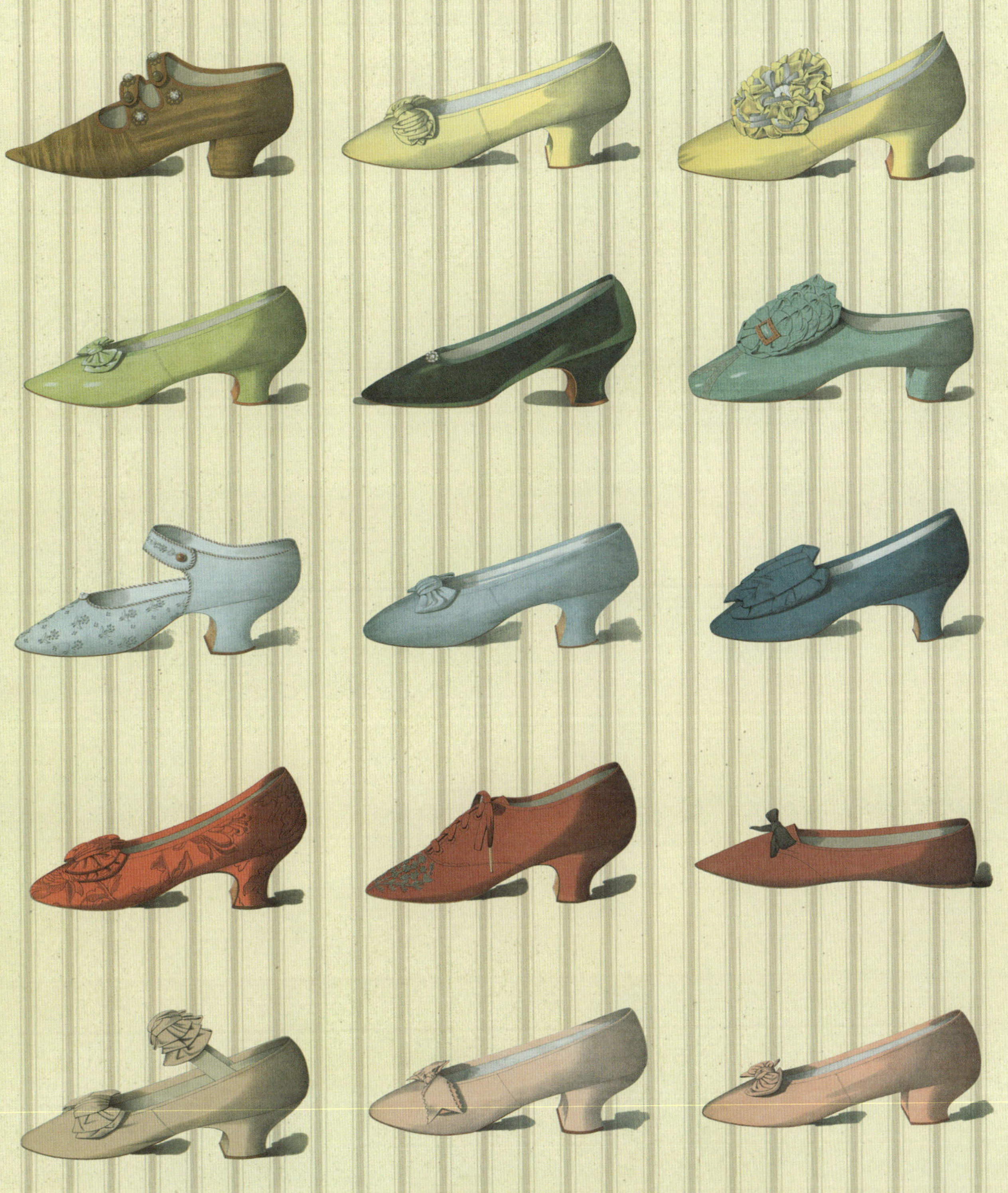

SHINE FAMILY PRIDE

CHRONICLE MORNING

team ABSOLUTE LARGE

Materials DAILY

band ROCK MORE

MAKING EDIT

GENIUS EXCURSION NOTES

Journal Romance

DALL Brand Premium

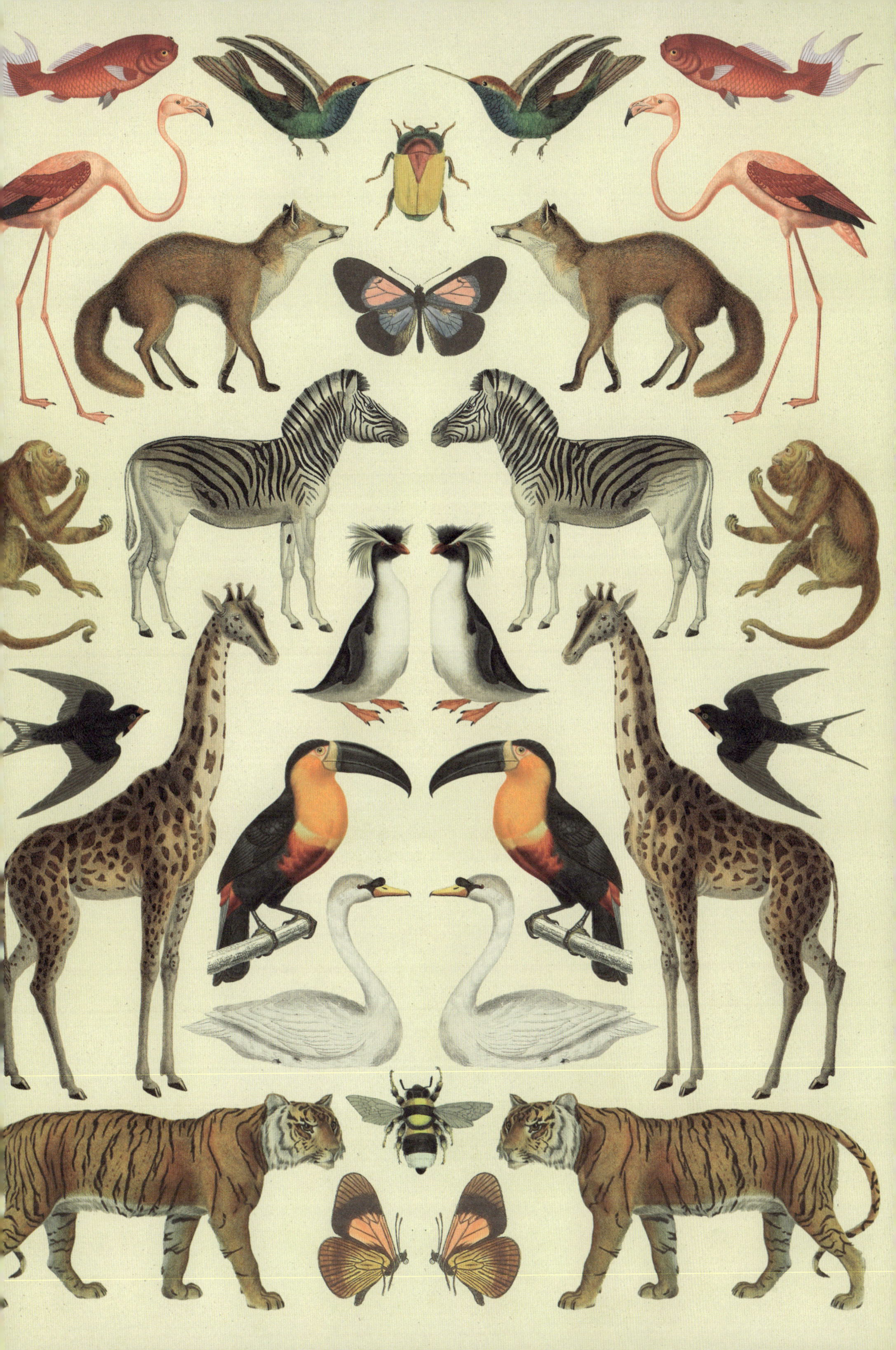

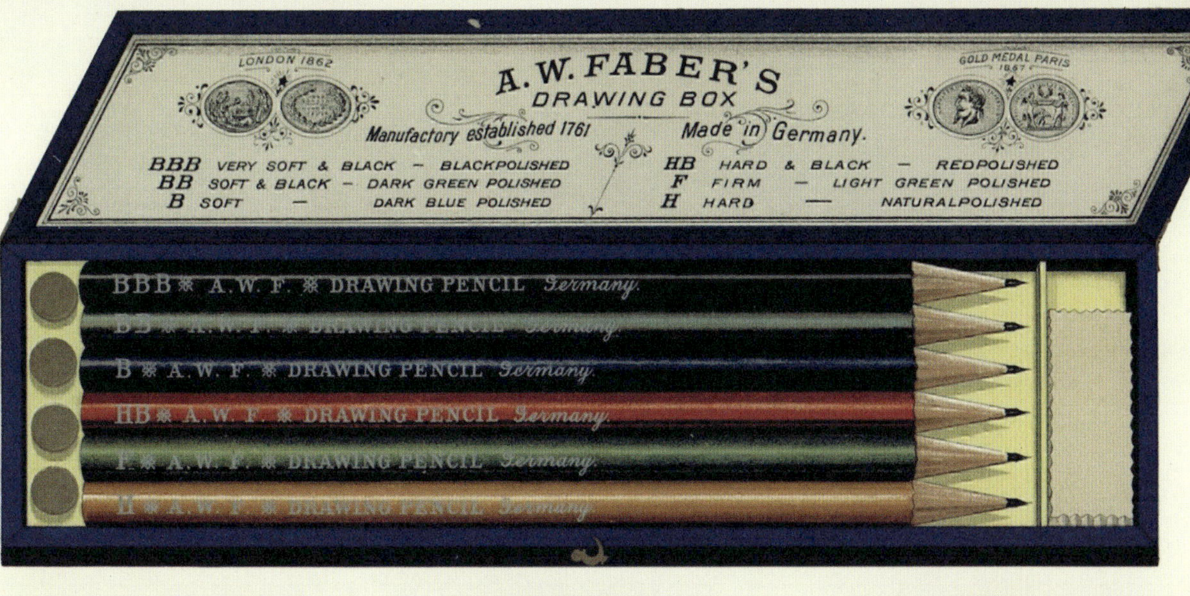
LONDON 1862
GOLD MEDAL PARIS 1867
A.W. FABER'S
DRAWING BOX
Manufactory established 1761   Made in Germany.
BBB VERY SOFT & BLACK - BLACK POLISHED   HB HARD & BLACK - RED POLISHED
BB   SOFT & BLACK - DARK GREEN POLISHED   F FIRM - LIGHT GREEN POLISHED
B   SOFT - DARK BLUE POLISHED   H HARD - NATURAL POLISHED
BBB * A.W.F. * DRAWING PENCIL Germany.
BB * A.W.F. * DRAWING PENCIL Germany.
B * A.W.F. * DRAWING PENCIL Germany.
HB * A.W.F. * DRAWING PENCIL Germany.
F * A.W.F. * DRAWING PENCIL Germany.
H * A.W.F. * DRAWING PENCIL Germany.

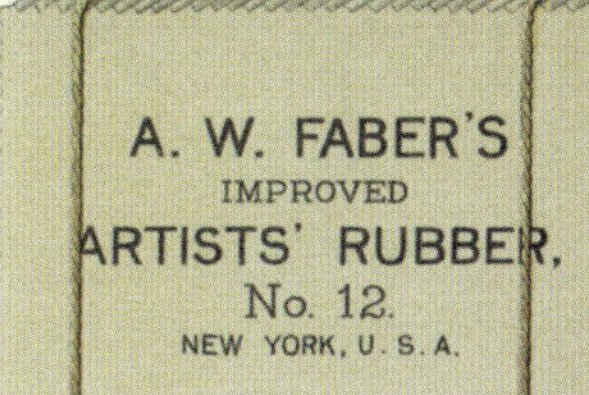
A. W. FABER'S
IMPROVED
ARTISTS' RUBBER,
No. 12.
NEW YORK, U.S.A.

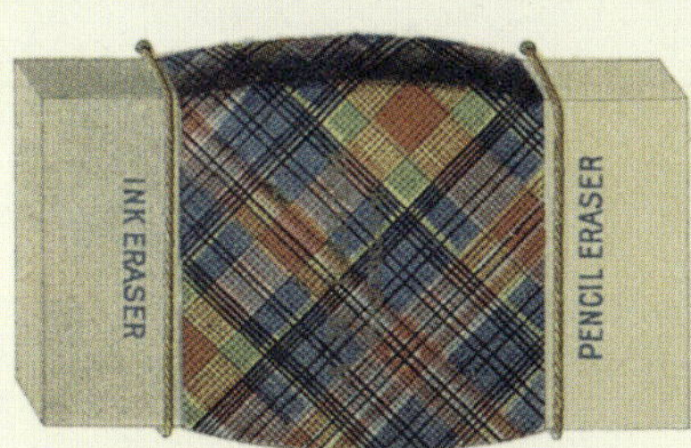
INK ERASER
PENCIL ERASER

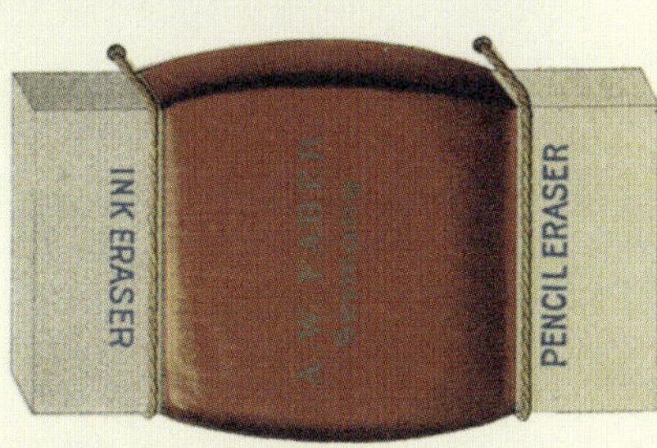
INK ERASER
PENCIL ERASER

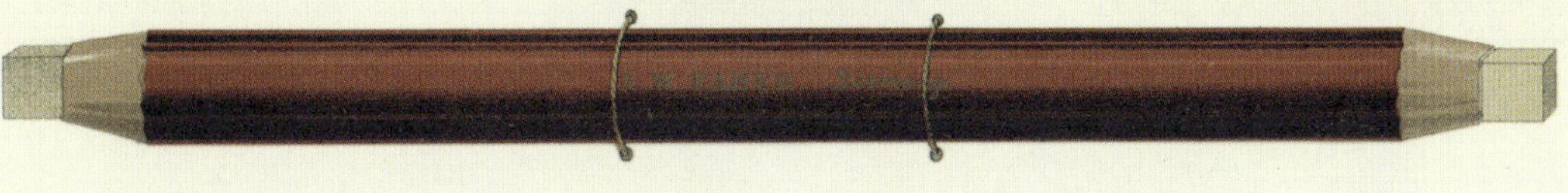

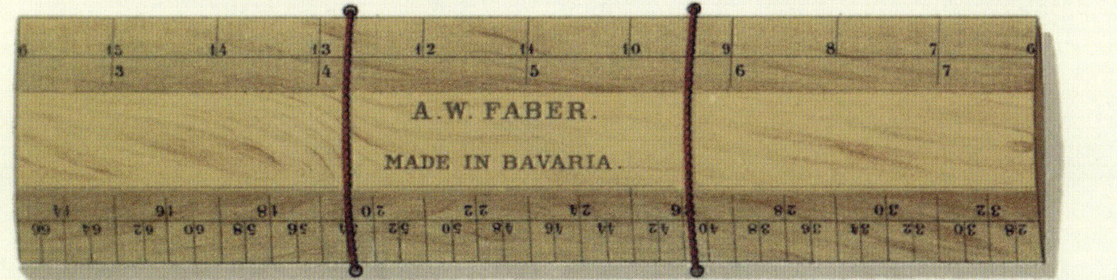
15 14 13 12 11 10 9 8 7 6
3   4   5   6   7
A.W. FABER.
MADE IN BAVARIA.

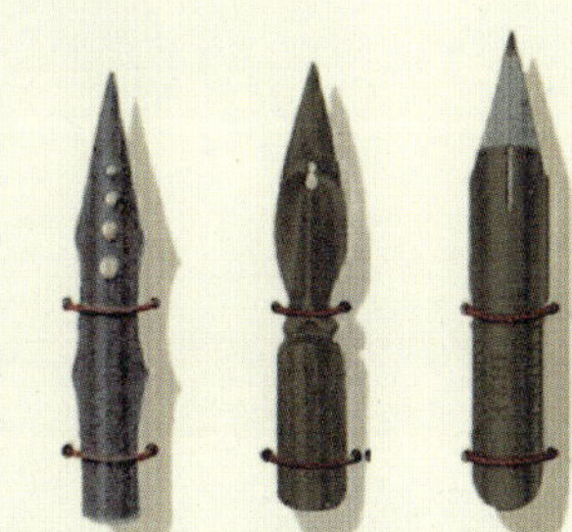

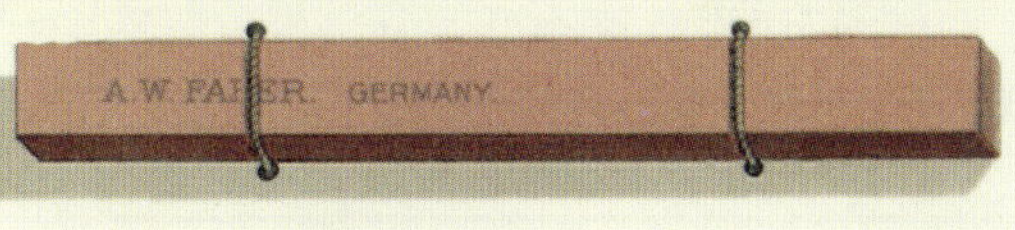
A.W. FABER. GERMANY.

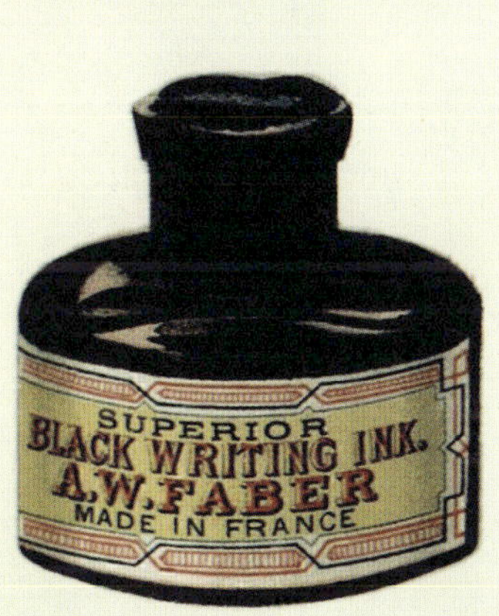
SUPERIOR
BLACK WRITING INK.
A.W. FABER
MADE IN FRANCE

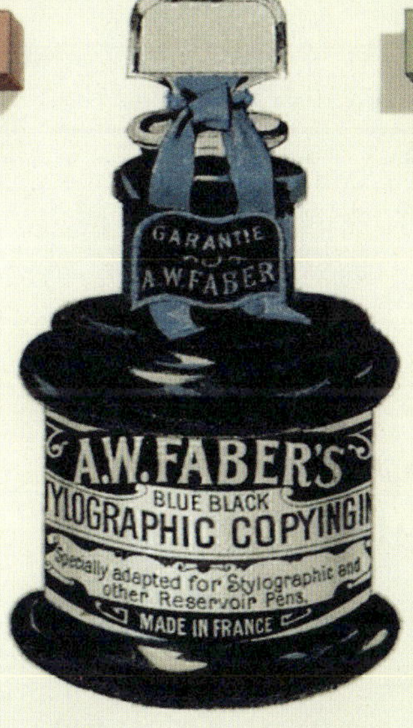
GARANTIE
A.W. FABER
A.W. FABER'S
BLUE BLACK
STYLOGRAPHIC COPYING INK
Specially adapted for Stylographic and
other Reservoir Pens.
MADE IN FRANCE

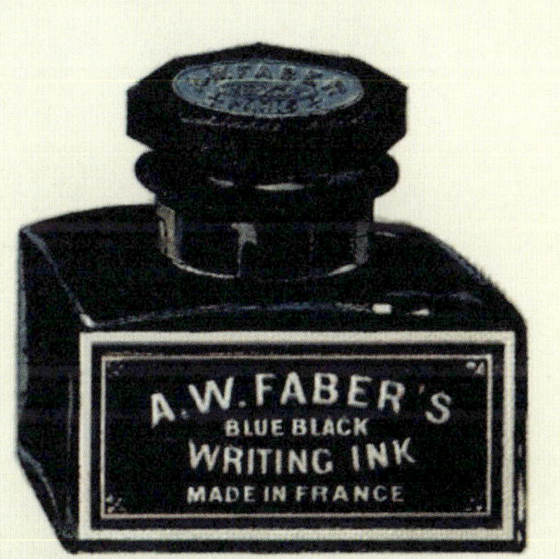
A.W. FABER'S
BLUE BLACK
WRITING INK
MADE IN FRANCE

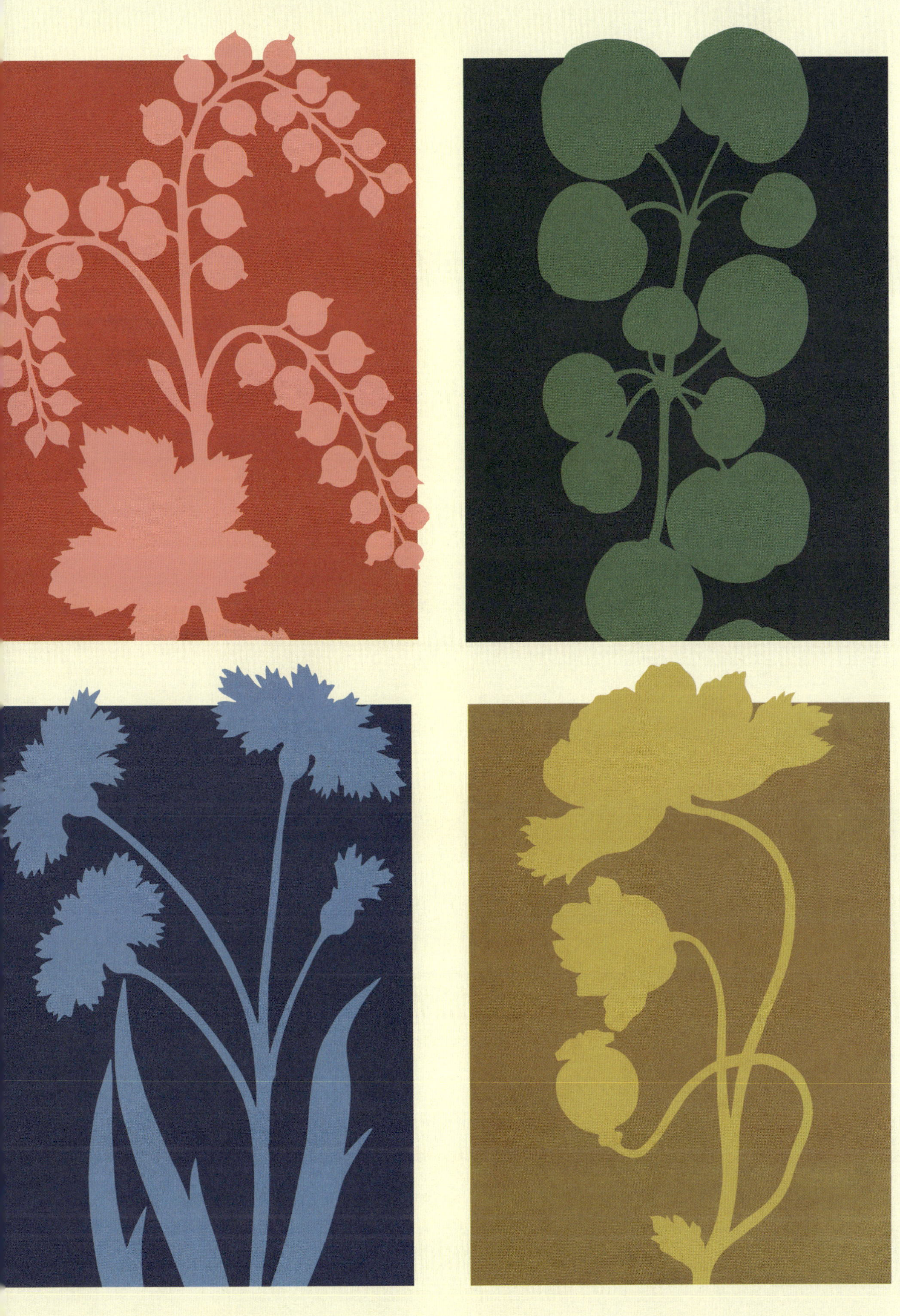

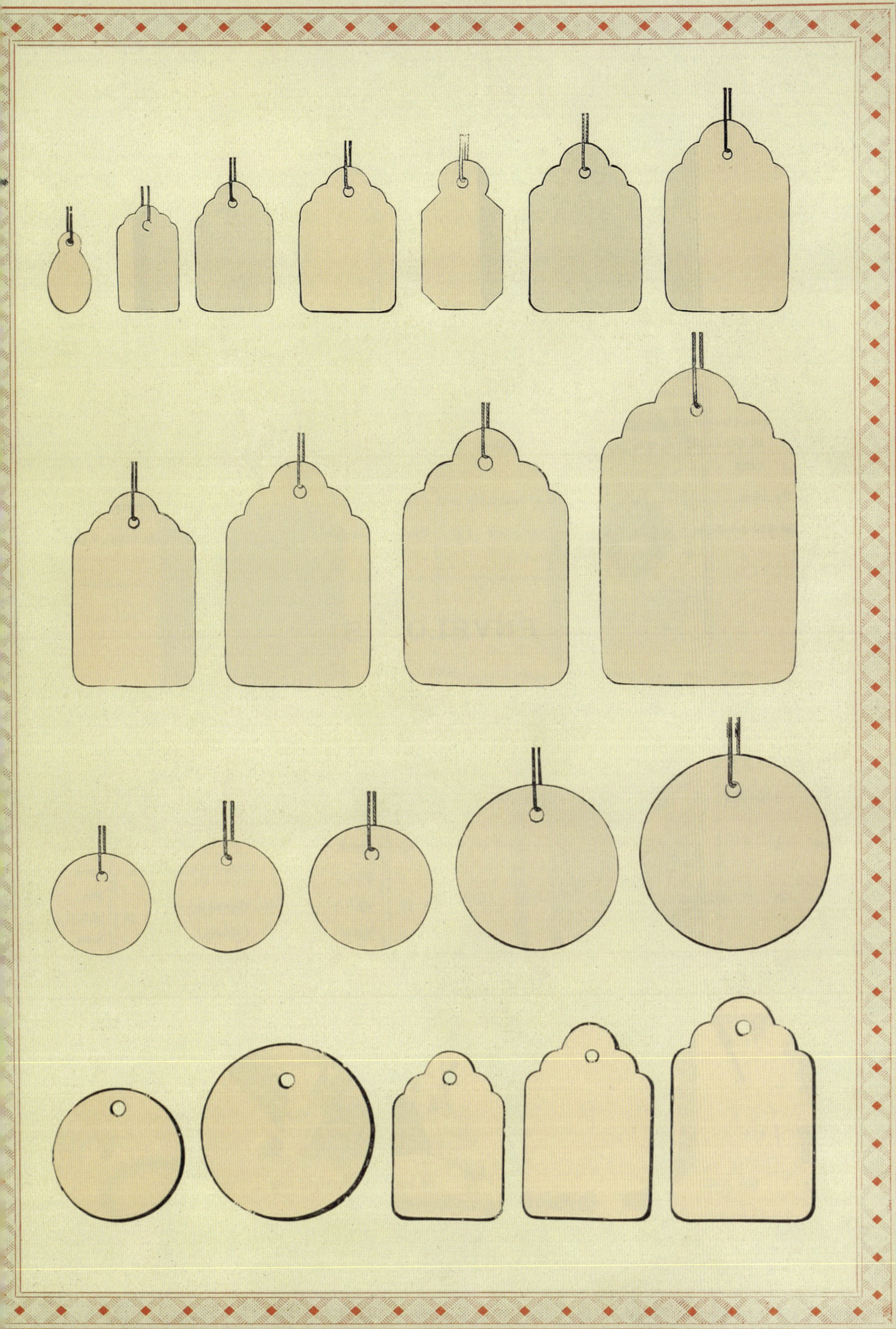

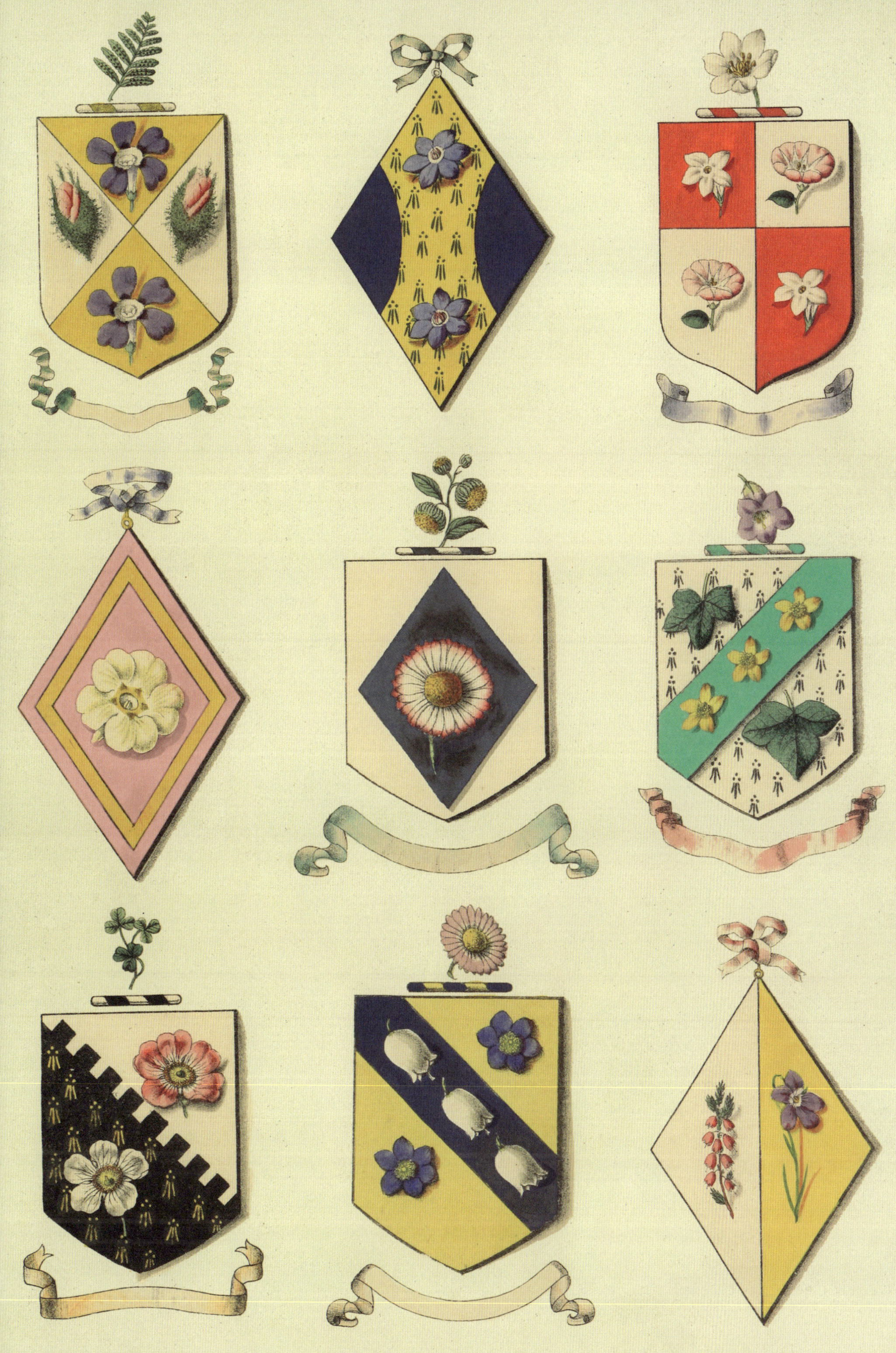

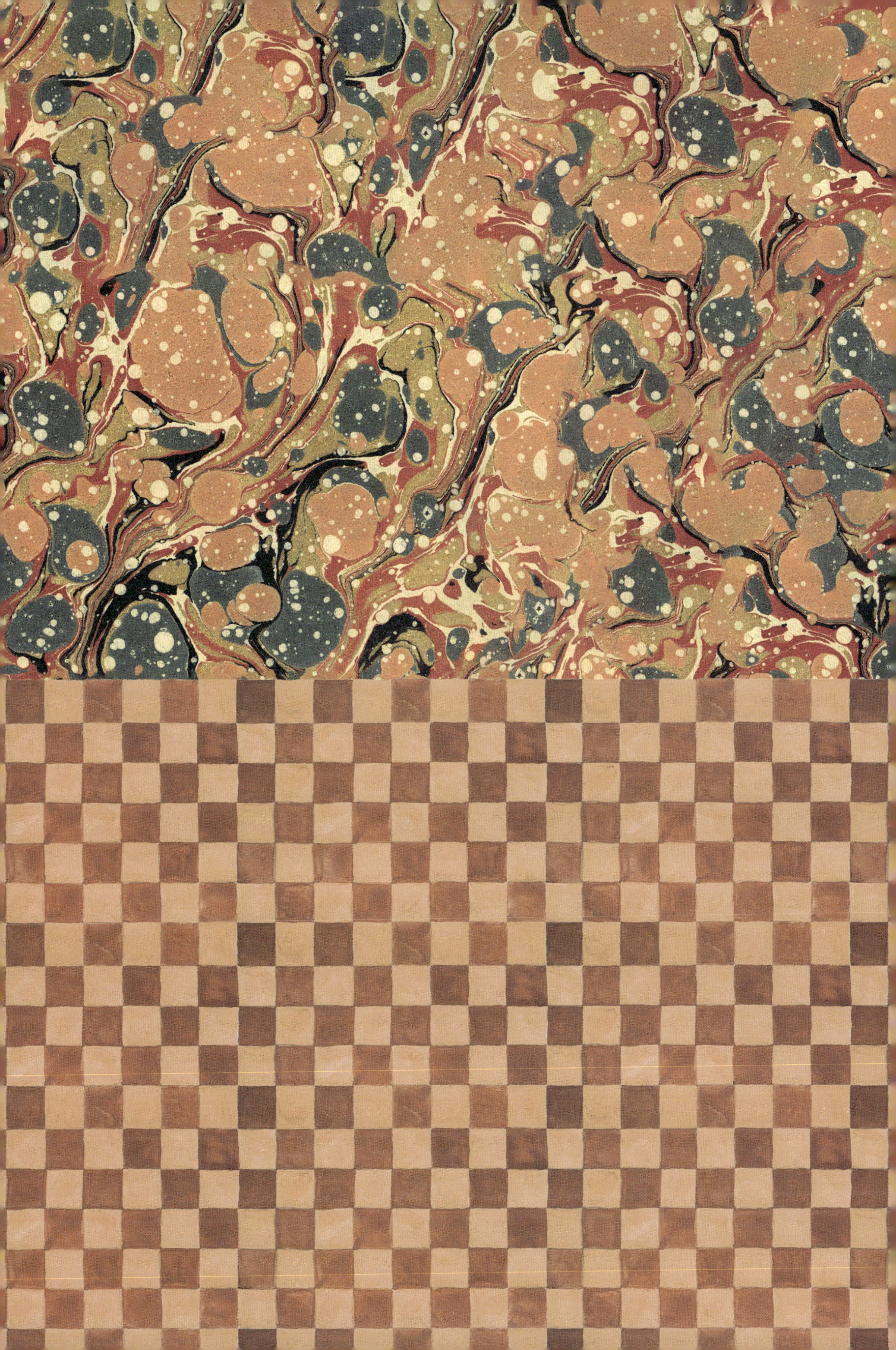

ABCDE
FGHIJK
LMNOP
QRSTU
VWXYZ

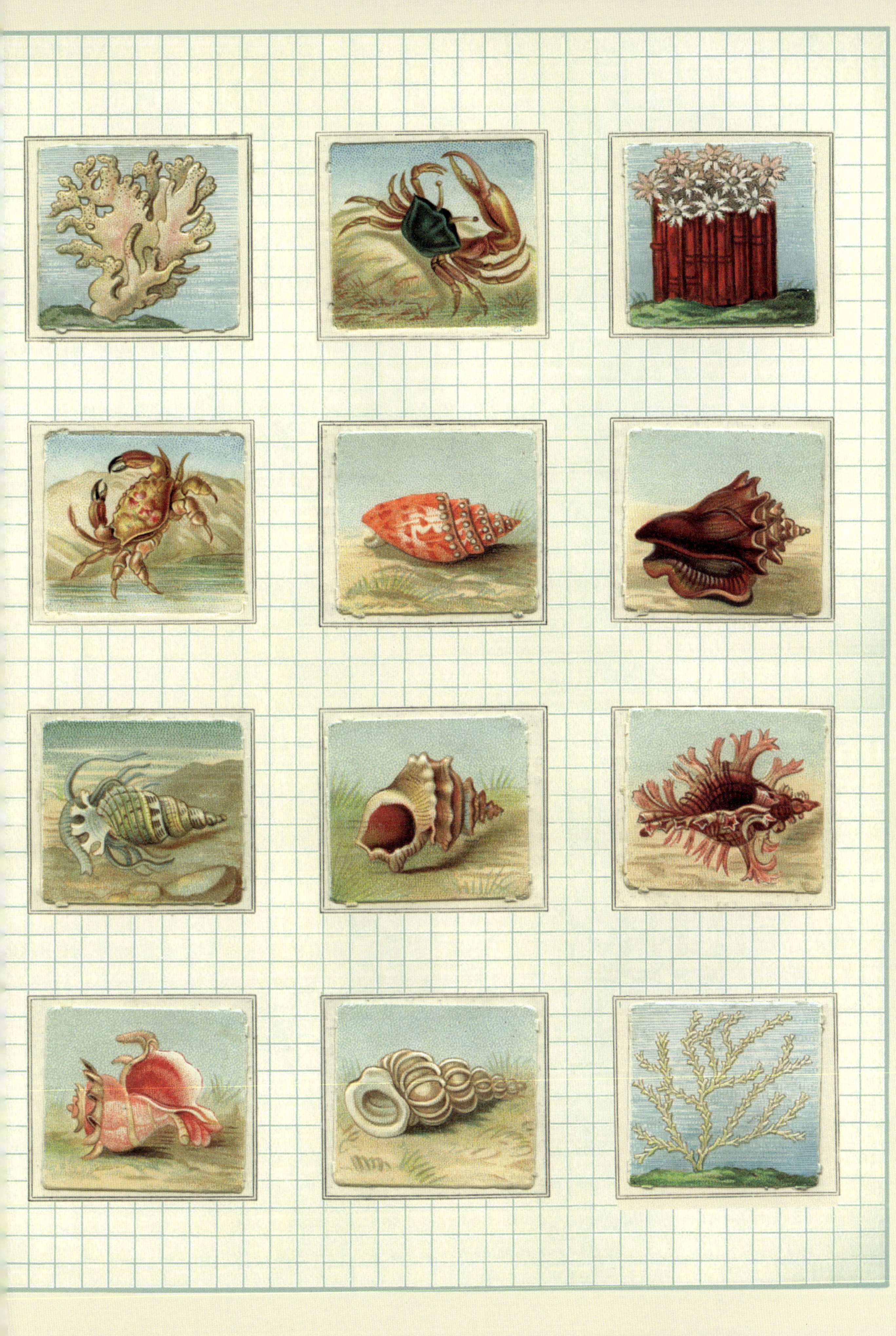

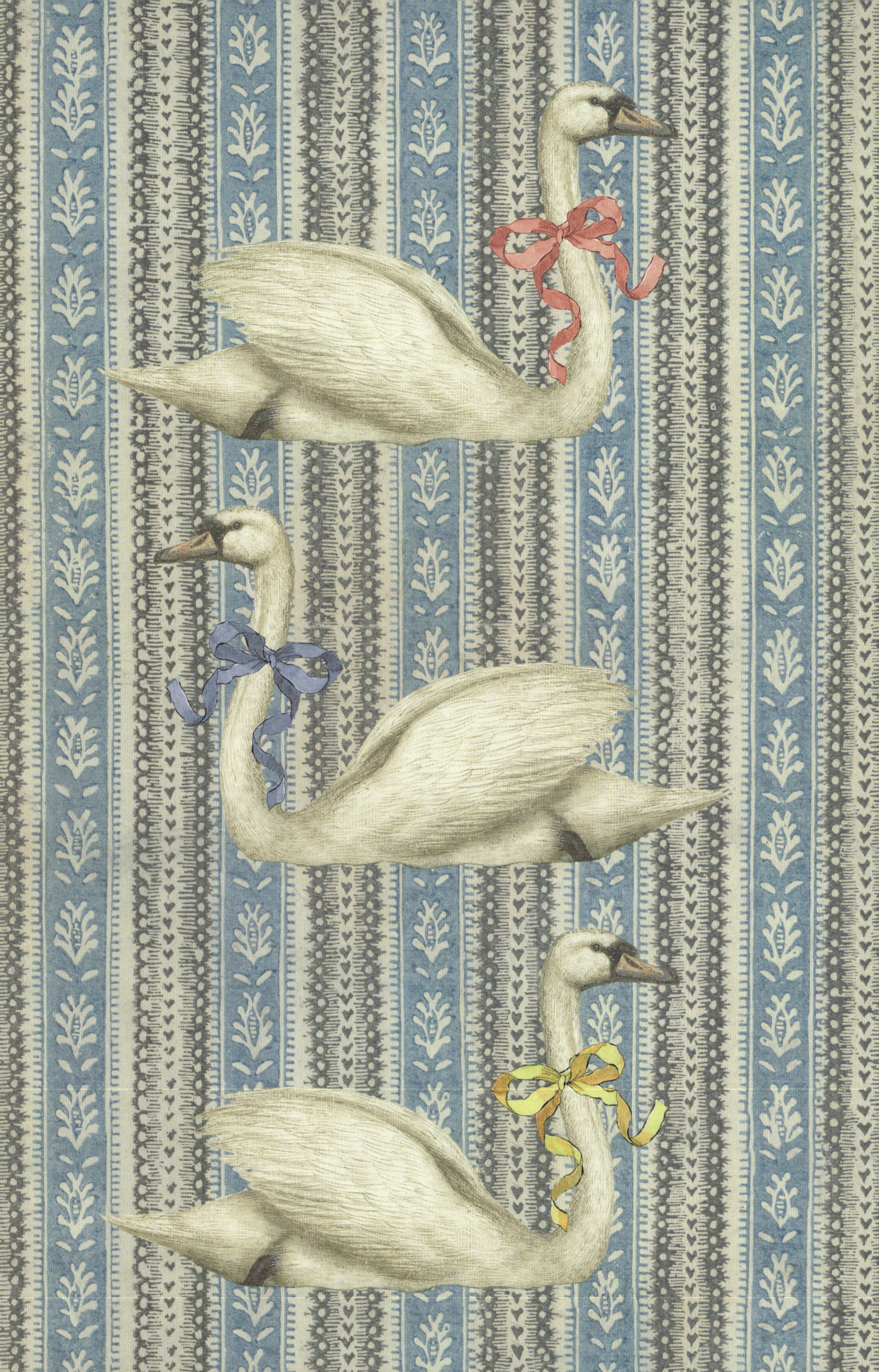

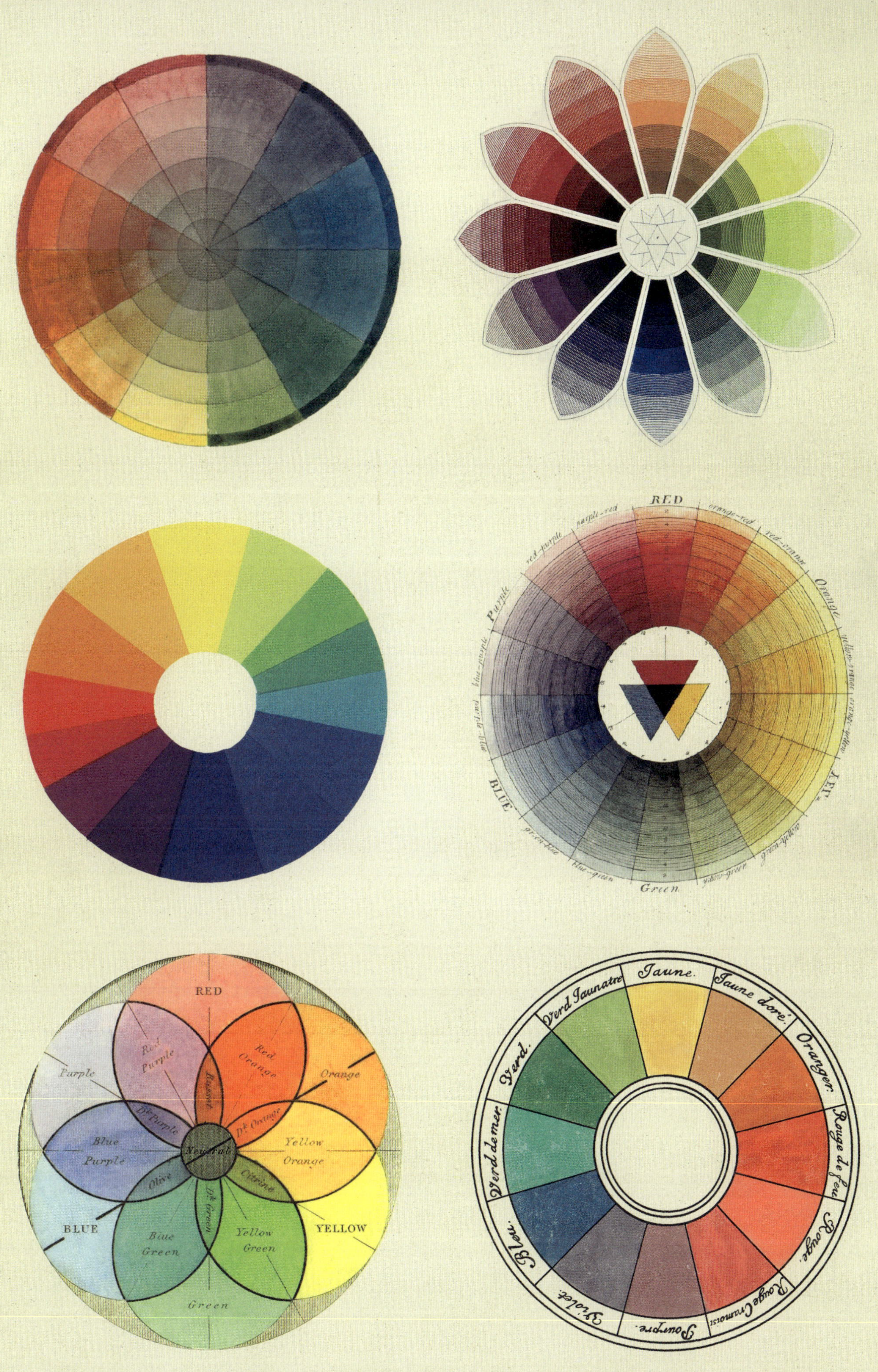
RED
purple-red
orange-red
red-purple
red-orange
Purple
Orange
blue-purple
yellow-orange
purple-blue
orange-yellow
BLUE
YEL.
green-blue
yellow-green
blue-green
green-yellow
Green.
RED
Purple
Red Purple
Red Orange
Orange
Df. Purple
Russet
Df. Orange
Yellow Orange
Blue Purple
Neutral
Citrine
Olive
Df. Green
BLUE
Blue Green
Yellow Green
YELLOW
Green
Jaune.
Verd Jaunatre
Jaune doré.
Verd.
Orangé.
Verd de mer.
Rouge de feu.
Bleu.
Rouge.
Violet.
Rouge cramoisi.
Pourpre.

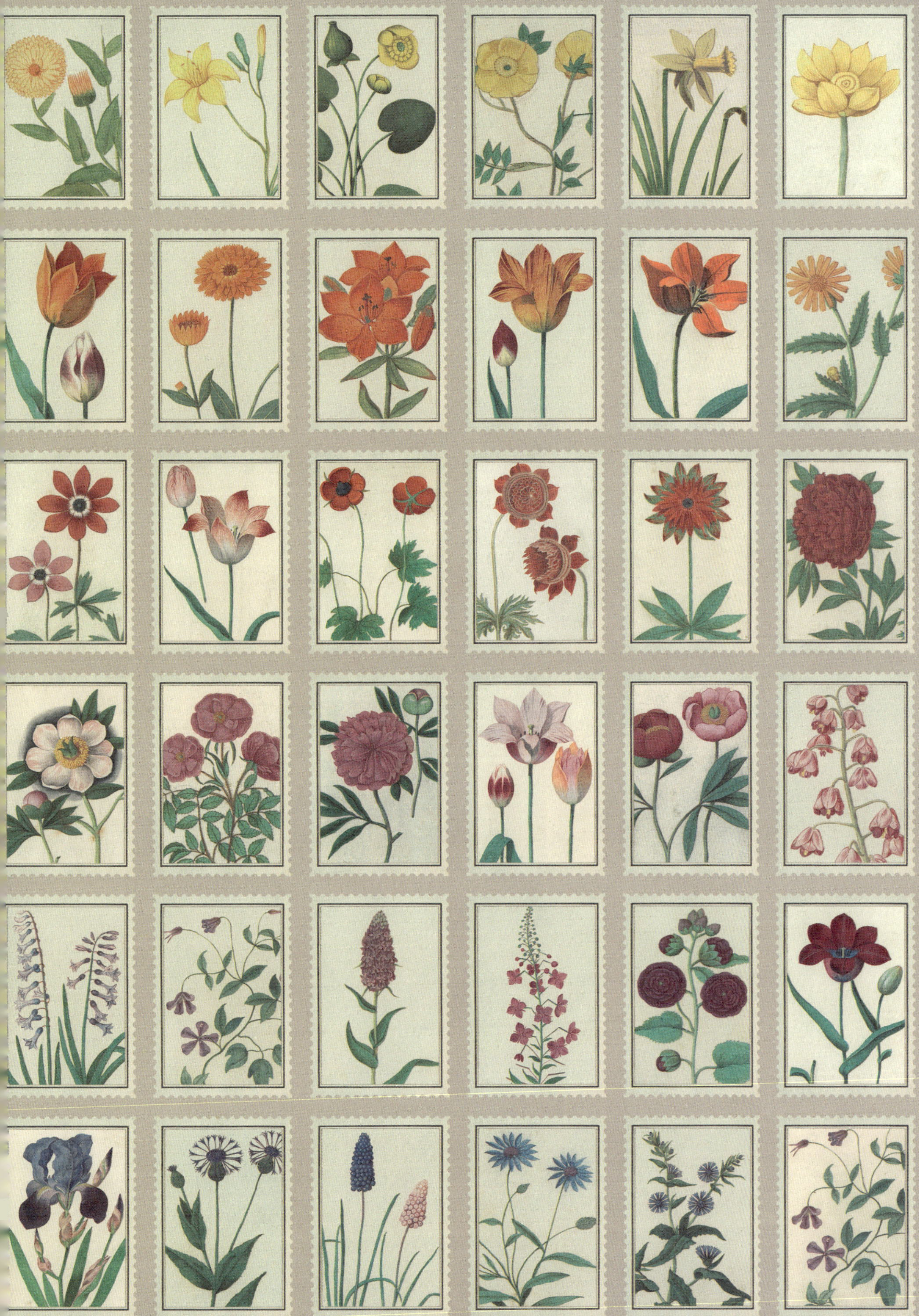

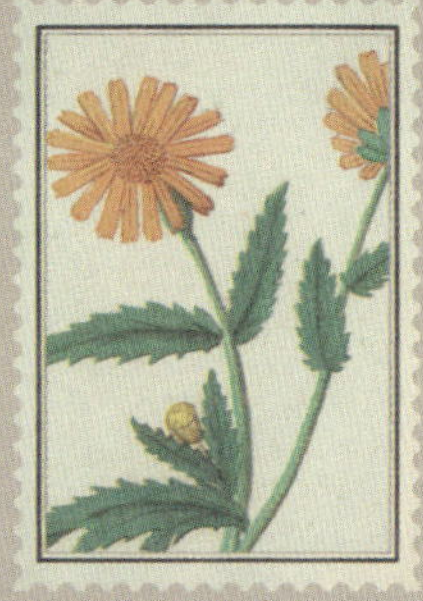

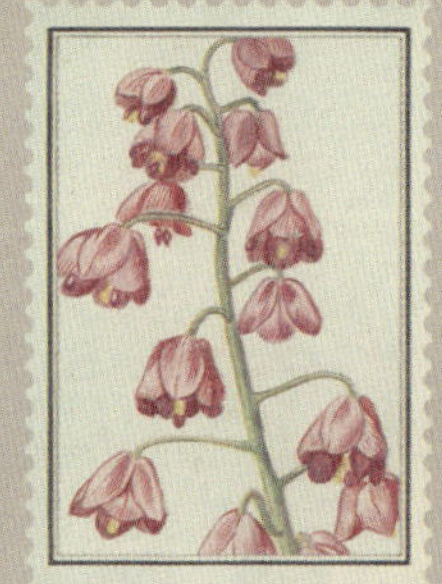
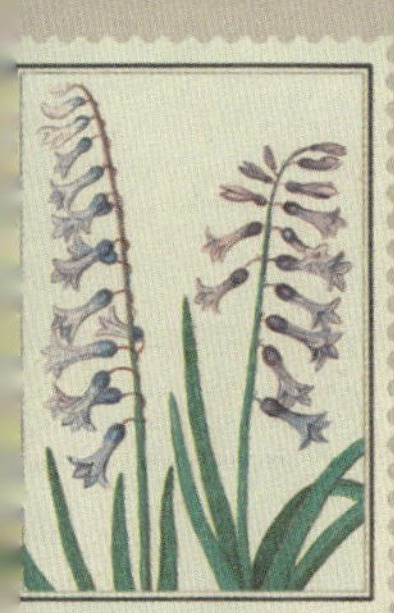
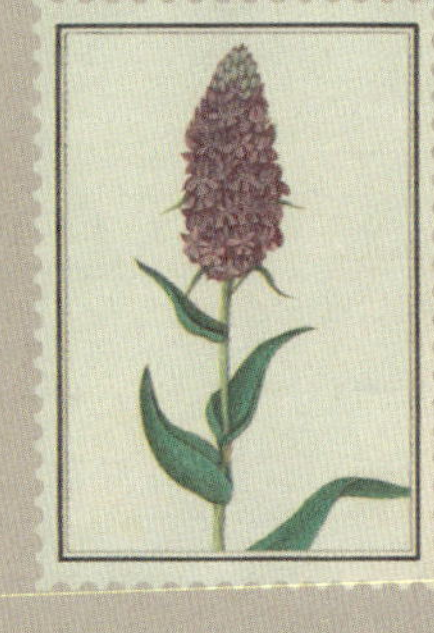
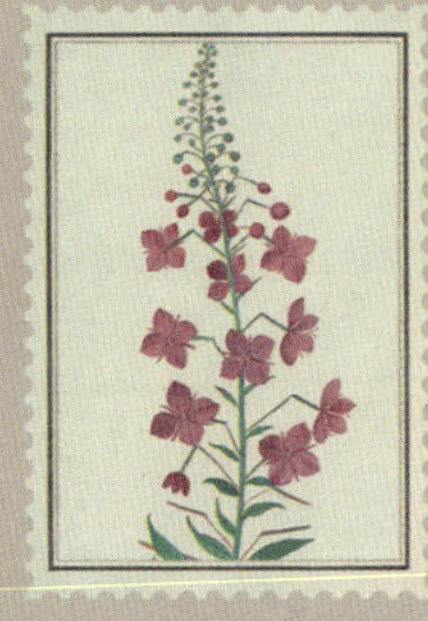

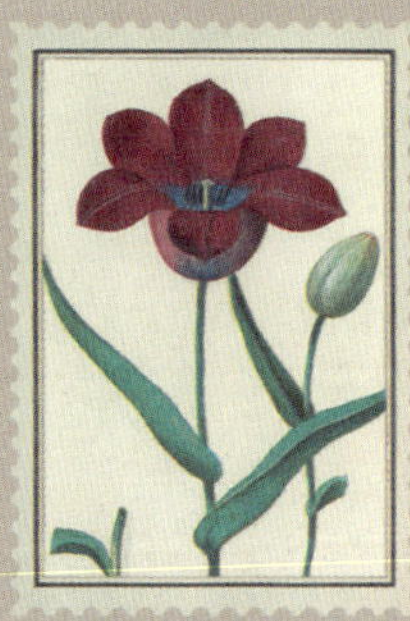
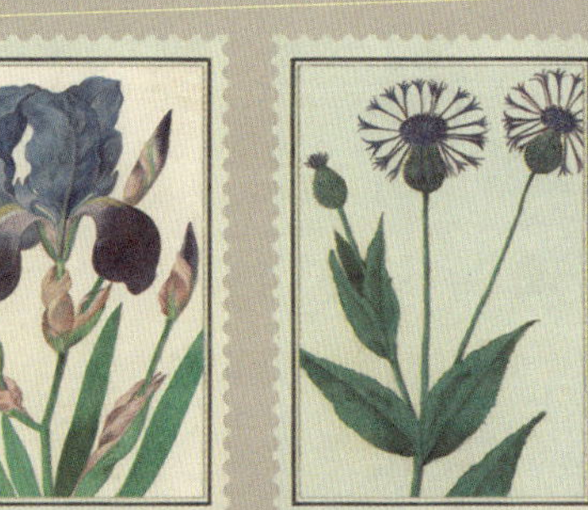
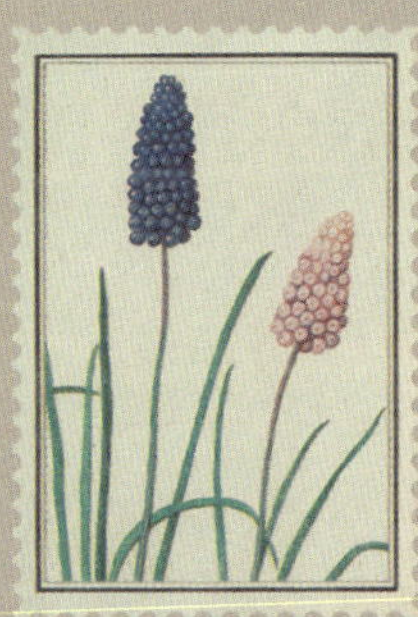

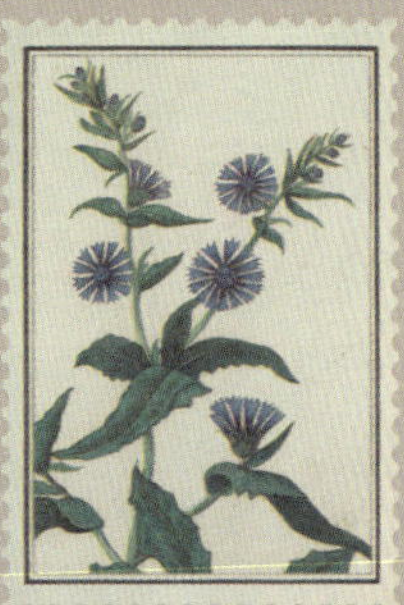

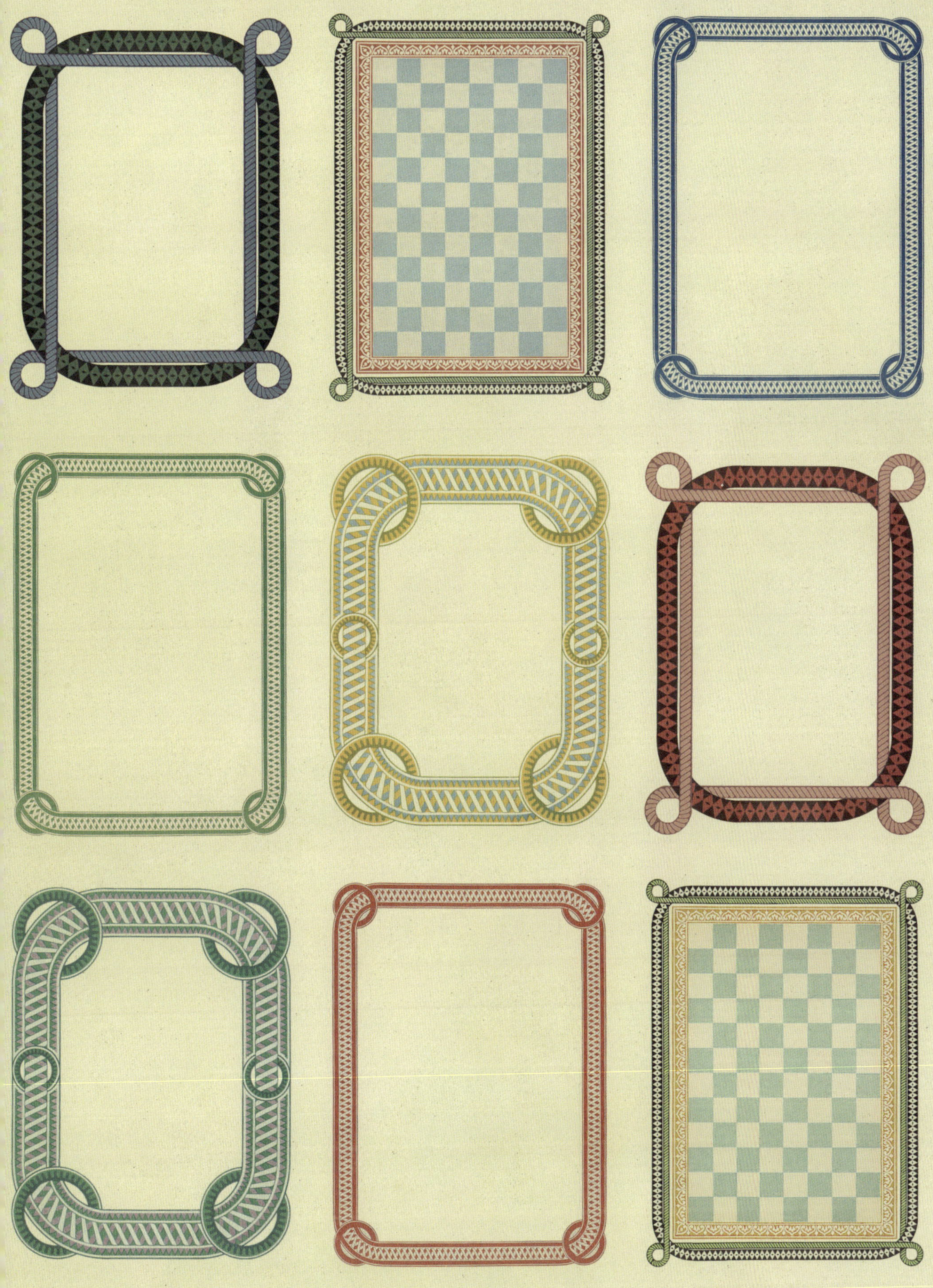

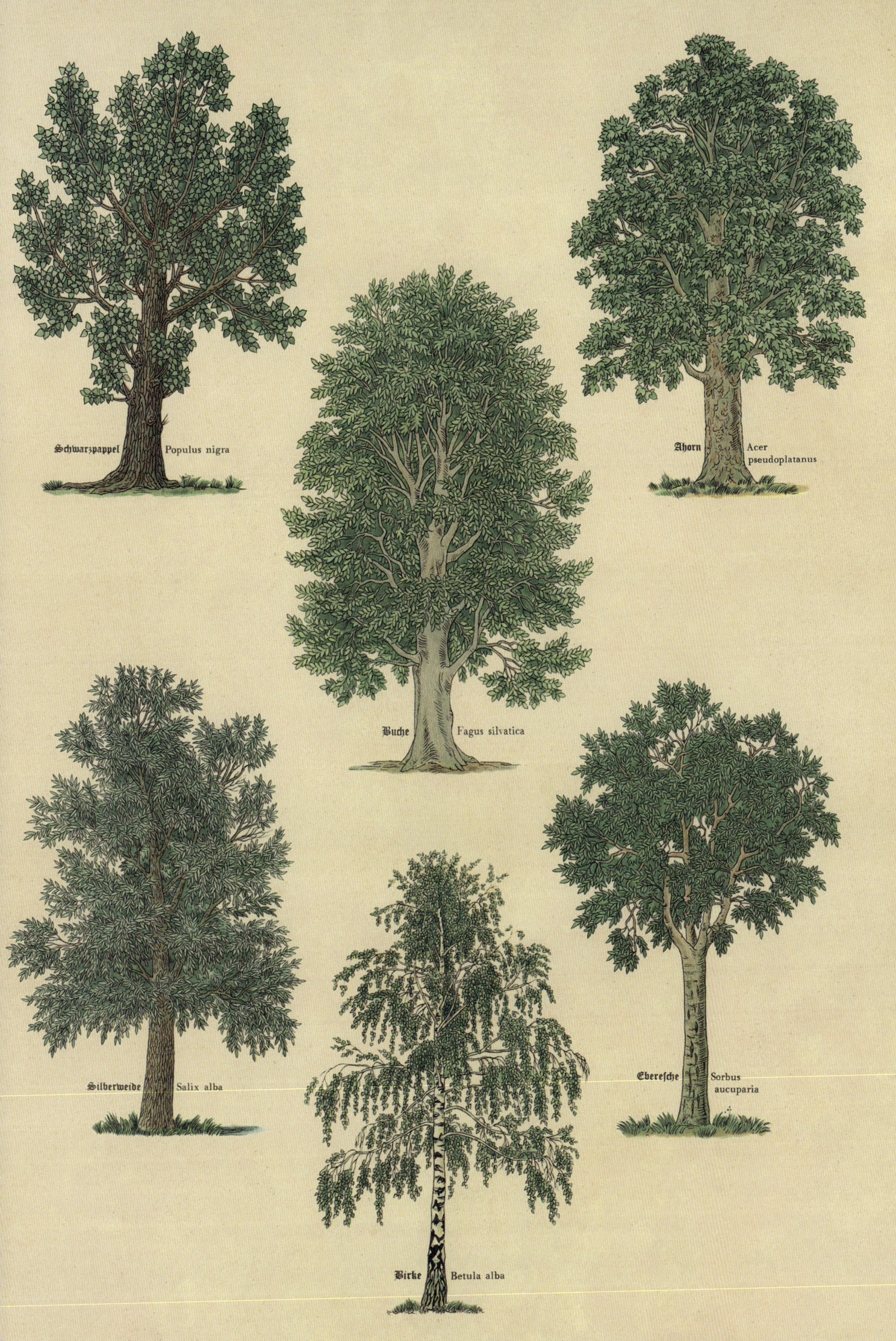

Schwarzpappel   Populus nigra

Ahorn   Acer pseudoplatanus

Buche   Fagus silvatica

Silberweide   Salix alba

Eberesche   Sorbus aucuparia

Birke   Betula alba

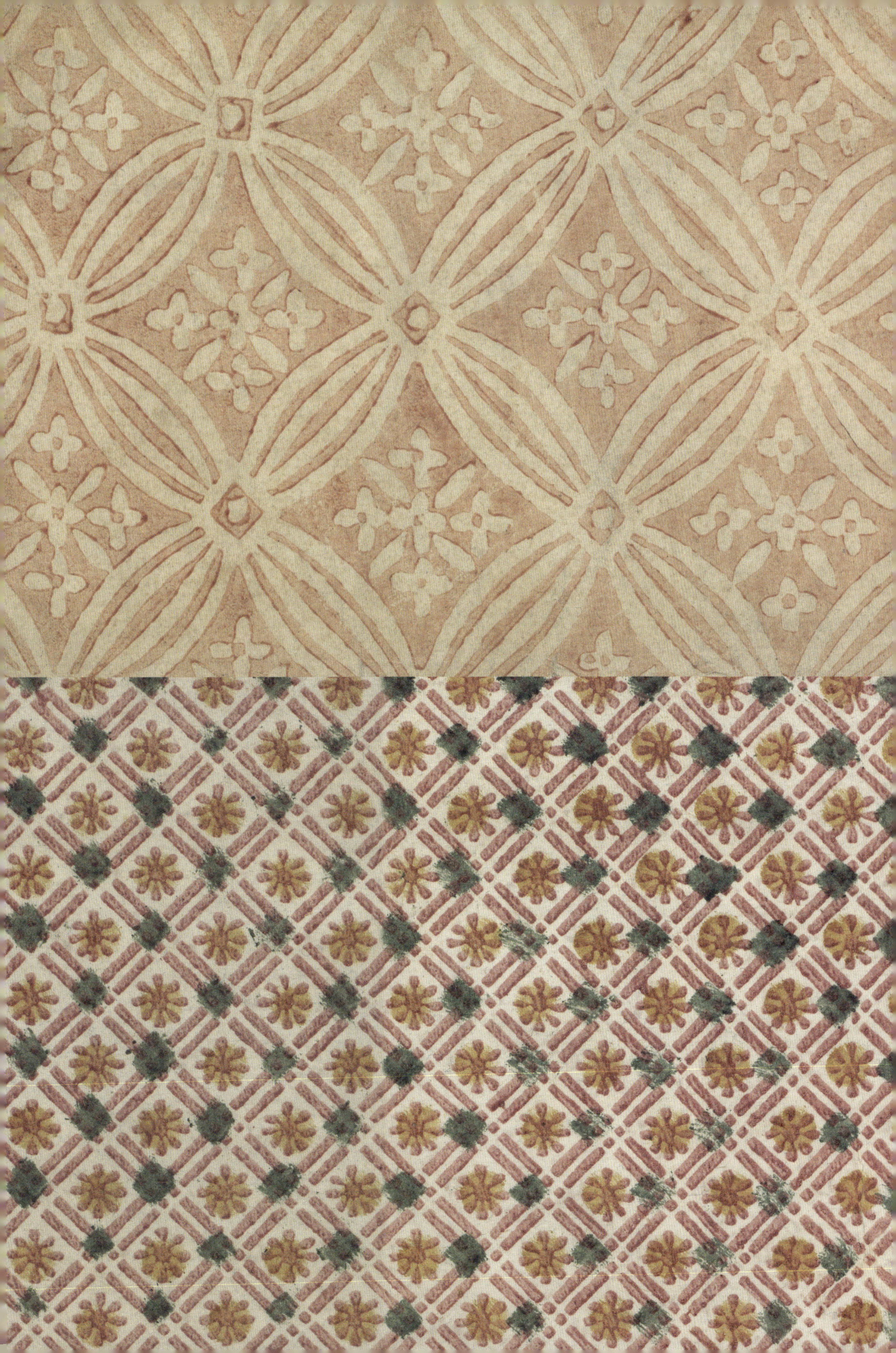

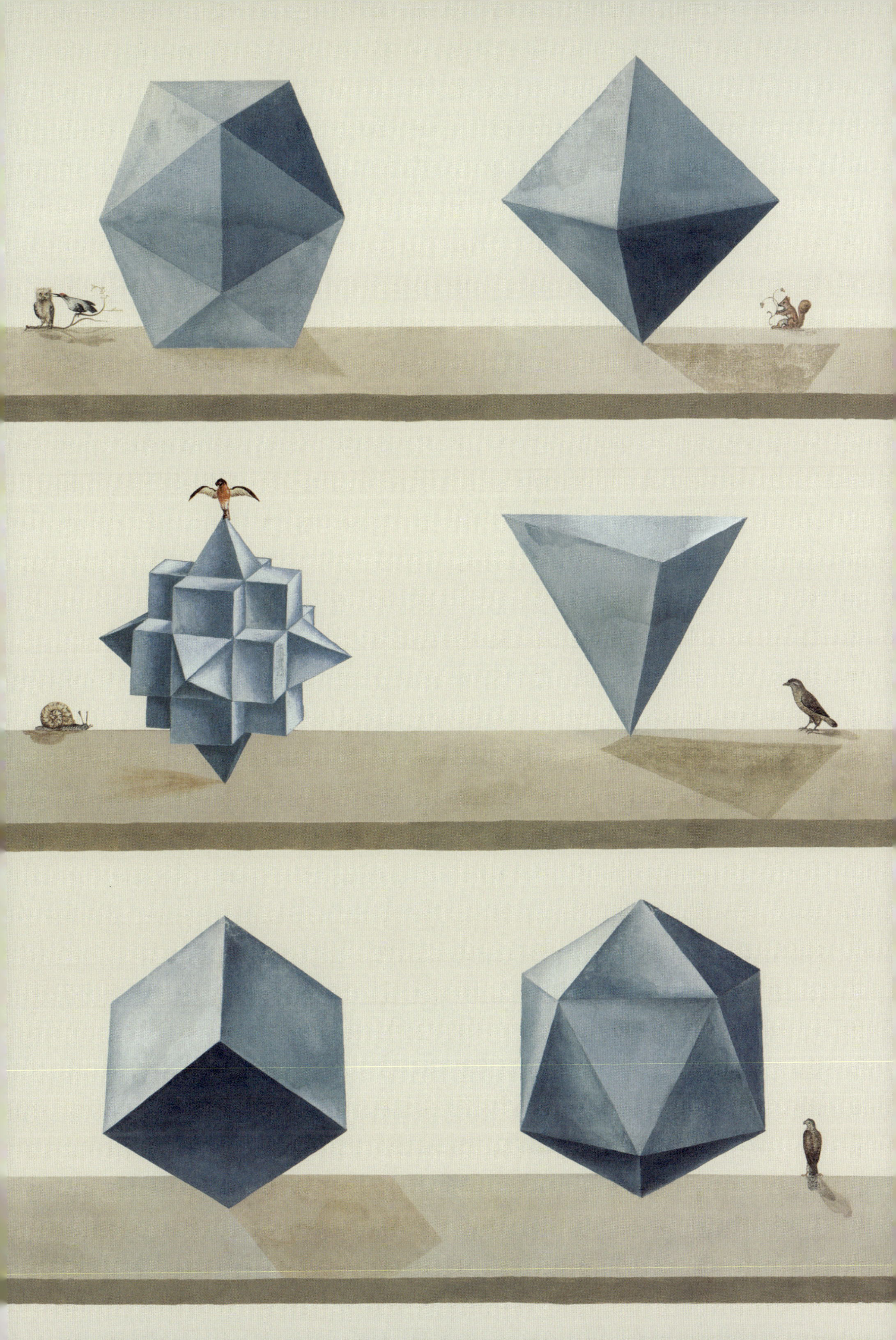

GRACIAS
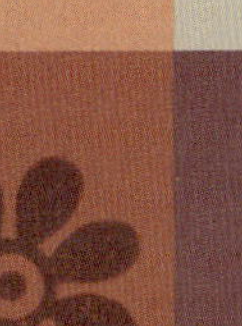
MERCI
THANKS
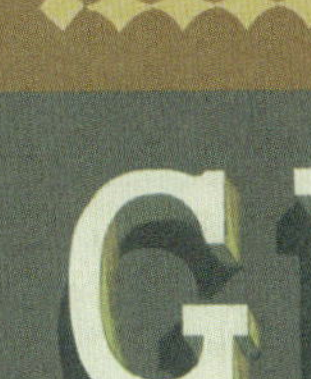
GRAZIE
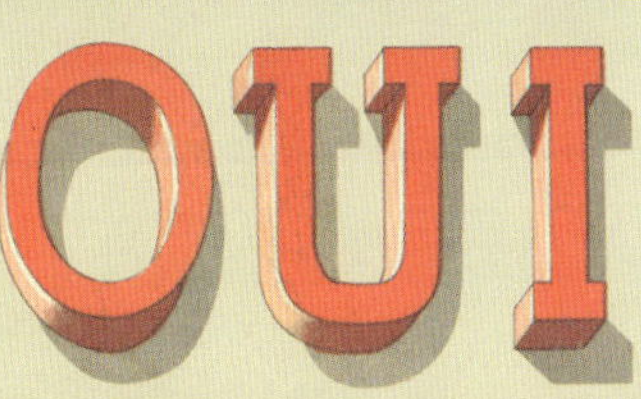
OUI
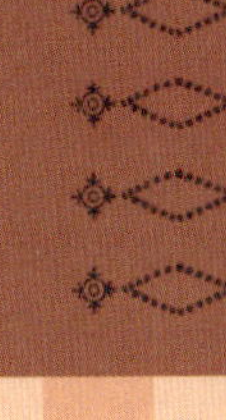
BISOUS

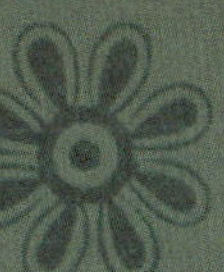

AMOUR
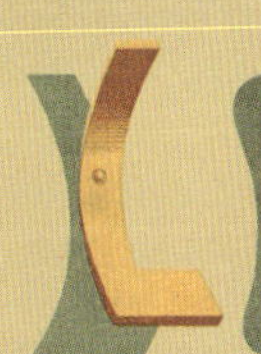
LOVE
AMOR

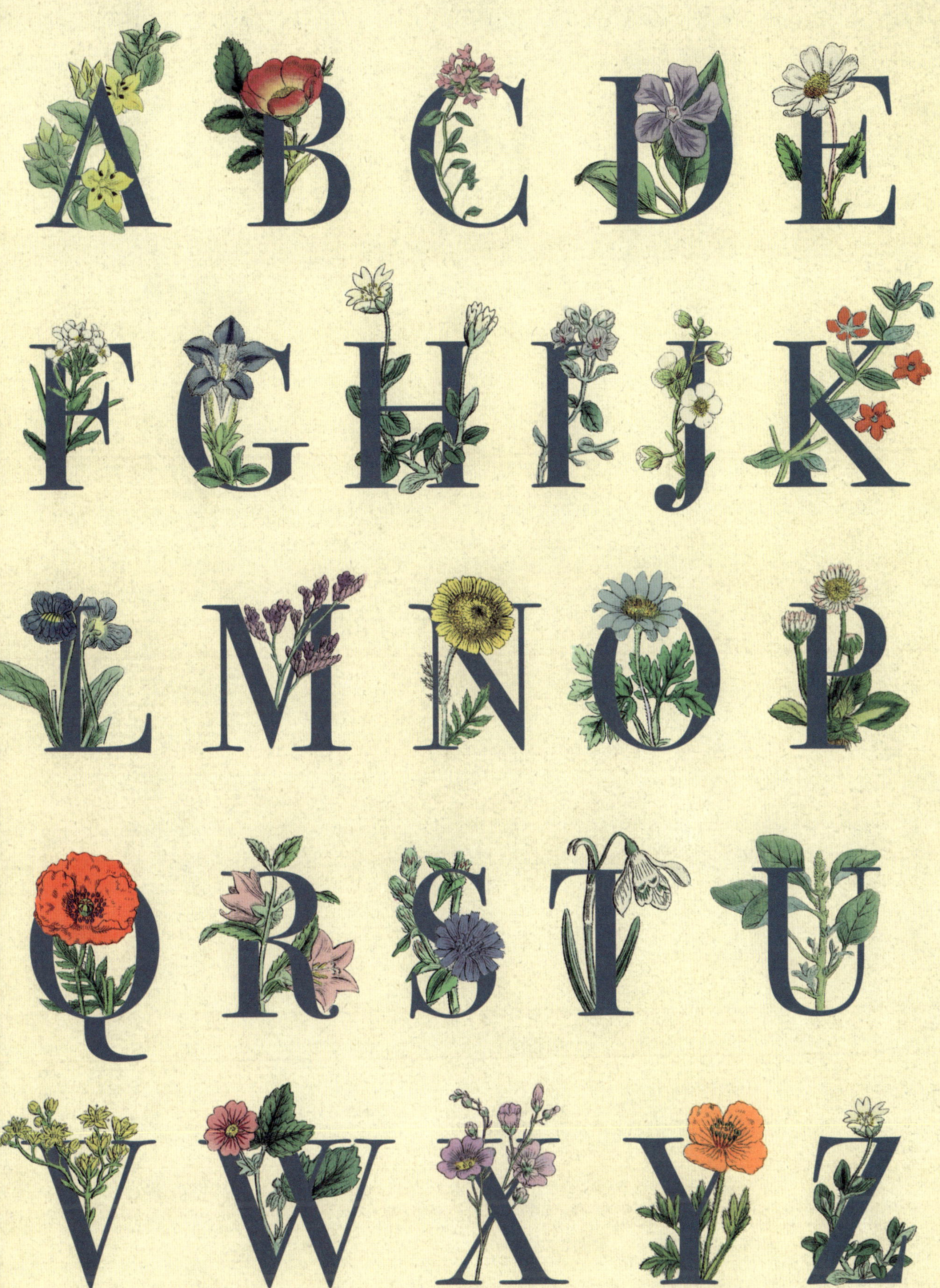

MAQUETTES POUR ARTISTES

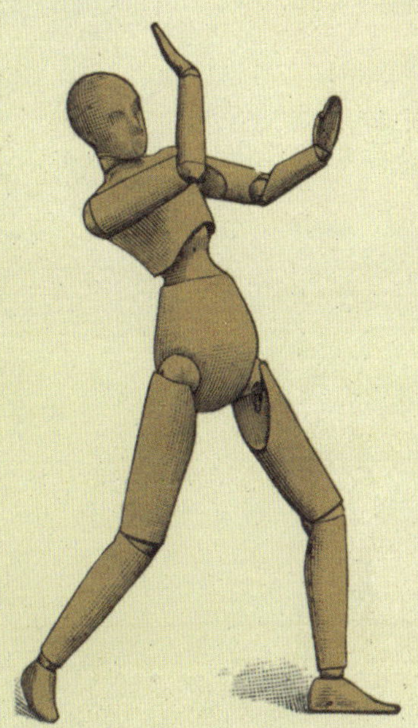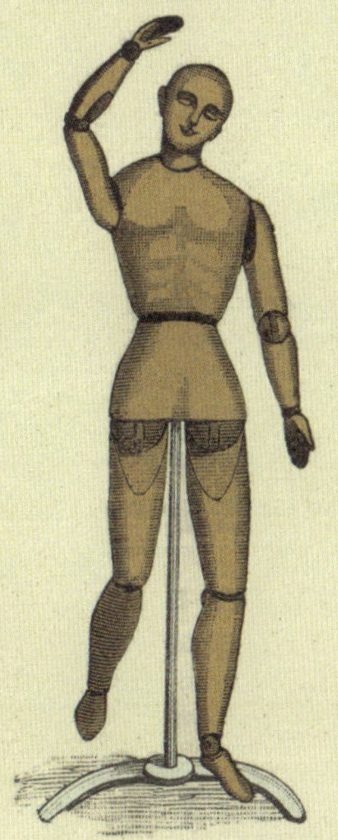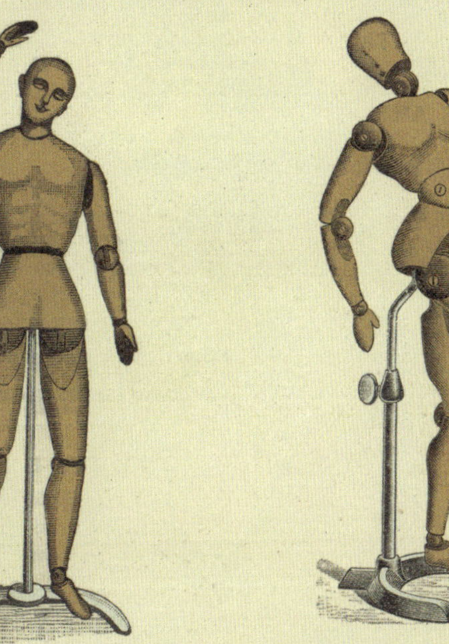

PALETTES

COULEURS

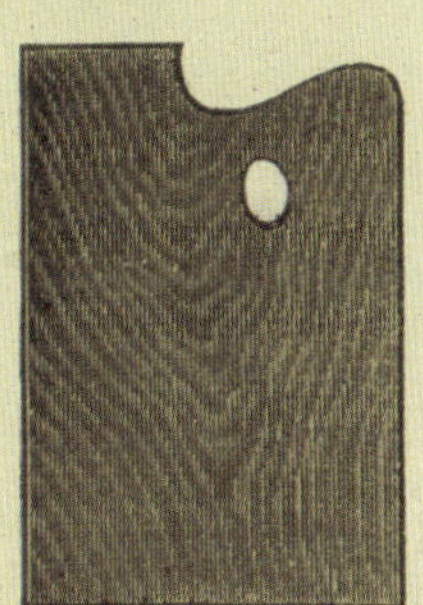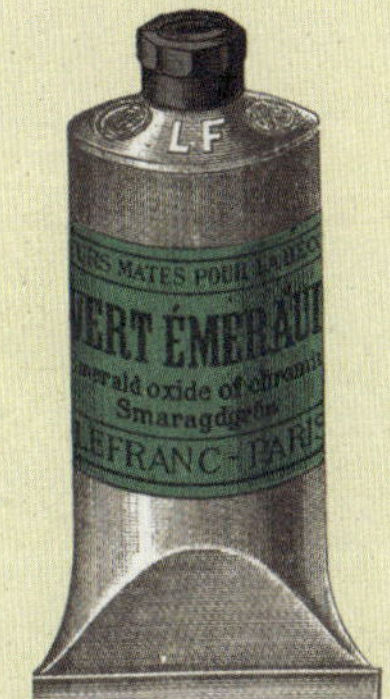

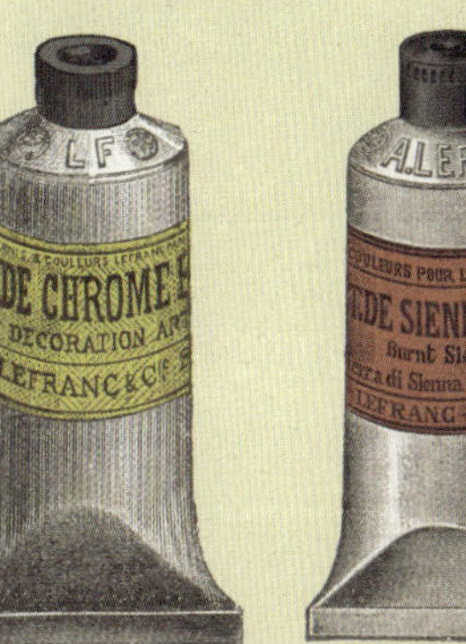

CRAYONS A DESSIN

GOMMES

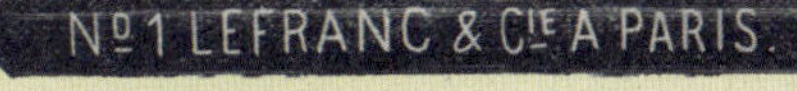

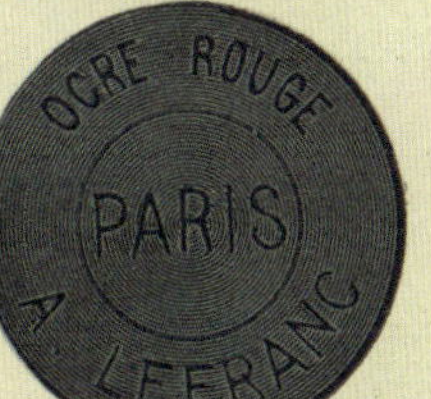

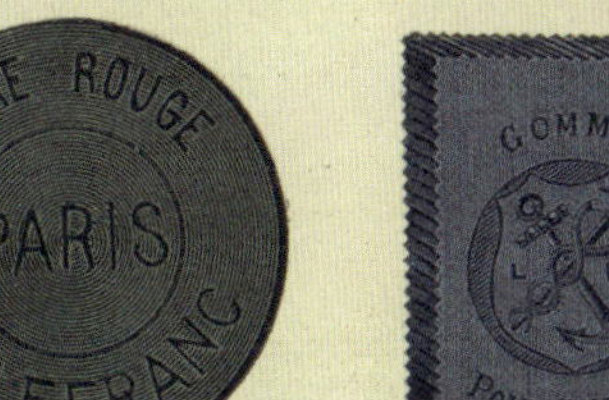

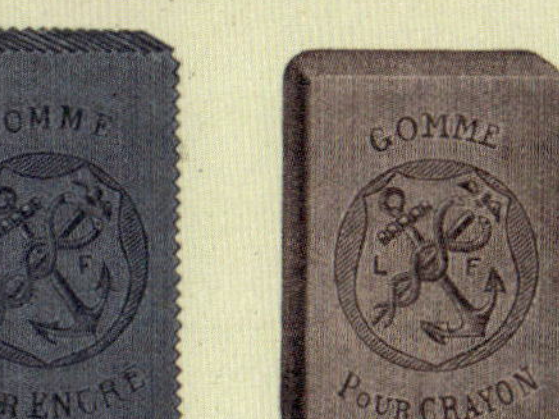

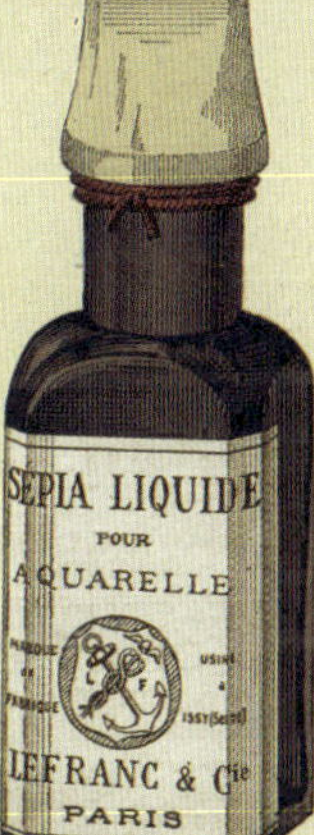

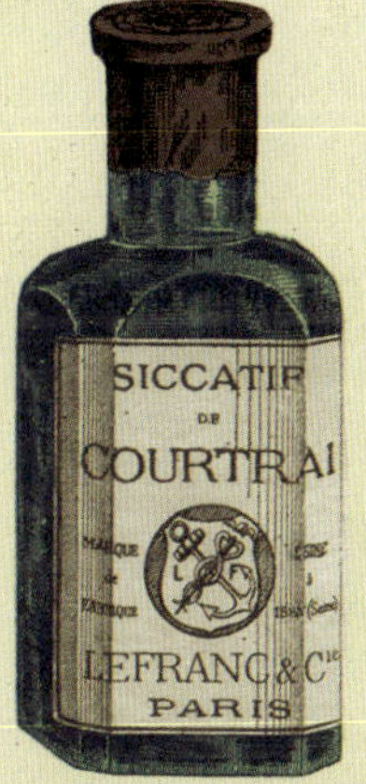

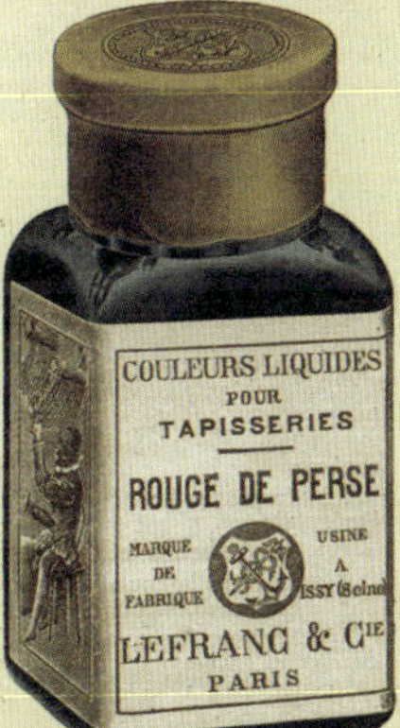

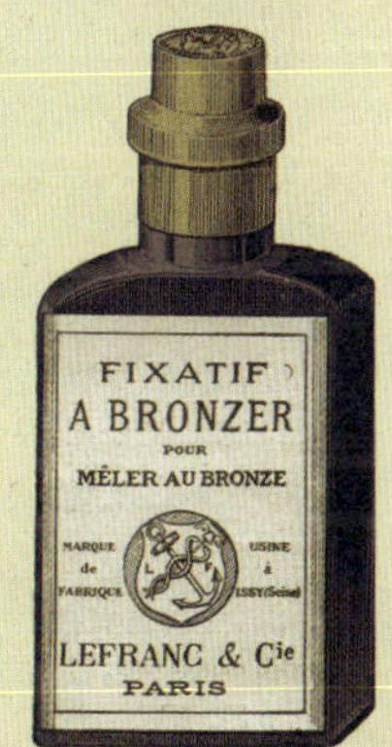

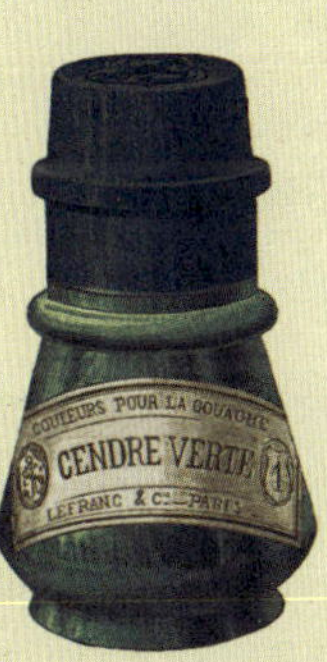

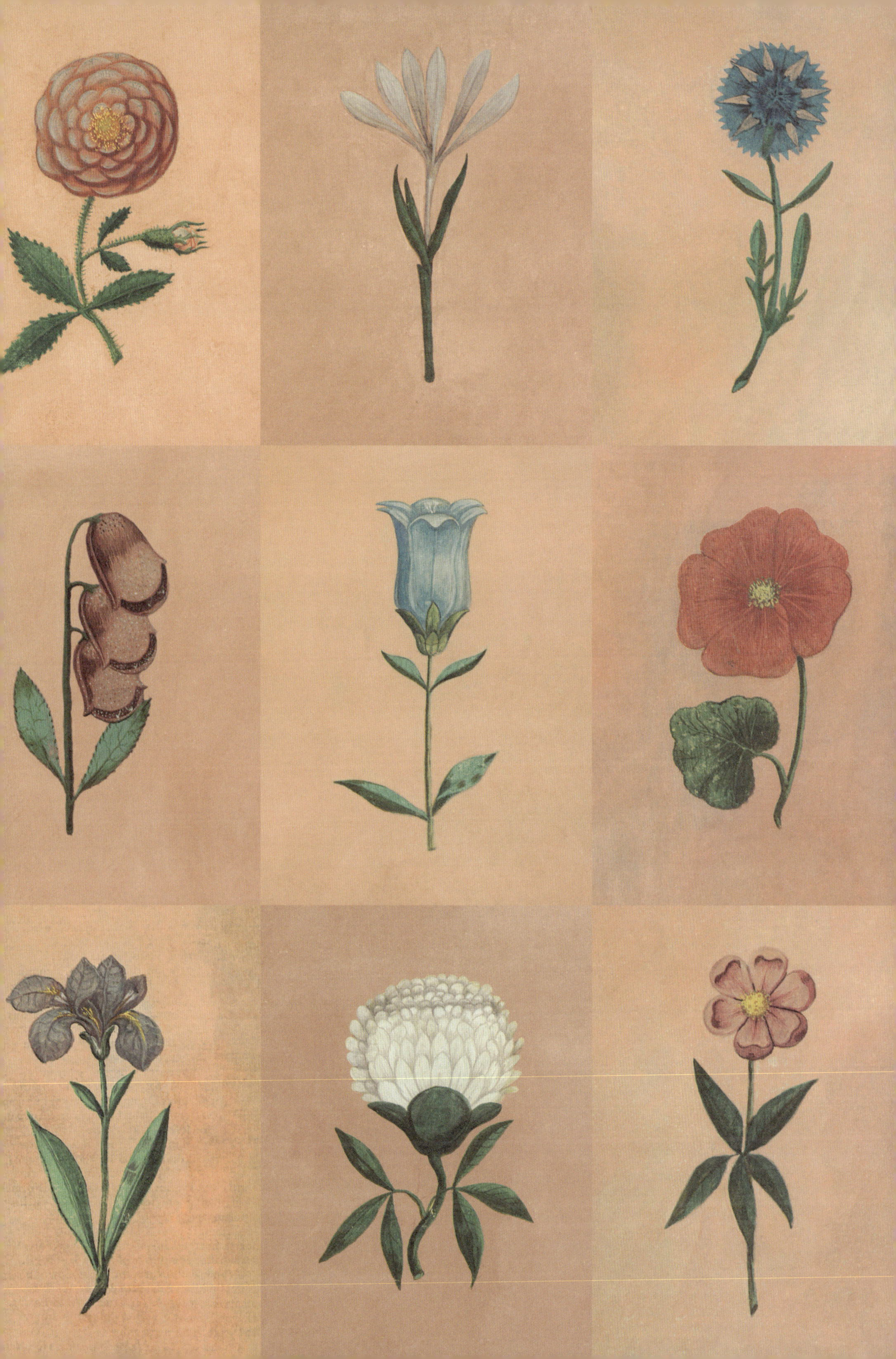

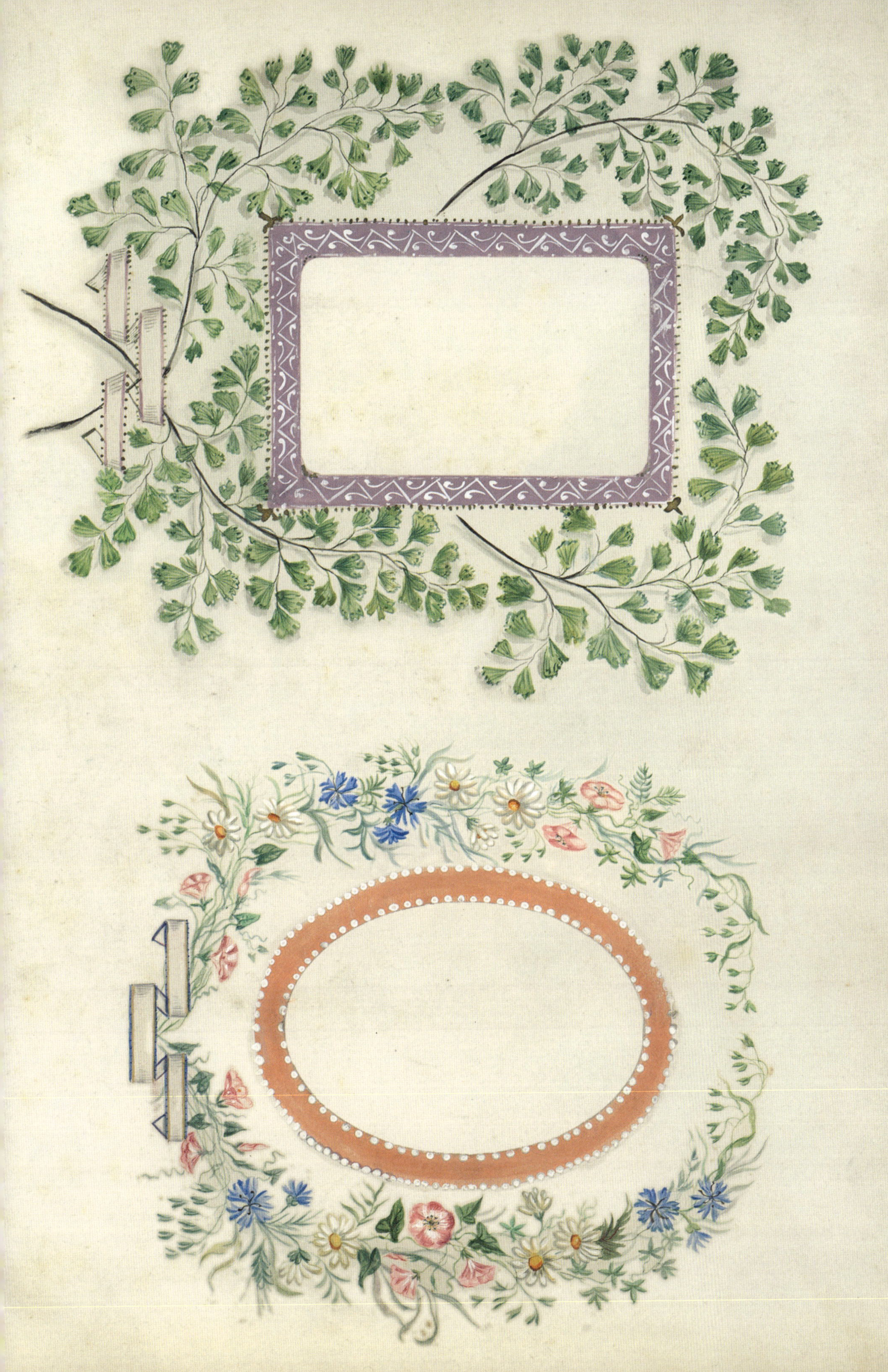

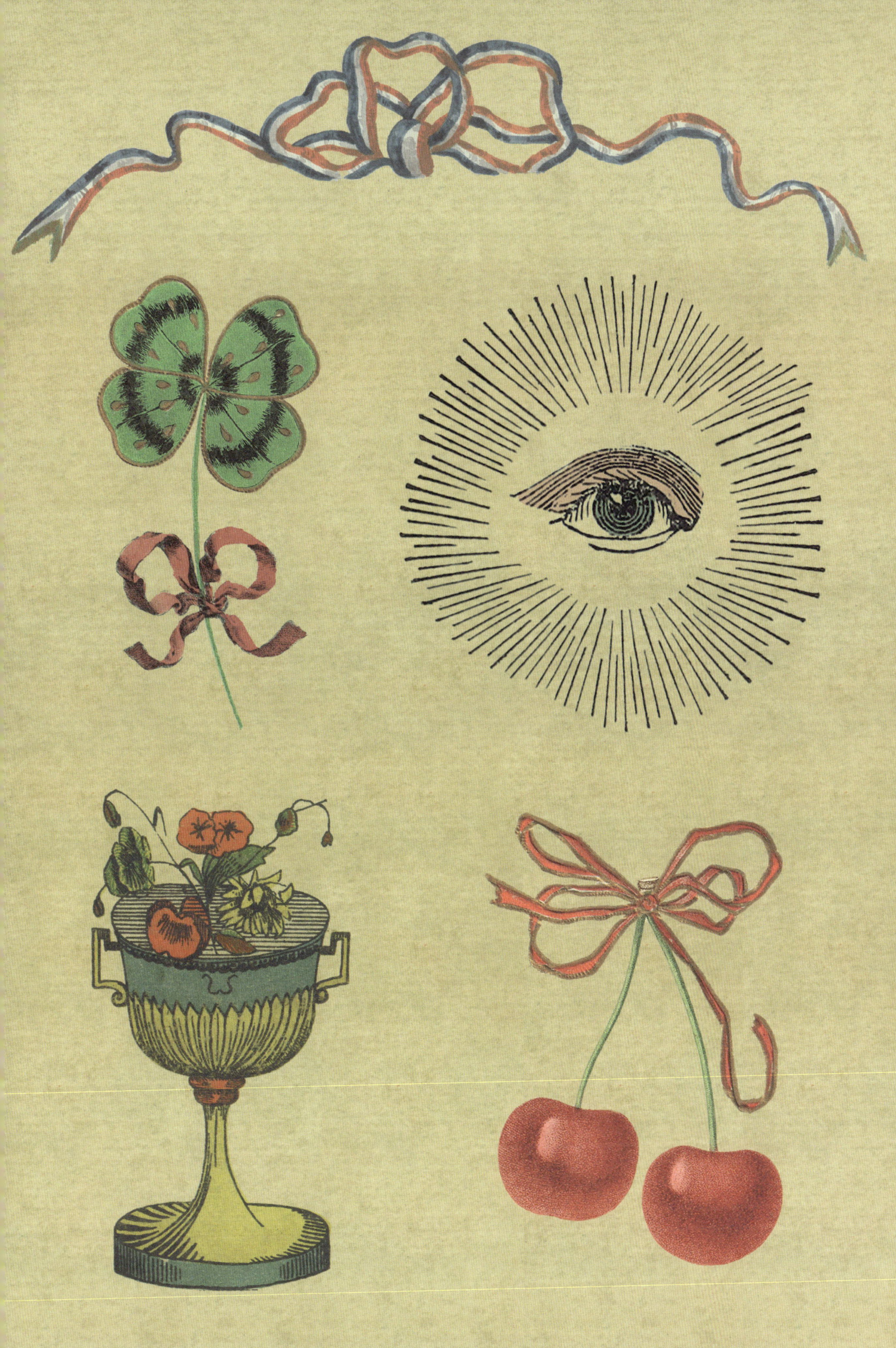

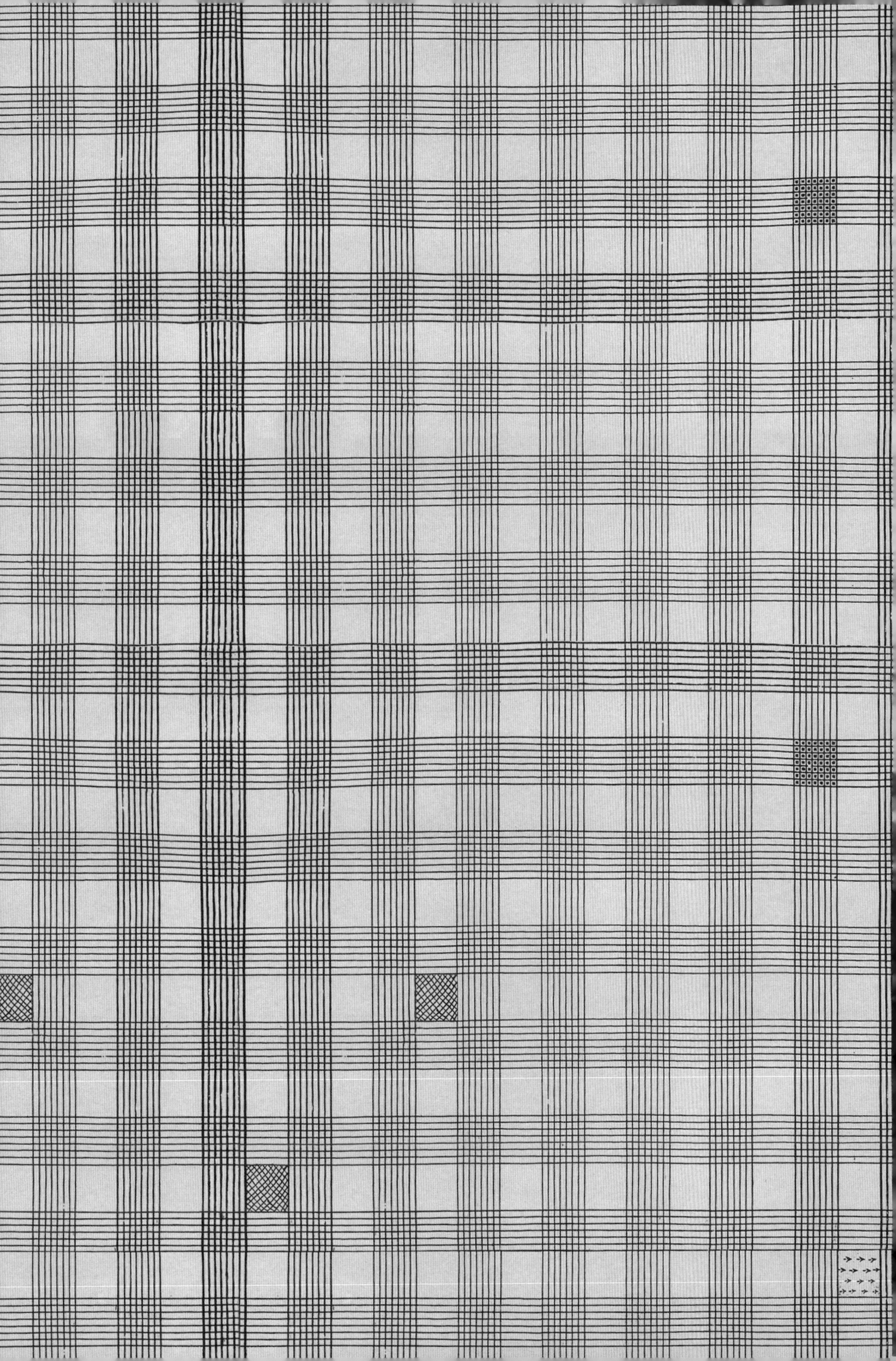

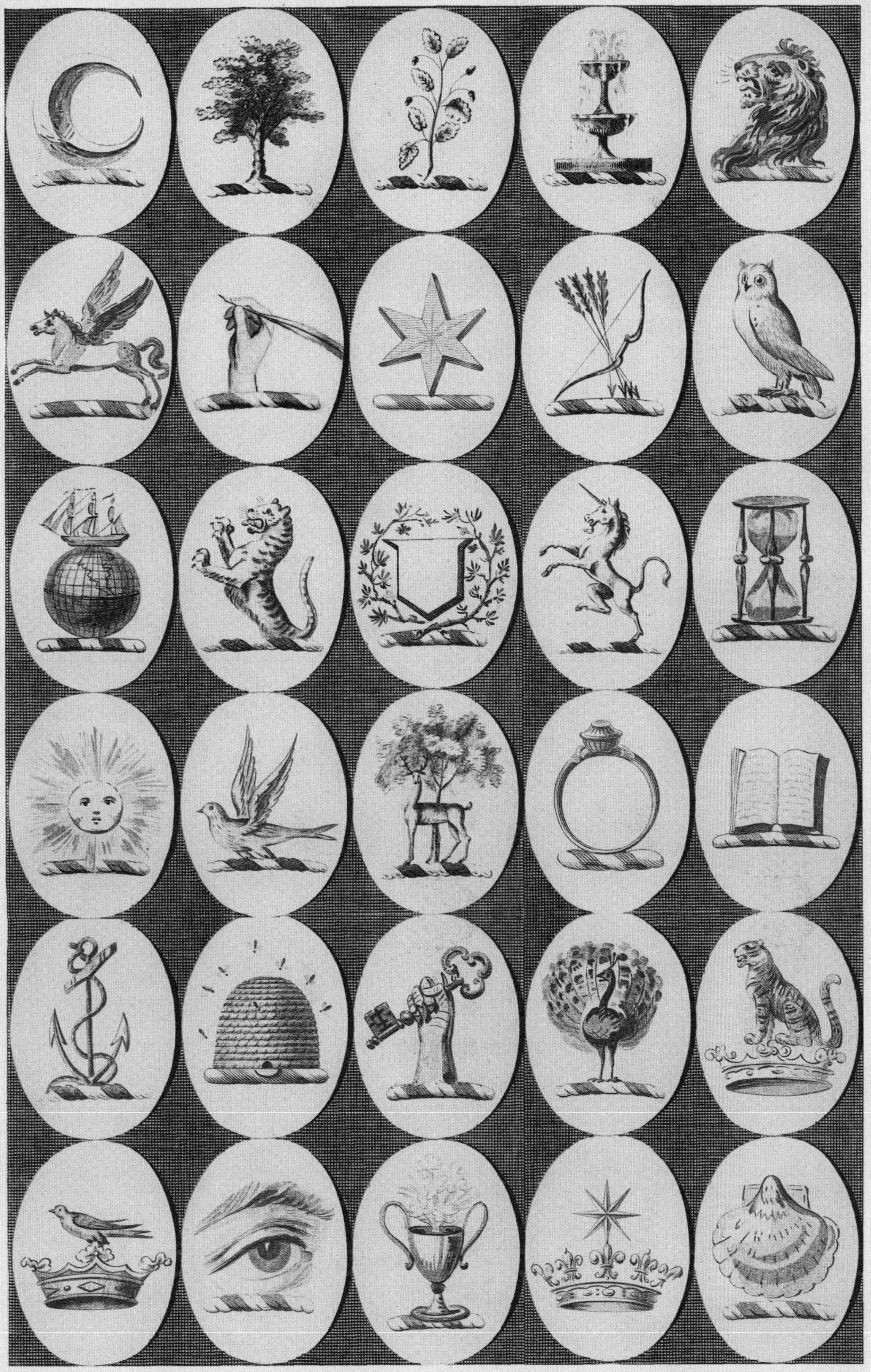

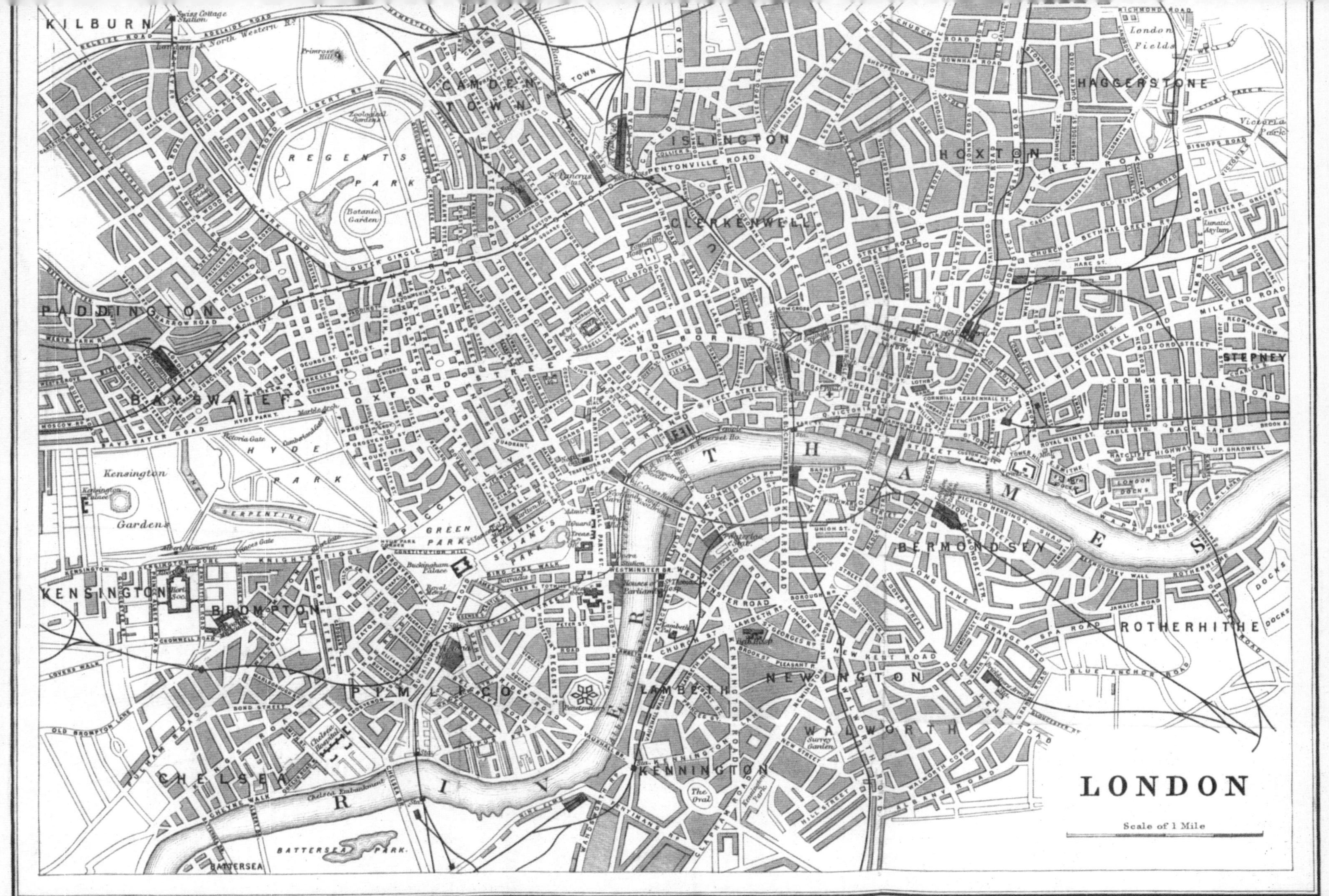

LONDON
Scale of 1 Mile
KILBURN
PADDINGTON
BAYSWATER
KENSINGTON
BROMPTON
CHELSEA
PIMLICO
CAMDEN TOWN
REGENTS PARK
Botanic Garden
Zoological Gardens
Primrose Hill
ISLINGTON
HOXTON
HAGGERSTONE
CLERKENWELL
STEPNEY
CITY
HOLBORN
OXFORD STREET
PICCADILLY
HYDE PARK
GREEN PARK
ST. JAMES'S PARK
Kensington Gardens
Kensington Palace
SERPENTINE
Buckingham Palace
FLEET STREET
THAMES
RIVER
BERMONDSEY
ROTHERHITHE
LAMBETH
KENNINGTON
NEWINGTON
WALWORTH
The Oval
BATTERSEA PARK
BATTERSEA
London Fields
Victoria Park
Lunatic Asylum

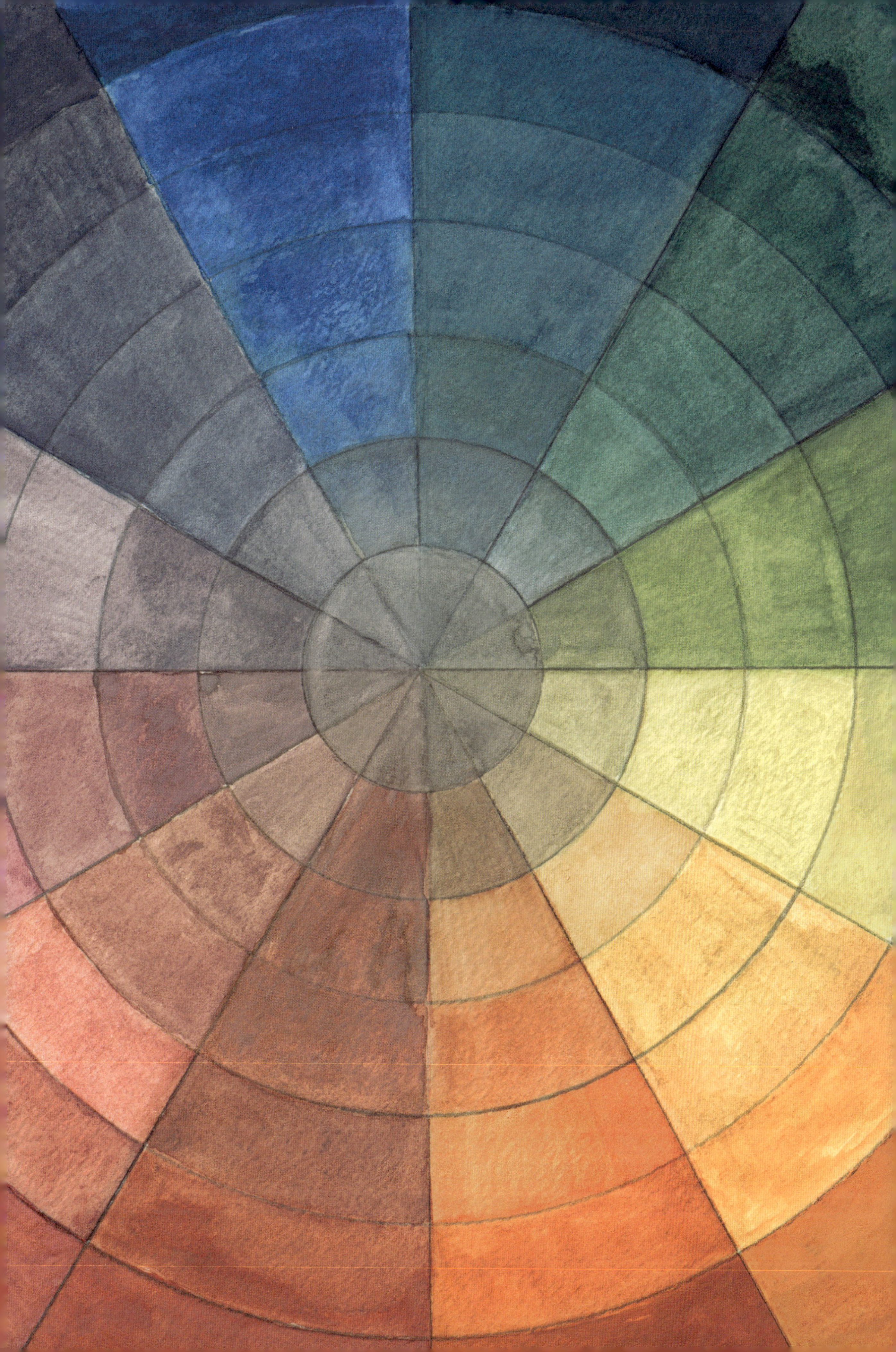

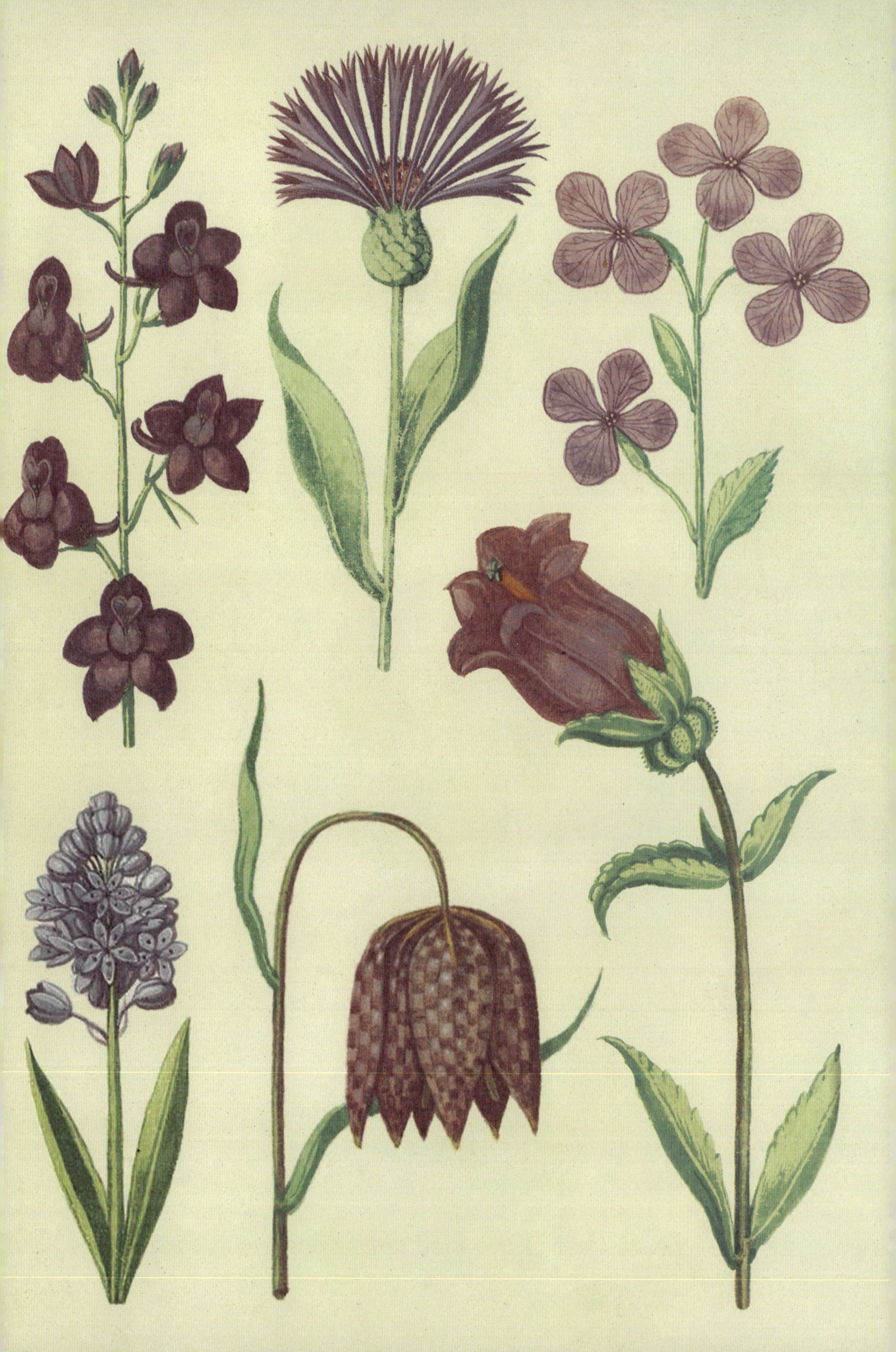

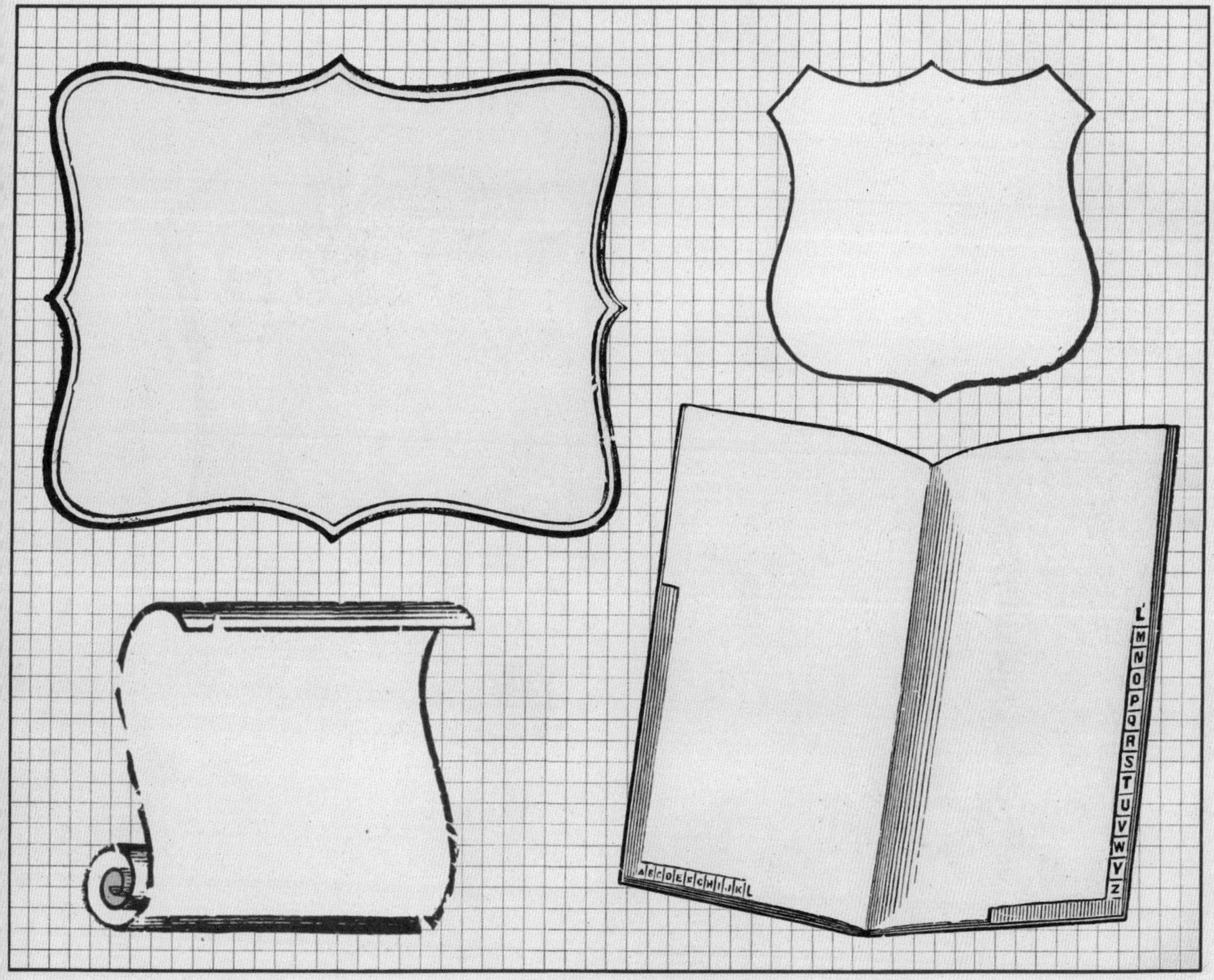

0 1 2 3 4 5 6 7 8 9

0 1 2 3 4 5 6 7 8 9

0 1 2 3 4 5 6 7 8 9

Su	Mo	Tu	We	Th	Fr	Sa
Su	Mo	Tu	We	Th	Fr	Sa
Su	Mo	Tu	We	Th	Fr	Sa
Su	Mo	Tu	We	Th	Fr	Sa

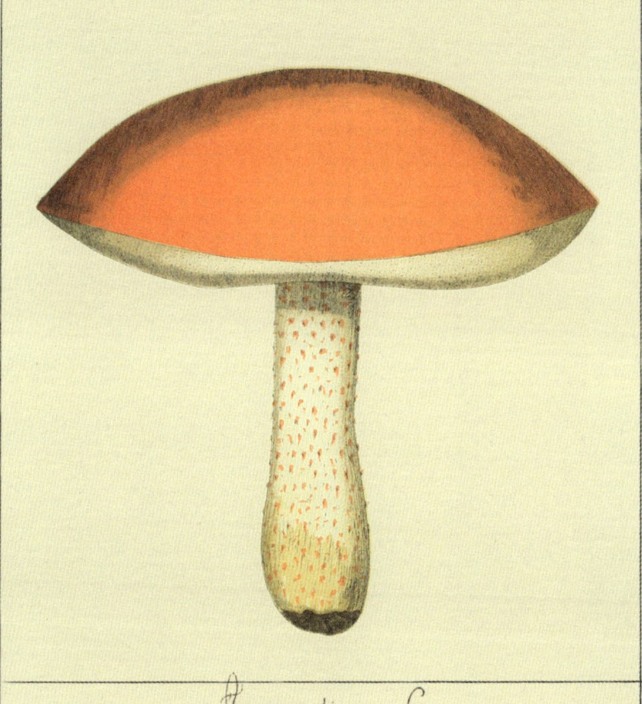

Aurantiacus, C

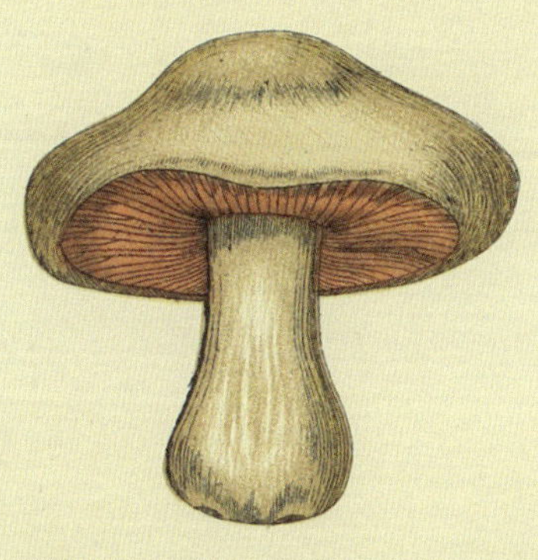

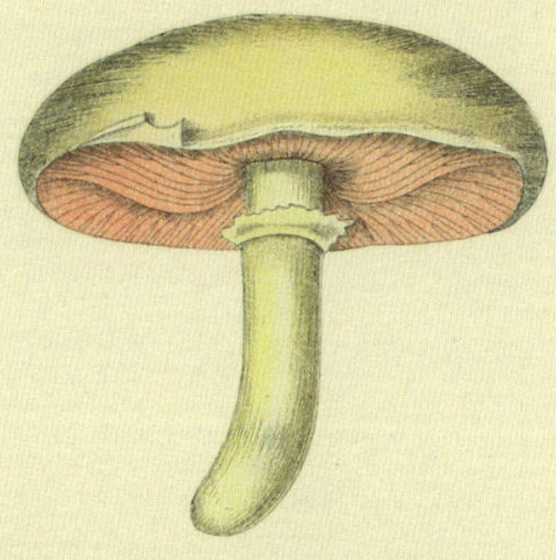

Squarrosus, C

Sinuatus, C

Campestris, C

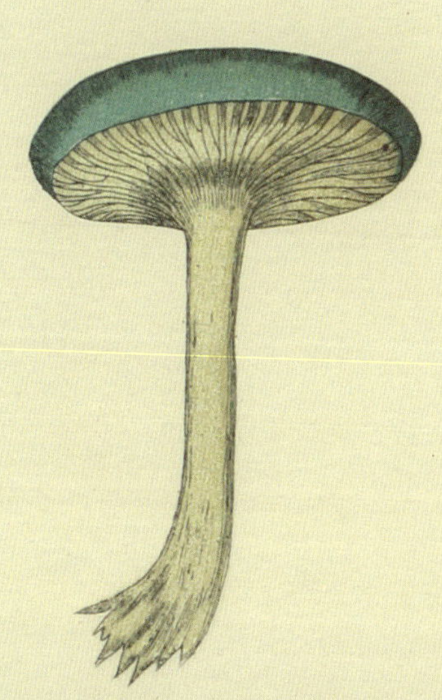

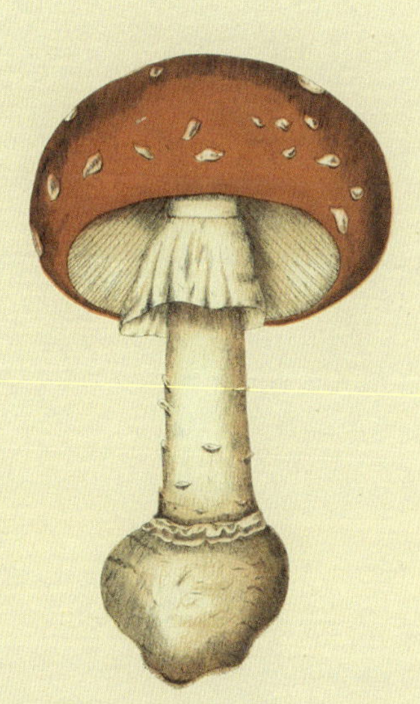

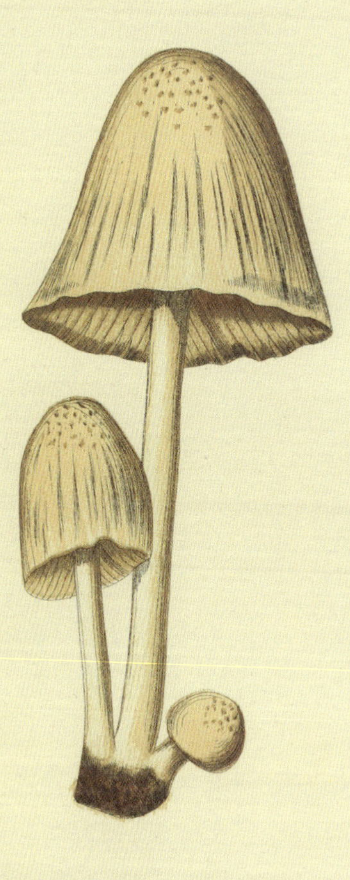

Odorus, C

Amanita Muscaria, V

Atramentarius, C

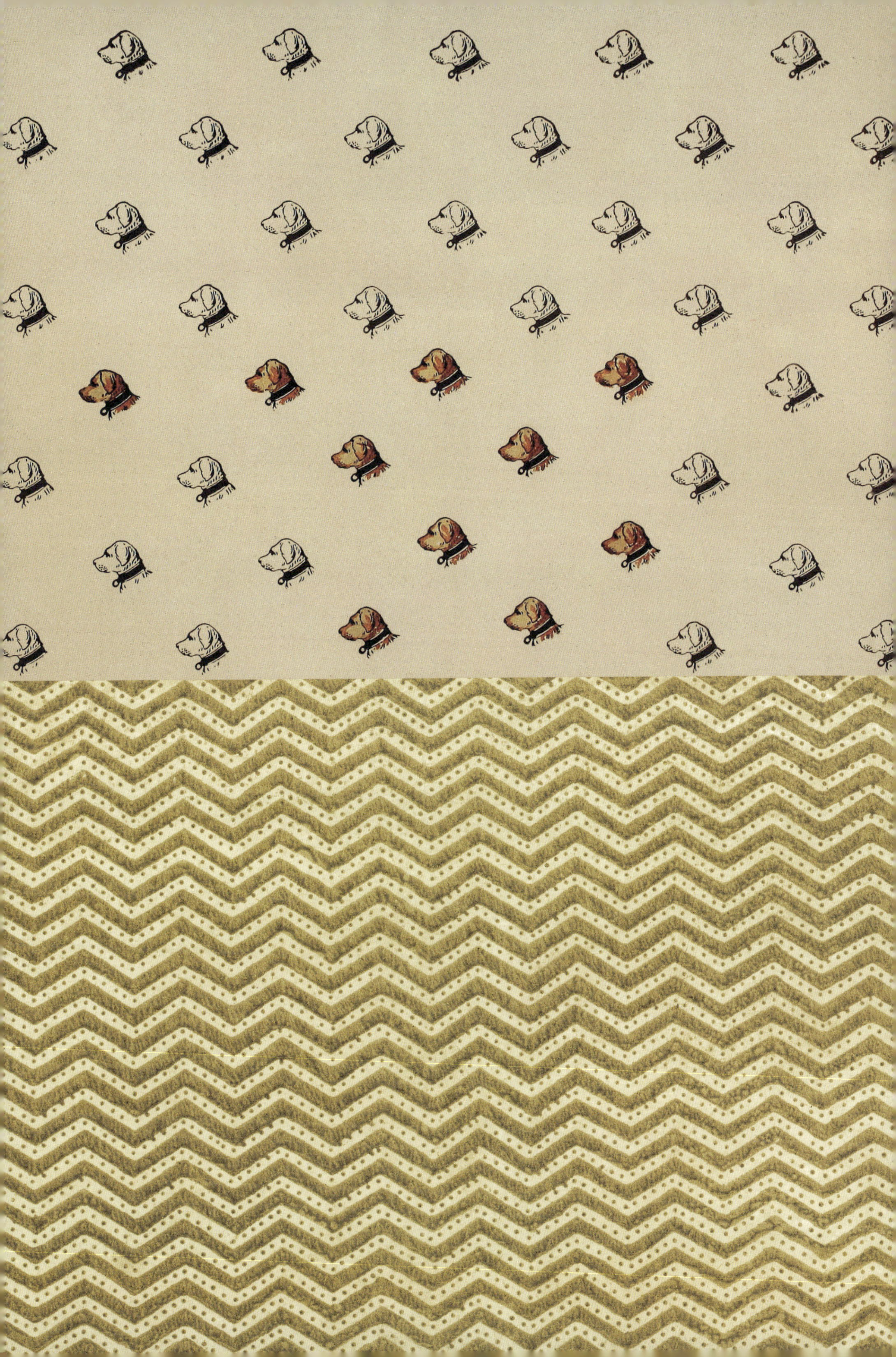

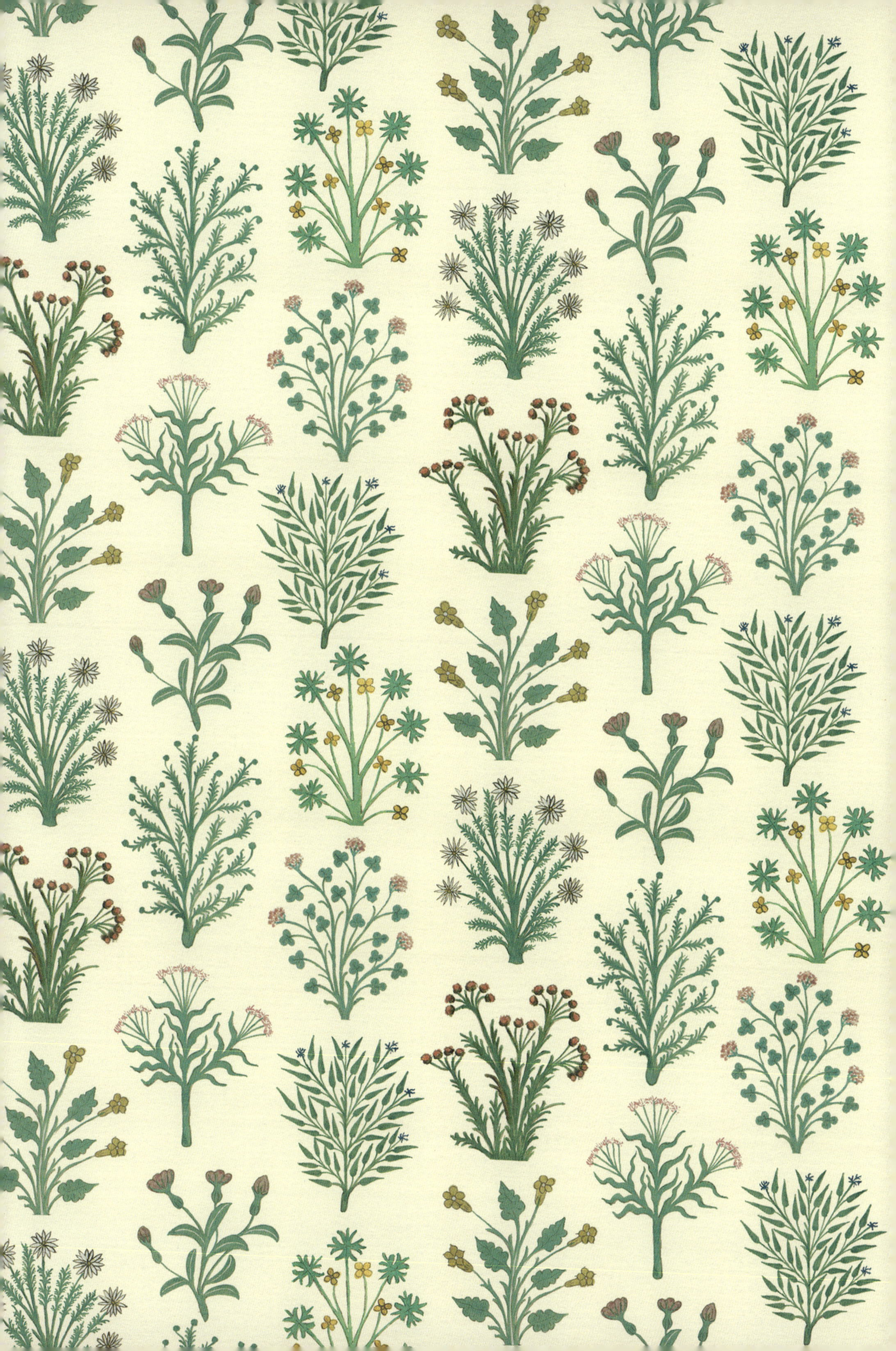

ABCDE
FGHIJK
LMNOP
QRSTU
VWXYZ

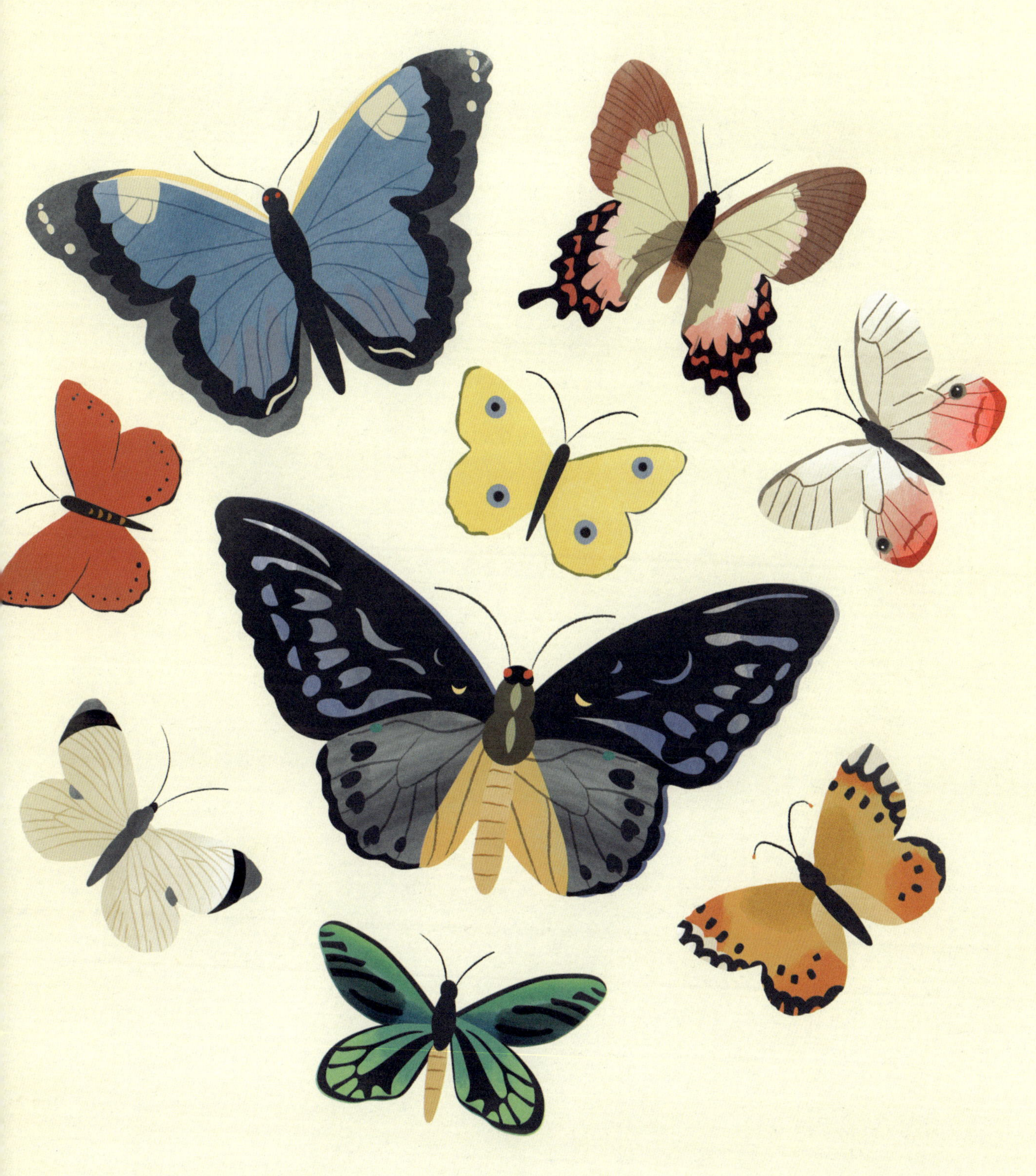

Image Credits

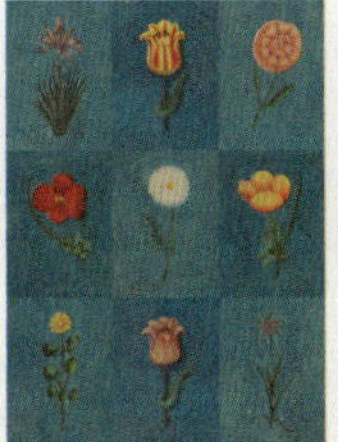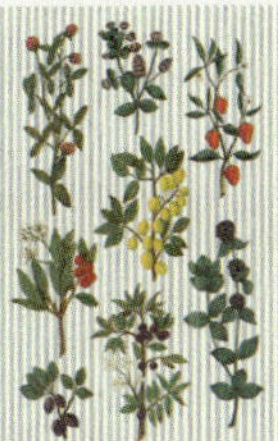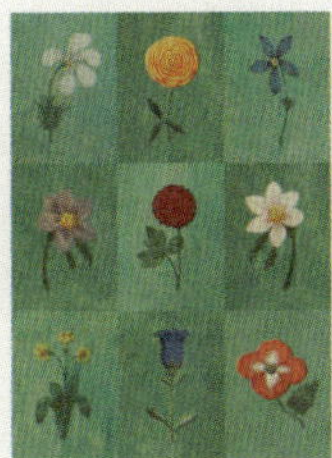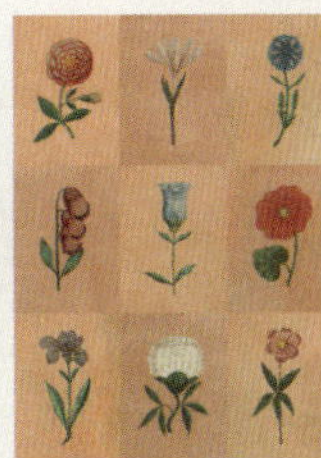

Pages 7, 11, 81, and 209: Dilich, Wilhelm, Artist, and Landgrave of Hesse-Kassel Moritz. Description of the *Christening of Lady Elisabeth of Hesse*, 1598. Library of Congress, World Digital Library, https://hdl.loc.gov/loc.wdl/wdl.8917.

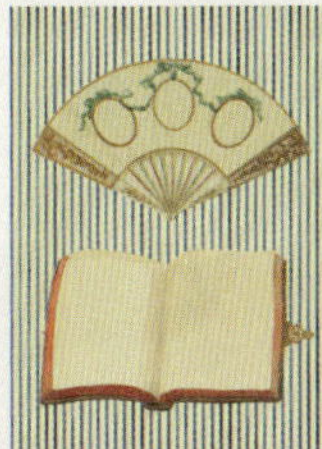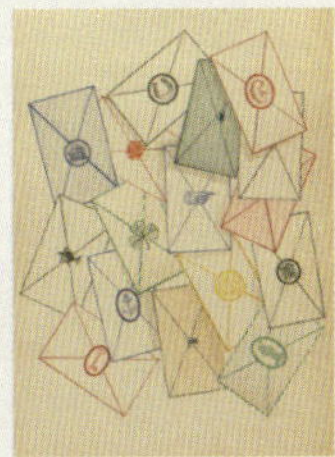

Pages 19 and 105: Fournier, Marie-Blanche Hennelle. *The Madame B Album*, 1870–1879. Art Institute of Chicago, https://www.artic.edu/artworks/185495 /the-madame-b-album.

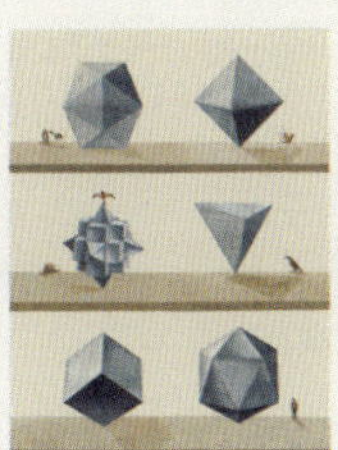

Page 201: Copyright © Herzog August Bibliothek.

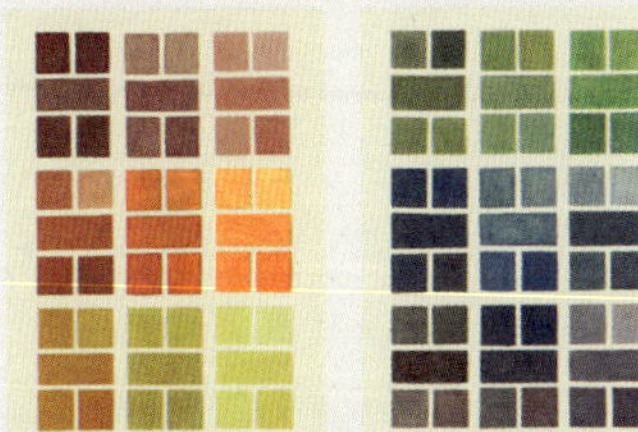

Pages 15 and 31: Boogert, A. *Traité des couleurs servant à la peinture à l'eau* (Treatise on colors used in watercolor painting), 1692. Méjanes Bibliotèques et Archives d'Aix-en-Provence, https://bibliotheque-numerique.citedulivre -aix.com/viewer/35315/?offset=#page=111&viewer=picture&o=bookmarks &n=0&q=.

Library of Congress Cataloging-in-Publication Data available.

ISBN 978-1-7972-4084-8

Manufactured in China.

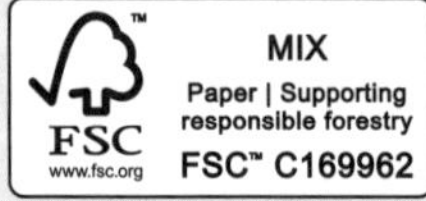

10 9 8 7 6 5 4 3 2 1

Chronicle books and gifts are available at special quantity discounts to corpora-
tions, professional associations, literacy programs, and other organizations. For
details and discount information, please contact our premiums department at
corporatesales@chroniclebooks.com or at 1-800-759-0190.

Chronicle Books LLC
680 Second Street
San Francisco, California 94107
chroniclebooks.com